## BEGINNING TO 1877

# AMERICA'S HISTORY
## LAND OF *Liberty*

### BY VIVIAN BERNSTEIN

CONSULTANTS

Dr. James E. Davis
Social Science Education Consortium
Lafayette, Colorado

Richard Jankowski
Social Studies Department Chairman
West Hills Middle School
Bloomfield Hills School District
Bloomfield, Michigan

Karen Tindel Wiggins
Director of Social Studies
Richardson Independent School District
Richardson, Texas

STECK-VAUGHN
COMPANY
ELEMENTARY · SECONDARY · ADULT · LIBRARY

## ABOUT THE AUTHOR

Vivian Bernstein is the author of *World History and You*, *America's Story*, *World Geography and You*, *American Government*, *Decisions for Health*, and *Life Skills for Today*. Bernstein is active with professional organizations in social studies, education, and reading. She gives presentations to school faculties and professional groups about content area reading. She received her Master of Arts degree from New York University and was a teacher in the New York City Public School System for a number of years.

## STAFF CREDITS

*Executive Editor:* Diane Sharpe

*Senior Editor:* Martin S. Saiewitz

*Senior Design Manager:* Pamela Heaney

*Photo Editor:* Margie Foster

*Electronic Production:* Jill Klinger

*Electronic Specialist:* Alan Klemp

## ACKNOWLEDGMENTS

pp. 20–21 Excerpt from *The Log of Christopher Columbus* by Christopher Columbus; translated by Robert H. Fuson. Copyright © 1987. Reprinted by permission of the McGraw-Hill Companies.

*Cartography:* GeoSystems, Inc.

*Charts, Graphs, and Tables:* Chuck Mackey

*Cover Photography:* (Eagle)© Daniel J. Cox/Tony Stone Images, (Flag)© Superstock

*Photo Credits:* (KEY: CP=Culver Pictures; GC=The Granger Collection; NP=National Portrait Gallery, Smithsonian Institution; NW=North Wind Picture Archive; SS=Superstock) pp. 2-3 St. Augustine Historical Society; p. 4 GC; pp. 5, 6 © SS; p. 8 NW; p. 9 GC; p.10 (left) NW, (center) © SS; p. 14 GC; p. 15 (both) NW; p. 16 © SS; p. 19 GC; p. 20 NW; pp. 22, 25, 26, 27, 28 GC; p. 30 New York Historical Society; pp. 31, 35, 37, 38, 39, 40, 43 GC; p. 44 © SS; p. 45 Colonial Williamsburg Foundation; p. 47, 49 © SS; p. 50 GC; pp. 56-57 © Charles D. Winters/Stock Boston; p 58 GC; p. 60 © Photri; pp. 61, 63 NW; p. 64 © SS; p. 68 GC; p. 69 (both) NW; p. 71 (top) © Daniel J. Cox/Tony Stone Images, (bottom) GC; p. 72 GC; p. 73 (center) © SS, (right) NW; p. 74 Courtesy, Museum of Fine Arts, Boston, Gift of Joseph W., William B., and Edward H.R. Revere; p. 78 © SS; p. 79 GC; p. 80 © SS; p. 81 NW; p. 82 © SS; p. 85 NP/Art Resource; p. 86 GC; p. 96 Abby Aldrich Rockefeller Folk Art Center, Williamsburg, VA; p. 97 GC; 98 (both) Independence Hall National Historic Park; p. 101 GC; p. 102 AP/Wide World; p. 103 NP; pp. 136-137 Lafayette College; p. 138 (all) Mt. Vernon Ladies Association; pp. 139, 140 GC; p. 141 The National Archives of the United States by Herman Viola, photographer, Jonathan Wallen; p. 143 NP; pp. 149, 150, 151, 152, 155 GC; p. 157 Arkansas History Commission; p. 159, 160, 161, 165, 166 GC; p. 167 (right) Wichita State University, (bottom) The Library of Congress; p. 168 (left, middle right) GC, (middle left) CP, (right) Sophia Smith Collection, Smith College; p. 171 GC; p. 172 NP; p. 176 North Museum, Franklin and Marshall College, photographer, © Runk/Schoenberger/Grant Heilman Photography; p. 177 Nebraska State Historical Society; p. 178 Texas State Archives; p. 181 (both) © SS; p. 182 Seaver Center for Western History Research, Natural History Museum of Los Angeles County; p. 183 CP; pp. 190-191 © Eric Sander/Gamma-Liaison; p. 192 © Alan Pitcairn/Grant Heilman Photography; pp. 193, 194 (both), 196 GC; p. 197 South Carolinian Library; p. 198 CP; p. 202 © Runk/Schoenberger/Grant Heilman Photography; p. 204 CP; p. 206 (both) GC; p. 207 NW; p. 208 Washington and Lee University; p. 212 CP; pp. 213, 214, 216, 217, 218 GC; p. 219 © SS; pp. 220 (both), 225 GC; p. 226 The Library of Congress; pp. 227, 228 GC; p. 230 © Bern Keating/Black Star; p. 231 GC.

ISBN 0–8172–6334–9

Copyright © 1997 Steck-Vaughn Company

# CONTENTS

Sherman's March to the Sea • Lincoln's Reelection • Final Battles of the Civil War • The Results of the Civil War

**CHAPTER 18 • THE RECONSTRUCTION YEARS**

Plans for Reconstruction • Congress and Reconstruction • The Impeachment of Johnson • The South During Reconstruction • African Americans in the South After the Civil War • The End of Reconstruction • The South After Reconstruction

## MAPS

## CHARTS, GRAPHS, AND TABLES

## To the Reader,

You are about to read the exciting story of a great experiment in history. As you read *America's History: Land of Liberty*, you will discover how people created a new nation in North America that was different from any other country. That nation, the United States of America, was the only nation at the end of the 1700s where people made their own laws and ruled themselves without a king or queen. It was a great experiment because no one knew if a nation with such a government could survive. You will learn how the new nation not only survived, but grew larger and stronger.

You will begin your study of American history by learning about Indians who had lived in America for thousands of years. Next, you will learn how people from Europe explored and settled North America. After the United States became independent from Great Britain, more states became part of the nation. Finally, you will find out how the States survived the difficult years of the Civil War.

As you explore your nation's past, use *America's History: Land of Liberty* to become a stronger social studies student. You will need a social studies notebook for assignments and writing activities. Begin by mastering new vocabulary words for each chapter and reviewing vocabulary from earlier chapters. Locate new places on a map and understand the ways geography can affect history. Read each chapter carefully. A second reading will improve your comprehension and recall. By working carefully on end of chapter activities, you will improve your vocabulary, critical thinking, writing, and social studies skills.

As you study American history, you will learn how many kinds of Americans built your nation. Think about the ways events of the past have created the nation that you are a part of today. An understanding of America's triumphs and mistakes in the past can help you work for a better future. As you journey through American history, remember that the story of the United States is your story, too!

*Vivian Bernstein*

# Unit 1

## AMERICA'S EARLY YEARS

**W**ould you travel through dangerous, unknown land to find gold and become rich? Imagine being told that somewhere in North America there are seven cities where jewels cover the houses and gold covers the streets. During the 1500s, people from Spain explored North America as they searched for the seven cities of gold. Although they never found the seven cities of gold, the Spanish did build an empire.

As you read Unit 1, you will learn how Europeans explored and settled America and changed the lives of the Native Americans who had been living there.

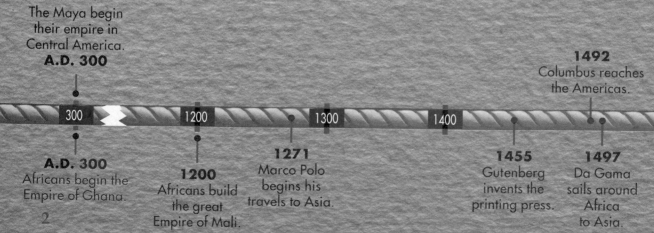

The Maya begin their empire in Central America.
**A.D. 300**

| 300 | 1200 | 1300 | 1400 |

**1492**
Columbus reaches the Americas.

**A.D. 300**
Africans begin the Empire of Ghana.

**1200**
Africans build the great Empire of Mali.

**1271**
Marco Polo begins his travels to Asia.

**1455**
Gutenberg invents the printing press.

**1497**
Da Gama sails around Africa to Asia.

2

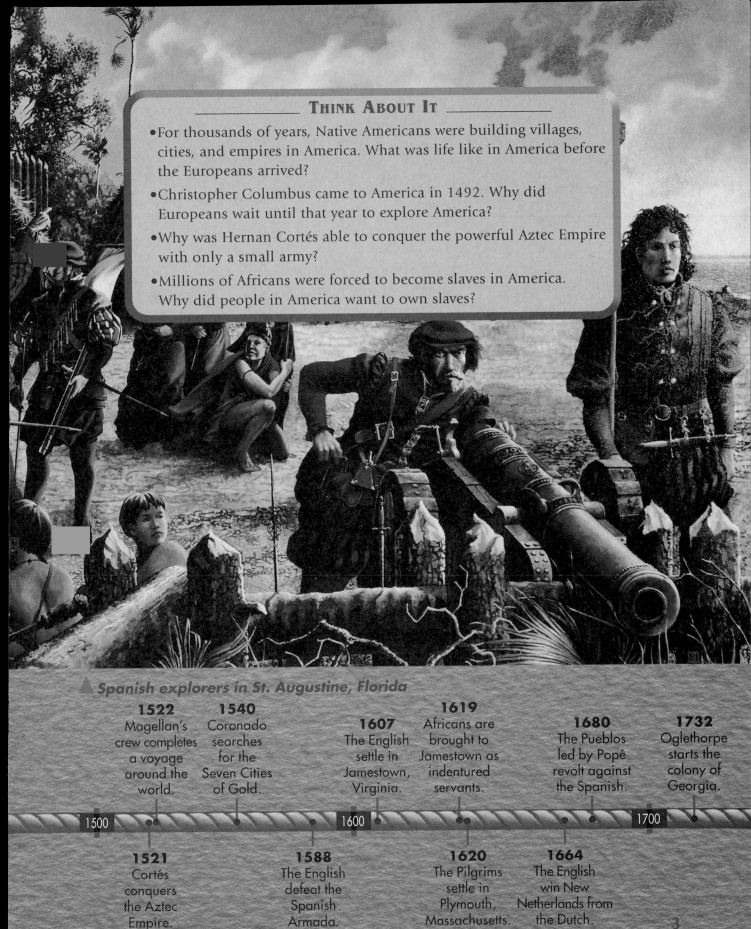

## THINK ABOUT IT

- For thousands of years, Native Americans were building villages, cities, and empires in America. What was life like in America before the Europeans arrived?

- Christopher Columbus came to America in 1492. Why did Europeans wait until that year to explore America?

- Why was Hernan Cortés able to conquer the powerful Aztec Empire with only a small army?

- Millions of Africans were forced to become slaves in America. Why did people in America want to own slaves?

▲ *Spanish explorers in St. Augustine, Florida*

**1522**
Magellan's crew completes a voyage around the world.

**1540**
Coronado searches for the Seven Cities of Gold.

**1607**
The English settle in Jamestown, Virginia.

**1619**
Africans are brought to Jamestown as indentured servants.

**1680**
The Pueblos led by Popé revolt against the Spanish.

**1732**
Oglethorpe starts the colony of Georgia.

1500 — 1600 — 1700

**1521**
Cortés conquers the Aztec Empire.

**1588**
The English defeat the Spanish Armada.

**1620**
The Pilgrims settle in Plymouth, Massachusetts.

**1664**
The English win New Netherlands from the Dutch.

3

# EARLIEST PEOPLE OF THE AMERICAS

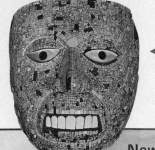

◀ *Mask of the Aztec god Quetzalcoatl*

### People

Native Americans •
Pueblos • Mound Builders •
Iroquois • Maya• Aztec •
Inca • Hiawatha •
Tadodaho • Peacemaker

### Places

Bering Sea • Mississippi
River • Rocky Mountains •
Great Plains • Ohio River
Mexico • Tenochtitlan •
Andes Mountains • Peru

### New Vocabulary

archaeologists • artifacts •
gatherers • culture •
irrigation canals • totem
poles • survive • tepees •
confederation •
civilization • pyramids •
human sacrifices •
empire • terraces

### Focus on Main Ideas

1. What is known about the first Americans?
2. How did Native American life differ in the Southwest, the Northwest, the Great Plains, and east of the Mississippi River?
3. What kinds of civilizations did Native Americans build in Mexico, Central America, and South America?

Imagine what America was like 50,000 years ago. It was a time called the Ice Age. The climate was much colder than it is today, and most of North America was covered with huge sheets of ice. Fifty thousand years ago, people had not yet come to America.

## The First Americans

**Archaeologists** believe that people first came to America between 20,000 and 50,000 years ago. People walked across a land bridge from Asia to North America. This land bridge was located where the Bering Sea is today. For several thousand years, groups of Asians continued to cross this land bridge. As time passed, Earth's climate became warmer and the Ice Age ended. As the huge sheets of ice that had covered North America melted, the level of the sea became higher. Finally the land bridge disappeared under the Bering Sea.

The first Americans did not have a writing system, so they left no books about their lives. Without written records no one really knows exactly how these people lived. But archaeologists have found bones from people who lived in America thousands of years ago. They have also found tools that these early people made. By studying bones, tools, and other **artifacts**, archaeologists have learned a lot about the earliest Americans.

The earliest Americans fished and hunted for food. These early people were also **gatherers**. They gathered wild berries, nuts, and plant roots for food. They moved from place to place as they hunted and gathered food. Their lives changed when they learned to plant seeds and grow their own food. Once they learned how to farm, they stayed in one place. As time passed these first Americans, or Native Americans, settled throughout North and South America. Their **culture**—how they lived, how they dressed, what they ate, and the language they spoke—often depended on where they lived.

## Native Americans West of the Mississippi River

Hundreds of years ago, the Pueblos built large apartment houses along the sides of steep cliffs. The Pueblos also lived in villages of stone buildings. The land where they lived is now the southwestern part of the United States. Parts of the Southwest do not get enough rain to grow crops. In order to grow crops, the Pueblos built **irrigation canals** that carried river water to their farms. The Pueblos worked

*Some Pueblo were cliff dwellers. They built apartments into cliffs like the one pictured here in Colorado. Some of the buildings were more than four stories tall. For safety, none of the doors were on the first floor. If the Pueblo were attacked, they pulled their ladders into the upper floors.*

*Totem poles were used by several Native American groups in the Northwest. Each part of the totem could represent a different person or event in a family's history.*

hard to grow corn and beans for food. Religion was an important part of Pueblo life. The people did religious dances so there would be rain and crops.

Getting food was easier for Native Americans who lived in what is today the Pacific Northwest of the United States. Native Americans who lived in forests near the Pacific Ocean always had plenty of food. There were fish from the oceans and the rivers. They also ate nuts and wild berries from the forests. They ate meat from the animals that they hunted. Native Americans of the Northwest were not farmers because it was easy for them to find food.

The people of the Northwest used the trees in the forest in many ways. They built wooden homes and put tall wooden **totem poles** in front of their homes. Trees from the forest were also made into long canoes. They used their canoes to fish in the ocean and the rivers and for traveling to trade with other nations. Even their clothing was made from trees. Native Americans took the bark off trees, made it very soft, and then made the bark into clothing.

Life was far more difficult for the Native Americans who lived on the plains between the Rocky Mountains and the Mississippi River. The flat land of the Great Plains had few trees and not much rain. It was terribly hot in the summer and very cold in the winter. Since it was difficult to be farmers on this dry, flat land, Native Americans hunted buffalo to **survive**. Millions of buffalo lived on the Great Plains. Native Americans ate buffalo meat, made clothes out of buffalo skin, and made tools from buffalo bones. Even their homes, which were tents called **tepees**, were made of buffalo skins and bones.

To hunt buffalo Native Americans moved from place to place to follow the herds. Since the Native Americans did not have horses, they hunted by walking and running after the buffalo. They used bows and arrows and long spears to kill the buffalo. It was hard, dangerous work.

## Native Americans East of the Mississippi River

Many forests covered the land that was east of the Mississippi River. Native Americans who lived near the Ohio and Mississippi rivers built huge mounds, or hills of dirt, that were sometimes fifty feet high. These Native Americans have been called Mound Builders. Temples were built at the top of some mounds. Important people who had died were buried inside the mounds. Archaeologists have found pots, bowls, and pearls in some mounds. Since the pearls came from the Pacific Ocean, which was thousands of miles away, archaeologists believe the Mound Builders were excellent traders. By the late 1500s, the Mound Builders were replaced by other Native American groups.

One group that replaced the Mound Builders was the Iroquois. They settled in the eastern forests. The Iroquois hunted animals in the forests. They were also farmers. To clear the land, they chopped down the trees. Then they burned the tree stumps. After the trees were gone, they planted corn, beans, and squash. These crops were so important that the Iroquois called them the "Three Sisters."

The Iroquois lived in homes called longhouses. As many as twenty families would live together in a longhouse. Each family had its own small apartment in the longhouse. All of the families were related to each other. The oldest woman in the longhouse became the leader of all the families in the house.

There were many different Iroquois nations, and they often had wars with each other. People of one nation were often attacked by another nation. After many years of war, five Iroquois nations joined together in a **confederation** to have peace. They formed the Iroquois Confederation

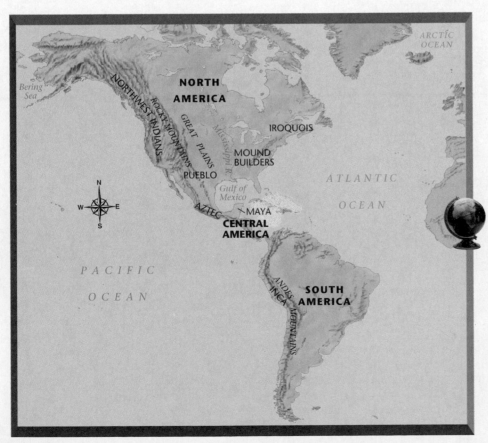

**Several Native American Cultures**
*Hundreds of different Native American cultures developed throughout North and South America. Which Native American group lived in the Andes Mountains?*

of Five Nations. All five nations sent chiefs to represent them at council meetings. The chiefs were chosen by women. At Council meetings laws were made and problems between nations were solved. The five nations remained independent, but they worked together for peace. When the United States became a free nation, it used the Iroquois's ideas about government to help plan the new American government.

## Native Americans of Mexico, Central America, and South America

Thick rain forests cover parts of Mexico and Central America. The weather in the rain forests is always hot and rainy. In these rain forests, people called the Maya built an amazing **civilization**. Between the years A.D. 300 and 900, the Maya built many beautiful cities. They studied math and invented a calendar. They were the first Native Americans to develop a system of writing. They used many small pictures to write their language.

The Maya built huge **pyramids** where they buried their dead kings. Temples were built on top of some pyramids. The Maya prayed to many different gods in these temples. The sun god was the most important Mayan god. The Maya believed they had to make **human sacrifices** to the

*Native Americans grew corn, beans, squash, potatoes, and many other types of products. The Iroquois cleared land in the eastern forests for their fields. Besides raising corn, the Iroquois also fished, hunted, and gathered to get food.*

sun god so that the sun would continue to shine. This means they killed people as a sacrifice to the sun god. About the year 900, the Maya left their cities and their civilization ended. No one knows why this happened. But people from ancient Mayan families still live in Mexico and Central America today.

The Aztec were Native Americans who built a great civilization in Mexico. The Aztec conquered and ruled a large **empire**. Perhaps eleven million people lived in this empire. Like the Maya, the Aztec developed a system for writing their language.

The Aztec were great builders. They built huge pyramids and temples. Their capital, Tenochtitlan, was built on an island on a lake. Bridges connected the city to the mainland. Large temples, houses, and government buildings were built in the city. Tenochtitlan was larger and cleaner than any city in Europe at that time.

The Aztec believed in many gods, but the sun god and the war god were the most important ones. The Aztec believed these gods needed human sacrifices. The Aztec sacrificed thousands of people each year. They went to war in order to capture people whom they could sacrifice.

The Inca were Native Americans who built an empire that extended through the Andes Mountains of South America. Their capital was in the country that is now Peru. People everywhere in the Inca Empire spoke the same language and obeyed the same king. The Inca built roads to connect cities throughout the empire. They also built bridges across deep valleys. Although they lived in very tall mountains, they learned how to grow food by making

The Aztec capital of Tenochtitlan in the Valley of Mexico was the center of an empire. More than 100,000 people lived in this city.

**terraces** on the sides of the mountains. They built irrigation canals to carry water to their farms. The Inca took care of their people, and poor people were not allowed to go hungry.

By the year 1492, millions of Native Americans were living throughout North, Central, and South America. They spoke hundreds of languages and had developed many different cultures. Until 1492 no one in Europe knew about the land we call America or the Native Americans who lived there. But in the year 1492, people from Europe began exploring America. As more and more people from Europe came to America, Native American life changed forever. Read on to learn what happened to Native Americans as people from Europe explored and settled America.

# BIOGRAPHY

## Hiawatha

Hiawatha was an Iroquois who helped bring peace to the five Iroquois nations.

For many years people from one Iroquois nation were often attacked and killed by people from another nation. Attacks among the five nations—Mohawk, Oneida, Cayuga, Seneca, and Onondaga—happened so often that it became unsafe to work on a farm or to hunt in the woods. One young Iroquois man, Hiawatha, believed the Iroquois should stop fighting and work together for peace. When Tadodaho, the leader of the Onondaga nation, heard Hiawatha's ideas about peace, he became so angry that he had all of Hiawatha's daughters killed.

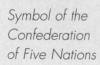

*Symbol of the Confederation of Five Nations*

Hiawatha was filled with grief after his daughters were killed. He was so unhappy that he left his home and went to live alone in a small house in the forest. One day he met a man from another Indian nation who also spoke about peace. His people called him Peacemaker. Hiawatha and Peacemaker decided to travel together to the different Iroquois nations to convince them to join a confederation that would work for peace. Since Hiawatha was an excellent speaker and Peacemaker was a poor one, the two men decided that Hiawatha would speak to the leaders of the nations. Hiawatha convinced four Iroquois nations to accept peace, but he wanted the Onondaga nation to join the Confederation, too. So Hiawatha faced his old enemy Tadodaho and spoke softly to him about peace. Tadodaho listened and agreed that the Onondaga nation would join the Confederation of Five Nations. The confederation kept peace among the Iroquois for about 300 years.

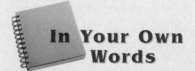

## In Your Own Words

Write a paragraph in the journal section of your social studies notebook that explains the importance of Hiawatha's work among the Iroquois nations.

# REVIEW AND APPLY

## CHAPTER 1 MAIN IDEAS

■ Native Americans first came to America from Asia between 20,000 and 50,000 years ago.

■ Native Americans developed many different cultures based on the geography and the climate of where they lived.

■ The Pueblos used irrigation to grow food in the dry Southwest.

■ Native Americans on the Great Plains depended on the buffalo to survive.

■ To keep peace, five Iroquois nations formed the Iroquois Confederation. Some ideas for the government of the United States are based on the ideas of the Iroquois Confederation.

■ The Maya, Aztec, and Inca developed great civilizations in Mexico, Central America, and South America.

## VOCABULARY

**Finish the Sentence** ■ **Choose one of the words or phrases from the box to complete each sentence. You will not use all the words in the box.**

1. An _____ studies old bones to learn how people lived long ago.

2. An _____ is a tool or object that was made by a person.

3. How people live, what they eat, and how they dress are all parts

   of the _____ of a group.

4. An _____ is a ditch that carries water to dry land so people can grow crops.

5. An _____ is land or people that are ruled by one nation.

6. A _____ is a tent that is made from animal skins and bones.

7. Native Americans of the Northwest used carved and painted _____ as symbols of their families.

8. The Iroquois joined together as a _____ to keep peace.

empire
culture
archaeologist
totem poles
tepee
irrigation canal
confederation
pyramids
artifact

## USING INFORMATION

Journal Writing ■ Write a paragraph in your journal that explains with which Native Americans you would want to live and why.

## COMPREHENSION CHECK

Finish the Paragraph ■ Use the words in the box to finish the paragraph. There is an extra word that you will not use.

| | | | |
|---|---|---|---|
| buffalo | Maya | gatherers | Bering Sea |
| | burning | cotton | villages |

Between 20,000 and 50,000 years ago, people first came to America by crossing the

_____ on a land bridge. These people were _____

because they moved from place to place searching for food. After people learned to farm,

they started to live in _____ . The Native Americans of the Great

Plains hunted _____ . In the eastern forests, Native Americans

farmed by first chopping down trees and then _____ the stumps.

The _____ built a civilization in Mexico and Central America.

## CRITICAL THINKING

Categories ■ Read the words in each group. Write a title for each group on the lines above each group. You may use the words in the box for all or part of each title. There is one title in the box that you will not need.

| | | |
|---|---|---|
| Pueblo | Iroquois | Inca |
| Aztec | Mound Builders | |

1. _____
   lived in longhouses
   planted corn, beans, and squash
   joined a confederation

2. _____
   lived in the Southwest of the United States
   built apartment houses
   built irrigation canals

3. _____
   their capital city was Tenochtitlan
   ruled an empire in Mexico
   believed in many gods

4. _____
   grew food on mountain terraces
   ruled a huge empire in South America
   built roads to connect cities

# SOCIAL STUDIES SKILLS

## Locating Oceans and Continents

Most of Earth is covered with water from four large bodies of water called oceans:

Pacific Ocean      Atlantic Ocean
Indian Ocean       Arctic Ocean

Earth also has very large bodies of land called continents:

Asia                Africa
North America       South America
Antarctica          Europe
Australia

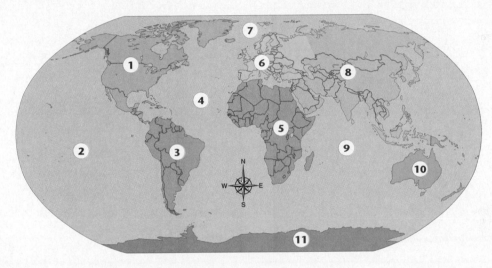

A. **Number your paper from 1 to 11. Next to each number, write the name of the ocean or continent represented by the numbers on the map above. Use the world map on page 236.**

B. **Write the answer to each question.**

1. Which ocean is located between Africa and South America?

   _____

2. Which ocean is located between Africa and Australia?

   _____

3. Which continent is connected to South America? _____

4. Which continent is connected to Europe? _____

5. Which continent is also one country? _____

# Chapter 2

# EUROPEANS EXPLORE THE AMERICAS

◀ *Astrolabe from Portugal from about 1555*

### People

Christopher Columbus •
Marco Polo • Queen
Isabella • Tainos • Amerigo
Vespucci • Ferdinand
Magellan • La Salle •
Estevanico • Zuni

### Places

England • Spain • France •
Portugal • Strait of Magellan •
Philippines • Canada •
St. Lawrence River •
Quebec • Gulf of Mexico •
Louisiana • Florida •
Mexico City

### New Vocabulary

technology • compass •
astrolabe • monarchs •
mainland • colonies •
circumnavigate •
tributaries • log

### Focus on Main Ideas

1. Why were Europeans ready for exploration in the 1400s?
2. How did Prince Henry help sailors from Portugal reach Asia 20 years after his death?
3. How did America get its name?
4. Why did explorers continue to look for new routes to Asia after Christopher Columbus came to America?

About the year 1000, Vikings sailed across the Atlantic Ocean and reached North America. The Vikings may have been the first people from Europe to reach America. But it was not until about five hundred years later that Christopher Columbus and others began to explore America.

### Why Did Europeans Become Explorers in the 1400s?

For hundreds of years, people in Europe knew little about other parts of the world. European mapmakers believed there were only three continents—Europe, Asia, and Africa. Europeans wanted more trade with Asia after they learned about the travels of Marco Polo. Marco Polo had left Italy in 1271 and had spent 24 years traveling in central Asia and China. He had returned to Europe with beautiful silks and jewels. He had written a book about his travels that made other people want to trade with Asia.

People in Europe also wanted to trade with Asian countries to get spices for their food. Spices were valuable because there were no refrigerators at that time, and spices helped food stay fresher and taste better. In order to trade with Asia,

Europeans had to make a long journey through dangerous lands. Because the journey over land was so long and dangerous, Europeans wanted to find an easier water route to Asia.

There were three reasons why Europeans were ready to start exploring for new ways to reach Asia. First, by the 1400s **technology** had improved ocean travel. Europeans had learned to build ships with better sails that could sail against the wind. They had learned to use the **compass**, which showed sailors which direction was north. Another instrument, the **astrolabe**, helped sailors know how far they were from the equator. Improved technology made it possible to travel and explore more than ever before.

Second, there was also great interest in learning new ideas at this time. Johannes Gutenberg invented a printing press in 1455, and many new books were printed. Through books people could spread ideas and information about travel and exploration.

A third reason was that England, Spain, France, and Portugal had become very strong nations that were ruled by powerful **monarchs**. Monarchs are kings and queens. These nations had the money and the power to send explorers on far off journeys. Each of these nations wanted to become more powerful than the others. By controlling trade with Asia, a nation could become rich and powerful.

*Prince Henry of Portugal brought together mapmakers and sailors from all over Europe to help sailors from Portugal explore the coast of Africa.*

*Vasco da Gama reached Asia by sailing around Africa. His father had been asked by the king of Portugal to lead the voyage. Da Gama took over after his father died.*

*Christopher Columbus presents his plans to Queen Isabella and King Ferdinand of Spain. Columbus had first gone to other rulers in Europe, but they had refused to help him.*

### The Portuguese Become Explorers First

Prince Henry of Portugal believed it was possible to reach Asia by sailing around Africa. So Henry started a school where men could learn to be sailors and learn how to build better ships. Europeans knew very little about Africa, so Prince Henry encouraged sailors to explore the west coast of Africa.

Finally in 1487, almost twenty years after Prince Henry "the Navigator" had died, a Portuguese explorer named Bartolomeu Dias sailed past the southern tip of Africa. Ten years later another Portuguese explorer, Vasco da Gama, sailed around Africa and through the Indian Ocean to India. At last Europeans had found a water route to Asia. Portugal became the leader in trade with Asia.

### Christopher Columbus Sails West

Christopher Columbus was born in Italy and became a sailor. He believed that sailing west across the Atlantic Ocean would be a shorter, faster way to reach Asia than sailing around Africa. Like other people at that time, Columbus did not know there were two American continents between Europe and Asia. He also did not know about the huge Pacific Ocean.

Columbus needed sailors and ships in order to sail west across the Atlantic Ocean. He asked the king of Portugal for ships, but the king refused because he thought Columbus's ideas were wrong. Then Columbus went to Spain where he presented his plans to Queen Isabella. After six years Isabella agreed to help Columbus. Isabella hoped Columbus might find gold in Asia so Spain would become a richer nation. She gave Columbus three ships and ninety sailors. Columbus's ships—the *Niña*, the *Pinta*, and the *Santa Maria*—began the long trip across the Atlantic Ocean in August 1492.

Columbus thought the Atlantic Ocean was much smaller than it really is, so the trip across the ocean took much longer than he expected. The sailors thought they were lost at sea because for weeks all they saw was the ocean all around them.

By October 9, 1492, the sailors were so frightened they told Columbus he must turn back to Spain. Columbus promised that he would turn back if they did not see land in three days. But three days later, on October 12, 1492, they reached land.

Columbus believed he had reached an island near India. He put a large cross and a Spanish flag on the island and said the land belonged to Spain. Columbus had reached the island of San Salvador in the Caribbean Sea. He did not know that he was on an island in the Americas. The Native Americans who lived on San Salvador were friendly people called Tainos. Columbus called the people he met Indians because he thought he was in India. To welcome Columbus the Tainos gave him presents that included small pieces of gold. Then Columbus explored other nearby islands as he and his crew searched for gold.

Christopher Columbus was a hero when he returned to Spain. He had forced six Tainos to go back to Spain with him, and they became slaves in Spain. Queen Isabella believed Columbus had reached Asia. She wanted him to return there and find more gold.

Columbus made three more trips to America. As he explored more islands in the Caribbean, he forced Indians to work as slaves to search for gold. Many Indians died from the cruel treatment they received. Columbus never found much gold.

Columbus always believed that the islands he was exploring were close to Asia's **mainland**, the land on the continent. Until the end of his life, Columbus always believed he had found a new way to reach Asia.

Since Spain and Portugal were both sending explorers to find new routes to Asia, the two nations began to argue about which one would rule new lands that were found. Both nations wanted to rule **colonies** in other parts of the world. By ruling colonies they would become more powerful. If gold and spices were found in the colonies, the ruling nation would be richer. The leader of the Roman Catholic Church, Pope Alexander VI, drew a line on a map from north to south that divided the Atlantic Ocean into two parts. The Pope said Spain would rule all new land that was found to the west of the line. Portugal would rule the land that was found to the east of the line. The Pope's decision was called the Treaty of Tordesillas. Portugal and Spain signed the treaty in 1494. When Portuguese explorer Pedro Cabral landed in the country we now call Brazil, the Portuguese said Brazil belonged to them because it was to the east of the Pope's line. Brazil became the only country in South America that was ruled by Portugal.

## Other Europeans Explore America to Reach Asia

Soon after 1492 other explorers tried to find water routes to Asia. Amerigo Vespucci came from Italy and sailed for Portugal. He explored the coast of South America. Vespucci realized that South America was not part of Asia as Columbus believed. Vespucci said the land was a new continent and he called it a "New World." The continent was a new world only to the people in Europe who never knew about South America. It was not a new world to the

Native Americans who had been there for thousands of years.

Vespucci wrote about his discovery, and a mapmaker read his work. When the mapmaker made a map that included the New World, the mapmaker decided to name the new continents America after Amerigo Vespucci.

Ferdinand Magellan was another explorer who tried to reach Asia by sailing west. He thought he could find a water route through America that went to Asia. Magellan sailed from Spain in 1519 with five ships and a crew of about 250 men. He reached South America and sailed south to a waterway that we now call the Strait of Magellan. The sea was so stormy it took more than a month to sail through the Strait of Magellan. After sailing through the dangerous waters, Magellan reached a huge calm ocean. Magellan named this ocean the Pacific, which means peaceful.

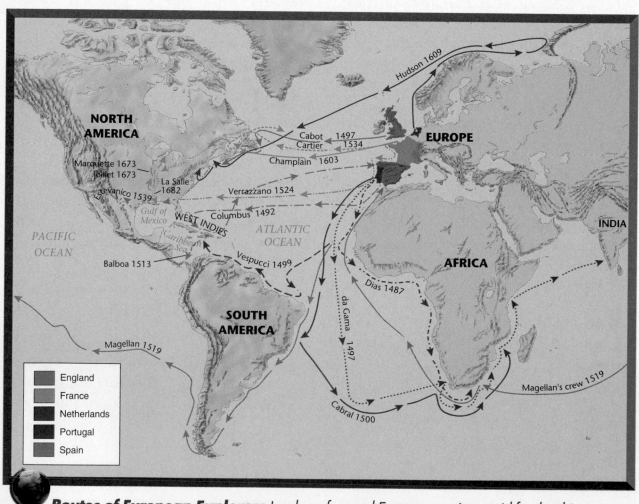

**Routes of European Explorers** Leaders of several European nations paid for the ships and crews of explorers. The colors on the map show for which country each explorer was working. Which explorers shown on the map were exploring for Spain?

Magellan did not know that the Pacific was much larger than the Atlantic Ocean. Magellan's trip across the Pacific was long and dangerous. For months the sailors did not see land. After they finished all the food on their ships, they ate all the rats they could find so they would not starve to death. Four ships were destroyed, and most of the sailors died along the way. Magellan was killed in a battle in the Philippines. After three years at sea, one ship with only eighteen men returned to Spain. These men who survived the voyage were the first to **circumnavigate**, or sail around, the world.

Some Europeans believed there was a Northwest Passage, or a northern water route, through North America to Asia. Many explorers tried to find the northern water route. The first was John Cabot who sailed for England. Cabot did not find the Northwest Passage, but he explored parts of Canada. Because of Cabot's work, England claimed the right to rule land in North America.

France also wanted to find a water route to Asia. Jacques Cartier searched for the Northwest Passage. He explored the St. Lawrence River and claimed all the land around that river for France. Samuel de Champlain made eleven trips to America for France. He started the French city of Quebec in Canada.

René-Robert Cavalier was another French explorer. He is also known by the name La Salle. He was born in France, and at age 23 he moved to Canada. In 1682 La Salle explored the entire Mississippi River, the longest river in the United States. He sailed from the north of the river in the

For 20 years La Salle explored parts of North America claiming land for France. In 1685 he set up a French colony on the Gulf of Mexico. The colony failed, and La Salle was killed by angry colonists.

area of the Great Lakes all the way south to the Gulf of Mexico. He claimed all the land around the river and its **tributaries**, or branches, for France. La Salle named this huge area Louisiana in honor of his king, King Louis XIV of France. France now claimed a large part of North America.

Before long, Europeans wanted to settle on and control the land in America. As Europeans tried to rule America, they fought with the Indians who were already there. In the next chapter you will learn how Europeans settled in America and what happened to the Indians who lived there.

# *Voices from the Past*

## The Log of Christopher Columbus

Christopher Columbus wrote about his first journey across the Atlantic Ocean in a log, or a journal. He wrote something about his travels every day. From his journal we learn that Columbus was a very religious man. The log also tells us that his goals were to find gold and to teach the Indians to be Christians. Here is part of his log for three days in October 1492.

### Thursday, 11 October 1492

I saw several things that were indications [signs] of land. At one time a large flock of sea birds flew overhead, and a green reed was found floating near the ship. The crew of the Pinta spotted some of the same reeds…they also saw what looked like a small board or plank. A stick was recovered that looks manmade.…But even these few made the crew breathe easier; in fact, the men have even become cheerful.…A special thanksgiving was offered to God for giving us renewed hope through the many signs of land He has provided.

… Then at two hours after midnight, the Pinta fired a cannon, my prearranged signal for the sighting of land.

### Friday, 12 October 1492

At dawn we saw naked people, and I went ashore…. I unfurled the royal banner and the captains brought the flags which displayed a large green cross with the letters F and Y at the left and right side of the cross. After a prayer of thanksgiving, I ordered the captains of the Pinta and Niña to witness that I was taking possession of this island for the King and Queen. To this island I gave the name San Salvador, in honor of our Blessed Lord.

People began to come to the beach… They are very well-built people, with handsome bodies and very fine faces. Many of the natives paint their faces; others paint their whole bodies; some, only the eyes or nose. Some are painted black, some white, some red; others are of different colors.

They are friendly… people who bear no arms except for small spears, and they have no iron. I showed one my sword, and through ignorance he grabbed it by the blade and cut himself. Their spears are made of wood, to which they attach a fish tooth at one end, or some other sharp thing. I want the

> *Then at two hours after midnight, the Pinta fired a cannon, my...signal for the sighting of land.*

natives to develop a friendly attitude toward us because I know that they are a people who can be made free and converted to our Holy Faith more by love than by force. I therefore gave red caps to some and glass beads to others. They hung the beads around their necks, along with some other things of slight value that I gave them.... They traded and gave everything they had with good will, but it seems to me that they have very little and are poor in everything.... This afternoon the people of San Salvador came swimming to our ships and in boats made from one log. They brought us parrots, balls of cotton thread, spears, and many other things....

They ought to make good and skilled servants, for they repeat very quickly whatever we say to them. I think they can easily be made Christians, for they seem to have no religion. If it please Our Lord, I will take six of them to Your Highnesses when I depart, in order that they may learn our language.

### Saturday, 13 October 1492

I have been very attentive and have tried very hard to find out if there is any gold here. I have seen a few natives who wear a little piece of gold hanging from a hole made in the nose.... I have learned that by going to the south, I can find a king who possesses a lot of gold.... I have tried to find some natives who will take me to this great king, but none seems inclined to make the journey. Tomorrow afternoon I intend to... look for gold and precious stones.

## Write Your Answers

**On a separate sheet of paper answer these questions.**

1. How did Columbus know he was near land?

2. How did Columbus describe the native people that he met?

3. Why did Columbus believe these people were peaceful?

4. What did Columbus want to do with the Indians?

5. How did Columbus expect to find gold?

# BIOGRAPHY

## Estevanico 1500(?)–1539

Estevanico was an African slave who explored for gold in Florida and in what is now the Southwest of the United States.

In 1528 the Spanish explorer Panfilo de Narváez led 400 men on a search for gold in Florida. They did not find gold, and they were attacked by Indians. So the Spanish tried to escape by building rafts and sailing to Mexico. Most of the men were killed in a hurricane off the coast of present-day Texas. Eight years later, four survivors of the doomed expedition reached Mexico City. Estevanico was one of those survivors.

Estevanico and the other three men had spent eight years trying to reach Mexico. They traveled through what is now Texas, New Mexico, and Arizona. Along the way Estevanico learned to speak several Indian languages. He was the first African the Indians had ever seen. They thought Estevanico might be a god, so they gave him gifts. They told Estevanico stories about a place called Cibola. In these stories Cibola had seven cities made of gold.

When Estevanico and the other three men reached Mexico City, they told the stories about Cibola. The Spanish wanted to find gold, so the governor of Mexico asked a priest, Father Marcos de Niza, to search for Cibola. Father Niza told Estevanico to help him since Estevanico had already traveled through the Southwest.

During the journey Estevanico was sent ahead of the group so that he could send information about Cibola back to Father Niza. Estevanico sent information to the priest about villages with tall houses that were covered with beautiful stones. Estevanico was killed by Zuni Indians in one of the villages he visited. After he died, the Zunis told legends about the tall African explorer. The Spanish later used what they learned from Estevanico to continue exploring the Southwest, but they never found cities of gold.

## In Your Own Words

Write a paragraph in the journal section of your notebook that describes Estevanico's travels and explorations.

# REVIEW AND APPLY

- New technology led Europeans to explore at the end of the 1400s.

- The Portuguese were the first Europeans to search for a water route around Africa to Asia.

- Christopher Columbus made four trips to America. He thought he had reached Asia.

- Columbus called the Taino who lived on the island that he explored Indians.

- America was named for the explorer Amerigo Vespucci.

- Ferdinand Magellan's crew was the first to circumnavigate the world.

- John Cabot explored parts of Canada for England.

- Jacques Cartier explored the St. Lawrence River for France.

- René-Robert Cavalier, also known as La Salle, explored the Mississippi River and claimed it for France. He named the region Louisiana for King Louis XIV of France.

## VOCABULARY

Analogies ■ Use a word in the box to finish each sentence. You will not use one word.

| tributary | log | technology |
|---|---|---|
| compass | mainland | circumnavigating |

1. Journal is to _____ as king is to monarch.

2. Branch is to tree as _____ is to river.

3. North America is to _____ as San Salvador is to island.

4. Scale is to weight as _____ is to direction.

5. Cartier's expedition is to river exploration as Magellan's expedition is to _____ Earth.

## USING INFORMATION

Essay Writing ■ There were three main reasons why Europeans began exploring in the 1400s. Write an essay that explains two of the reasons. Give one or two examples for each reason. Start your essay with a topic sentence.

## COMPREHENSION CHECK

Create an Information Chart ■ Create a chart about important explorers. Part of the chart has already been done for you.

| Explorer | For which Country Did He Explore? | What Did He Do? |
|---|---|---|
| Christopher Columbus | | |
| Pedro Cabral | | |
| Amerigo Vespucci | | Explored coast of South America; said it was a new continent |
| Ferdinand Magellan | | |
| John Cabot | England | |
| Robert de La Salle | | |

## CRITICAL THINKING

Drawing Conclusions ■ Read the paragraph below and the sentences that follow it. Put a check in front of the conclusions that can be drawn from the paragraph. You should find 3 conclusions.

Christopher Columbus explored the Caribbean islands of the Americas for Spain. Soon after Columbus's voyages, the Spanish began to settle in the Americas. Ferdinand Magellan tried to find a water route to Asia by sailing west. Three years later, only one of Magellan's five ships returned to Spain after it sailed all the way around the world. Other explorers of North America included John Cabot of England and Jacques Cartier of France.

_____ 1. Because of Columbus, Spain would claim colonies in the Americas.

_____ 2. Brazil would become Portugal's colony.

_____ 3. Magellan's trip was very dangerous.

_____ 4. Magellan's trip proved it was possible to sail around the world.

_____ 5. America was named for Amerigo Vespucci.

# Chapter 3
# EUROPEANS SETTLE AMERICA

◀ Gold coin from Spain

## People

Hernan Cortés •
Moctezuma • Francisco
Pizarro • Ponce de León •
Hernando de Soto •
Francisco de Coronado •
Father Junípero Serra •
Popé • Henry Hudson •
Bartolomé de Las Casas

## Places

New Spain • St. Augustine •
Santa Fe • West Africa •
New France • Great Lakes •
Hudson River • Manhattan

## New Vocabulary

conquistadors •
smallpox • settlement •
plantations • Creoles •
mestizos • mulattoes •
viceroys • missions •
revolt • civil wars •
peasants • Huguenots

### Focus on Main Ideas

1. What were the goals of the Spanish, French, and Dutch as they settled in the Americas?
2. What happened to Indians as more settlers came from Europe?
3. What did Europeans and Indians learn from each other?

**W**hy would people in Europe make the dangerous trip across the Atlantic Ocean to settle in the Americas? There would be hardships during the voyage and more hardships once they reached America. But there was also the chance to earn riches and build empires. As people from Europe settled in the Americas, life changed in many ways for them and for the Indians who lived there.

### The Conquistadors Build an Empire for Spain

Spain was the first nation to build an empire in America. The Spanish came to America to find gold, to teach the Catholic religion to the Indians, and to make Spain a more powerful nation. Brave but often cruel men called **conquistadors**, or conquerors, explored and conquered land in America for Spain.

Hernan Cortés was the conquistador who conquered Mexico for Spain. He landed in Mexico with about 500 soldiers in 1519. Then he led his army through thick jungles in order to reach the Aztec capital called Tenochtitlan. Cortés wanted to conquer the Aztec Empire and find gold for Spain.

Moctezuma, the Aztec emperor, thought Cortés might be one of the Aztec's gods. So Moctezuma did not try to capture Cortés.

*Hernan Cortés meets Moctezuma in this Aztec drawing. At first the Aztec gave Cortés presents, but later Cortés conquered them.*

Instead Moctezuma gave him gifts of gold. By 1521 Cortés and his army had conquered Mexico and destroyed the entire city of Tenochtitlan. Mexico City was built where the Aztec capital had been. The Spanish called their colony New Spain.

Why was Cortés and his small army able to defeat the huge Aztec Empire? The Spanish had horses, guns, and iron weapons to use against the Aztec. The Aztec did not have these powerful weapons. The most important reason was that Cortés and his army brought diseases from Europe like **smallpox** and measles and, which were new to the Indians. The diseases spread rapidly among the Indians and thousands died.

Francisco Pizarro, another conquistador, climbed the tall Andes Mountains with 180 soldiers. Then they attacked and conquered the Inca in 1530. The Spanish forced the Inca to work as slaves in gold and silver mines throughout the Andes. Ships carried the gold and silver back to Spain. Spain quickly became a very wealthy nation.

Ponce de León explored Florida in 1513 in order to find gold. He also searched for the Fountain of Youth. Stories were told that people who drank from this fountain would never grow old. Ponce de León did not find gold or the Fountain of Youth, but Florida became another Spanish colony. The Spanish built a **settlement** in Florida called St. Augustine. It is the oldest European settlement in the United States.

The Spanish heard stories about an amazing place called Cibola, the Seven Cities of Gold. They learned about Cibola from the African explorer, Estevanico. Conquistadors explored North America in order to find Cibola.

Hernando de Soto, another conquistador, started his search for Cibola in 1539. Hundreds of soldiers joined de Soto as they explored what is now the Southeast of

## Famous Spanish Conquistadors

| Conquistador<br>Dates of Exploration and Conquest | What Did the Conquistador Do? |
|---|---|
| Ponce de León<br>1513 | Explored Florida |
| Hernan Cortés<br>1519–1521 | Explored Mexico, conquered Aztec Empire |
| Francisco Pizarro<br>1530–1532 | Explored Peru, conquered Inca Empire |
| Hernando de Soto<br>1539–1542 | First European to see Mississippi River, explored Southeast of the United States |
| Francisco de Coronado<br>1540–1542 | Explored Southwest of the United States |

the United States. He began his search in Florida and then traveled to the Mississippi River. He became the first European to see the river that La Salle would later claim for France. De Soto never found gold, but the Southeast became a Spanish colony.

Francisco de Coronado, another conquistador, searched for Cibola from 1540 to 1542. With 300 soldiers he explored what is now the Southwest of the United States. He finally reached the place that was supposed to be Cibola. Instead of finding gold, Coronado found Indian villages that were made of mud and clay. Spain claimed a large colony in the Southwest and started a settlement called Santa Fe in 1610.

## Spanish Missions and Settlements

By 1542 Spain ruled a huge empire in America. Most of the Spanish settled in Mexico, Central America, and South America where gold and silver were found. Settlers also started huge sugar cane and tobacco **plantations**. Fewer settlers came to North America because gold had not been found there.

The Spanish needed workers for their mines and plantations. At first Indians who were forced into slavery did most of the work. But millions of Indians died from diseases and poor treatment. When the Spanish needed more workers, they

Hernando de Soto's search for Cibola began near Tampa Bay in Florida. After exploring the Southeast, he reached the Mississippi River. After exploring farther west, De Soto became sick and died. His men buried him in the Mississippi River.

*Father Junípero Serra started the first Spanish missions in California. The first mission was located near San Diego, California.*

brought slaves from West Africa to work in the colonies. In Chapter 4, you will read more about Africans in America.

As time passed there were different classes of people in the Spanish colonies. The highest class was the rich nobles who were born in Spain. They held the highest government jobs in the colonies. The next class was the **Creoles**, Spanish people who were born in America. Then came **mestizos**, people who had both Native American and Spanish parents. Indians, Africans, and **mulattoes** were considered the lowest class of people. Mulattoes had African and Spanish or African and Native American parents.

The king of Spain chose governors called **viceroys** to rule different parts of the empire. The viceroys carried out laws that Spain wrote for the colonies. These laws told settlers what crops to grow, where they could build towns, and how they should treat Indians. The viceroys were very strict rulers who gave the people very little freedom.

One of Spain's goals was to teach the Indians to be Catholics. The Spanish built **missions** where priests taught their religion. These missions were located throughout what is now the southeastern and southwestern parts of the United States. Forts were built near the missions to protect priests from attacks by Indians. Although Indians had followed their own religions for hundreds of years, the Spanish did not respect their beliefs. Instead they forced Indians to live at the missions, work for the priests, and become Catholics.

In 1769 Father Junípero Serra, a Spanish priest, started a chain of missions in California. Father Serra traveled on foot from one mission to another. He always made sure Indians were treated fairly. At the missions, priests taught Indians how to raise sheep, goats, and cattle in addition to teaching them the Catholic religion.

Many Indians were angry about being forced to live at the missions. Popé, a Pueblo Indian, led a **revolt** against the Spanish in 1680. During that revolt 8,000 Indians attacked the Spanish in New Mexico. They destroyed the missions and forced the Spanish to leave Santa Fe. These Indians began to practice their own religions again. The Spanish did not control Santa Fe again until 1696.

As Indians and Spanish settlers lived together, there was an important exchange of cultures. The Spanish learned about many types of foods that Europeans did not have. The Indians taught them how to grow these crops. The Spanish brought horses and other animals that were not known by the Indians. The use of horses spread throughout the Great Plains. This changed the way the Indians there hunted buffalo. Riding horses made it easier to hunt buffalo and to follow the herds as they moved across the plains.

The Spanish also gave new technology to the Indians, such as guns and metal tools. The chart on this page shows what these two groups of people learned from each other.

## The French Settle in America

The Spanish had settlements in America for about one hundred years before other European settlers came. The French had not been ready to start colonies in America because they were fighting in wars against other nations in Europe. There were also civil wars in France between Catholics and Protestants. But the king of France became jealous that Spain had built a huge empire in America. So he sent people to explore and settle North America. Like Spain, France's goals in America were to find wealth and to teach the Catholic religion to the Indians.

French explorers searched for gold but did not find any in North America. Instead they found a different way to become rich. At that time people in Europe enjoyed wearing hats made of beaver fur. By selling beaver furs in Europe, the French could become very rich. So the French learned

to trap beavers in the North American forests. They also traded with Indians for beaver furs.

The French Empire in North America was called New France. New France was a huge colony. It included all the land around the Mississippi River, the Ohio River, the Great Lakes, and the St. Lawrence River. The colony's rivers and lakes made it possible to travel by canoe from place to place. French settlements began when Samuel de Champlain started Quebec in 1608. As the French explored the St. Lawrence River and the Great Lakes, they built forts and trading posts.

The French king wanted settlers in New France, but few people came. Only French nobles were allowed to own land in America so French peasants, or poor people, did not want to be settlers. French law did not allow the Huguenots, or French Protestants, to settle in America. Only

## The Exchange of Cultures

| What Did the Indians Give to the Spanish? | What Did the Spanish Give to the Indians? |
| --- | --- |
| potatoes | horses |
| tomatoes | cows |
| corn | goats |
| turkeys | chickens |
| tobacco | sheep |
| squash | metal tools |
| cocoa | guns |
| peanuts | bananas |
| sweet potatoes | wheat |
| pumpkins | oranges |
| ponchos | printing presses |

French Catholics were allowed to be settlers. So the population of New France remained small, and the settlements were often far from each other.

The king of France chose governors to rule New France. Like the Spanish viceroys, the French governors were very strict. People had little freedom in New France.

Indians had better relationships with the French than with the Spanish. The French started missions to teach the Catholic religion to the Indians. But French priests did not force them to live and work at the missions. They did not force Indians to be their slaves. Instead the French often lived in the woods with Indians as they trapped beavers. The French learned to speak Indian languages and often married Indian women. From Indians the French learned to build canoes, trap beavers, and make snowshoes.

Although the French got along well with most Indians, they became enemies of the Iroquois nations. This problem began when Samuel de Champlain joined with other tribes against the Iroquois. In Chapter 7 you will learn how these problems with the Iroquois helped France lose its empire in America.

### The Dutch Settlement in America

Henry Hudson was an explorer who tried to find the Northwest Passage for a small country in Europe called the Netherlands. He explored the river in New York that is now called the Hudson River. The Dutch, the people of the Netherlands, claimed the right to rule the land around the Hudson River. The Dutch wanted to

*Henry Hudson explored for both the Dutch and the English. As a result of his trips, both countries claimed land in North America.*

become rich from the fur trade. They built trading posts along the Hudson River, and they traded with Indians for beaver furs.

The Dutch colony was called New Netherlands. The Dutch started a town on the island of Manhattan called New Amsterdam. In 1626 the Dutch bought Manhattan from the Indians for only $24 worth of knives, beads, and other goods. People from many countries settled in New Amsterdam. Before long 18 languages were spoken in the colony. But the population of New Netherlands grew slowly. In 1664 England won control of the colony and its name became New York.

As the Spanish, the French, and the Dutch settled in America, Indians lost their lands. Millions of Indians died from European diseases. While the Indian population grew smaller and smaller, the European population grew larger. Europeans would continue to win more control of America.

# BIOGRAPHY

## Bartolomé de Las Casas 1474–1566

Bartolomé de Las Casas became famous for speaking out against using Indians as slaves.

Las Casas was born in Spain. As a teenager he sailed with Columbus on his third voyage to America. He became a landowner in America, and the Indians who lived on his land were his slaves. Las Casas decided to become a priest. In 1510 he was the first person to become a Catholic priest in America.

As Las Casas read the Bible, he became convinced that slavery was wrong and evil. In 1514, at the age of 40, Las Casas decided that he would no longer own slaves. All of his Indian slaves were given their freedom.

Las Casas began to speak out against slavery and the terrible treatment of Indians by the Spanish. His speeches made other Spanish landowners angry. They believed they needed slaves to earn wealth in America.

Church leaders were also angry with Las Casas. They felt he was destroying their efforts to turn Indians into Christians. He believed Indians were the children of God and should be protected by the Catholic Church and by the Spanish government. Las Casas said the Indians, not the Spanish, were the true Christians in America.

Las Casas traveled to Spain and advised the Spanish king, Charles I, to end Indian slavery. King Charles did write laws to end slavery, but it was difficult to carry out those laws in the colonies. When Las Casas returned to America, he wrote books calling for better treatment of Indians. When he was almost 80 he wrote his most famous book, *In Defense of the Indians*.

Las Casas lived to be 92 years old, and he continued working to help Indians until the end of his life. King Charles gave Las Casas the title "Protector of the Indians."

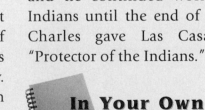

## In Your Own Words

Write a paragraph that explains how Las Casas's work and treatment of Indians differed from the treatment they received from other Spanish colonists.

# REVIEW AND APPLY

■ Hernan Cortés conquered Mexico, and Francisco Pizarro conquered the Inca Empire in Peru.

■ Francisco de Coronado explored the Southwest, and Hernando de Soto explored the Southeast of what would become the United States.

■ The Spanish forced Indians to live at the missions, learn the Catholic religion, and work as slaves.

■ The French built a large empire in North America called New France.

■ The Dutch ruled a colony called New Netherlands.

■ Indians gave Europeans foods such as potatoes, tomatoes, corn, and turkey. From the Spanish, Indians got horses, cows, sheep, wheat, and metal tools.

■ European diseases caused a decline in Indian population.

## VOCABULARY

**Matching** ■ Match the vocabulary word or phrase in Group B with the definition in Group A. You will not use all the words in Group B.

| Group A | Group B |
|---|---|
| _____ 1. This is the Spanish word for a person who conquered and explored an area. | A. revolt |
| | B. mestizos |
| _____ 2. This disease killed many Indians. | C. peasant |
| _____ 3. This was a large farm where crops such as tobacco and sugar were grown. | D. conquistador |
| _____ 4. This was a place where priests taught the Catholic religion to Indians. | E. mulattoes |
| | F. viceroy |
| _____ 5. This was a fight against the government. | G. plantation |
| _____ 6. This was a person who was poor. | H. smallpox |
| _____ 7. These people had Indian and Spanish parents. | I. mission |
| _____ 8. These people had African and Spanish or African and Indian parents. | |

## COMPREHENSION CHECK

Who Said It? ■ Read each statement in Group A. Then match the name of the person in Group B who might have said it. There is one name you will not use.

Group A

_____ 1. "I conquered the Aztec Empire in Mexico and destroyed the city of Tenochtitlan."

_____ 2. "I started missions in California where Indians were treated fairly."

_____ 3. "In 1608 I started the city of Quebec for France."

_____ 4. "I explored a river in New York for the Netherlands."

Group B

A. Francisco Pizarro

B. Henry Hudson

C. Samuel de Champlain

D. Father Junípero Serra

E. Hernan Cortés

## CRITICAL THINKING

Fact or Opinion ■ A fact is a true statement. An opinion is a statement that tells what a person thinks about something. Write F on the blank next to each statement that is a fact. Write O on the blank if the statement is an opinion. If the statement gives both a fact and an opinion, write FO on the blank. Then draw a line under the part of the sentence that is an opinion. The first one is done for you.

___FO___ 1. Moctezuma gave Cortés gifts, but he should have tried to capture Cortés.

_____ 2. The Spanish found gold and silver in the Inca Empire.

_____ 3. De Soto was a better explorer than Ponce de León was.

_____ 4. The Spanish king chose viceroys to rule regions of the Americas, but the viceroys were too strict.

_____ 5. The French should have allowed peasants to own land in America.

## USING INFORMATION

Writing an Opinion ■ Many people believe the Spanish were cruel to the Indians. Write a paragraph that tells your opinion about the Spanish treatment of Indians. Give two or three reasons for your opinion.

# SOCIAL STUDIES SKILLS

## Using a Compass Rose and a Map Key

A **compass rose** is used to show directions on a map. The four main, or **cardinal**, directions are north, south, east, and west. There are also four in-between directions. These **intermediate** directions are northeast, southeast, northwest, and southwest. Often cardinal directions are shortened to N, S, E, W, and intermediate directions to NE, SE, NW, SW.

Maps often use **symbols,** or little pictures, to show information on a map. A **map key** tells what the symbols mean. Sometimes the map key will show what different colors on a map mean.

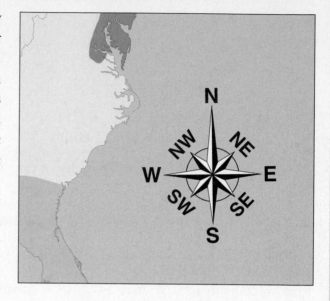

Look at the map key and the compass rose for the map below. Read each question and draw a circle around the correct answer.

1. New France is in the _____ .

   north        south        west

2. Florida is in the _____ .

   northeast      southeast      northwest

3. The Dutch settlements were in the _____ .

   northwest      southwest      northeast

4. There are _____ missions on the map.

   20      10      7

5. The French settlements included _____ .

   Florida      New France      Mexico

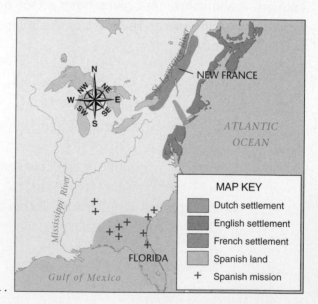

# Chapter 4

# AFRICANS IN AMERICA

◀ *Mansa Musa*

**People**

Muslims • Mansa Musa •
Africans • English •
Olaudah Equiano

**Places**

Ghana • North Africa •
Mali • Timbuktu •
Songhai • West Indies •
Barbados • Philadelphia

**New Vocabulary**

Muslims • converted •
Islam • rum •
Middle Passage •
indentured servants •
fare • contracts •
prejudice

**Focus on Main Ideas**

1. Which empires did Africans build in western Africa?
2. Why did Europeans start the slave trade?
3. What were the five steps in the slave trade?
4. Why was the Middle Passage so difficult for Africans?
5. What was slavery like in the Spanish and English colonies?

**M**illions of people came to America with chains on their legs and with fear in their hearts. These people were not like the Spanish and the French who wanted to become rich in America. Instead they were forced to come to America as slaves from their homes in Africa. The slave trade lasted almost 400 years. During that time, more than 10 million Africans were forced to come to the Americas as slaves.

## Empires of West Africa

Hundreds of years before Europeans were ready to explore Asia and America,

Africans had built empires in West Africa. They developed cultures that were rich with music, dancing, and storytelling. People in these empires created beautiful art work made from wood and metals. They also used iron to make strong tools and weapons.

The first empire in West Africa was the Empire of Ghana. It lasted from about A.D. 300 to 1200. The empire was rich in gold. So people in Ghana traded their gold for salt, cloth, and horses from North Africa.

**Muslims** conquered Ghana and built the Empire of Mali that lasted from 1200 to 1400. Mali had a powerful leader named Mansa Musa. He used his army to make

Mali larger, and he captured valuable salt mines that made Mali richer. Mansa Musa had **converted** to the religion of **Islam**, and he had become a Muslim. After that Islam became an important religion in West Africa. The large city of Timbuktu became Mali's center of trade and learning. In this city Africans built a large university where they studied history, law, and Islam. After Mansa Musa died, Mali began to lose its power.

The Empire of Mali was replaced by the Songhai Empire. This empire remained powerful until about 1600. Trade, farming, and Islam were important in Songhai. Timbuktu continued to be an important city. After 1600 the Songhai Empire became weaker and ended.

## The Beginning of the European Slave Trade

Slavery had existed in the West African empires and in other parts of Africa for hundreds of years. Slavery in Africa was different in many ways from the kind of slavery that would develop in America. A person captured in war could be made a slave. Africans who could not pay their debts also became slaves. African slaves were often treated as part of the slave owner's family. A slave could marry the master's son or daughter. Children of slaves were not considered slaves. Slaves could earn their freedom through hard work. After winning their freedom, slaves could get important jobs and even become

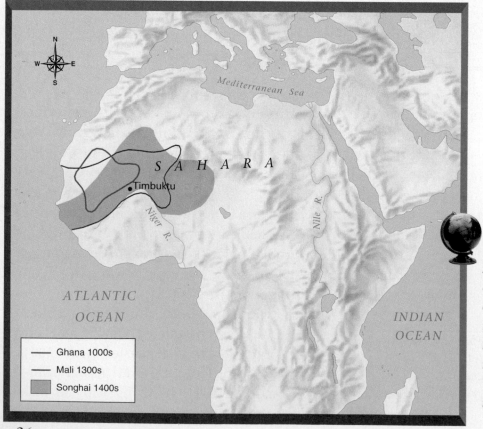

Mediterranean Sea

S A H A R A

•Timbuktu

Niger R.

Nile R.

ATLANTIC OCEAN

INDIAN OCEAN

— Ghana 1000s
— Mali 1300s
▨ Songhai 1400s

*Empires of West Africa* Mali, Ghana, and Songhai were three empires of West Africa. Each empire used its location as a center of trade for West Africa. Which river was a border for two of the empires?

leaders of their tribes. Much of this changed after the European slave trade began in Africa.

The European slave trade first began in 1442 when two Portuguese ships went to Africa and returned to Portugal with ten African slaves. These slaves became workers in Portugal. After the Portuguese began settling in Brazil, they began to bring African slaves to this colony. They were the first African slaves in the Americas.

The Spanish brought Africans to America, too. An African sailed with Christopher Columbus in 1492. Cortés, Pizarro, and other conquistadors brought African slaves with them. In 1501 the Spanish king passed a law that said Africans could be used as slaves in the Americas. Before long the Spanish were bringing 10,000 African slaves a year to their colonies. By the year 1600, there were almost 1 million African slaves in Spain's colonies.

---

### Steps in the Slave Trade

The slave trade was carried out by traders from Spain, Portugal, the Netherlands, France, and England. The two goals of the slave traders were to earn large profits by selling African slaves and to provide the colonies with the workers they needed.

There were five steps in the slave trade. First, Africans captured people from different tribes to be sold as slaves. Slave traders depended on these Africans to capture people for them. Slave traders paid for the slaves with European guns, bullets, **rum**, and other products. Second, the captured Africans were forced to march long

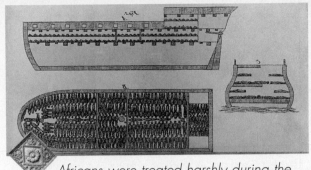

*Africans were treated harshly during the Middle Passage. This diagram was drawn to show ship owners how to fit in the most slaves.*

distances to the African coast. They marched with iron collars around their necks and with chains around their arms or legs. Many Africans died while they were forced to march.

Third, when they reached the coast of Africa, the captured Africans were held in prisons. They stayed there until they were forced to board ships that would take them on the long trip to America. The fourth step was the long trip from Africa to America, which was called the **Middle Passage**. Slaves were forced to remain in chains in the dark, hot, crowded space below deck.

The Middle Passage often took more than three months. Many slaves died on board the ships during the Middle Passage. They became sick and weak because they were given only small amounts of food and water. On the ships slaves were packed very close together. Diseases spread quickly and many slaves died. Only the strongest people were able to survive the Middle Passage.

The last step in the slave trade took place in the Americas. After slave ships landed at the West Indies, the Africans were sold as slaves. Other Africans were sold in Spanish and English colonies in North and South America.

## Slavery in Spanish America

The Spanish needed large numbers of workers for their plantations. At first the Spanish forced Indians to be slaves. But as millions of Indians died from disease, other workers were needed. So the Spanish began using African slaves as plantation workers. These slaves worked on tobacco and sugar cane plantations in Mexico, on islands in the Caribbean Sea, and in Central and South America.

Many slaves in the Spanish colonies tried to run away from their masters, so the Spanish hired Indians to hunt for them. These Indians often helped the Africans to escape. About one tenth of all Africans in Spain's colonies were able to escape because they were helped by Indians.

The Catholic Church tried to protect African slaves in several ways. African men and women were allowed to get married in churches. Families remained together after children were born. Spanish slave owners were not allowed to take children away from their mothers and sell them to different owners.

## Africans in the English Colonies

Why did the English bring slaves to America? In Chapter 5 you will read about

*European slave traders bought African slaves from other Africans. Often these slaves were captured and brought to the coast in chains connected to iron collars around their necks. The Europeans then kept the slaves in prisons until a ship arrived to take them on the Middle Passage to the Americas.*

the growth of plantations in some of the English colonies. At first the English tried using **indentured servants** as their plantation workers. Indentured servants were people who wanted to come to America but did not have enough money to pay the **fare**. So they signed **contracts** agreeing to work three to seven years for the people who paid their fares. However, not enough people came to America as indentured servants to supply the plantations with all the workers that they needed.

The first Africans were brought to the English colonies in 1619 as indentured servants. After their working period ended, these Africans were free to leave their masters and live where they pleased. But plantation owners needed many workers, and they began to use African slaves. As more plantations were started, more slaves were needed.

By the 1700s the English had taken control of most of the slave trade. Each year the English brought more slaves to America on the Middle Passage. Because of the slave trade, the population in the English colonies of the West Indies became about 90 percent African. In some southern colonies of what is now the United States, more than half the people were Africans.

By the 1700s most Africans in the English colonies were slaves. As slaves they could never be free and their children would also be slaves. Slave owners could take children away from their mothers and sell them to other plantation owners. Slaves were thought of as property; they did not have the same rights as other people. Free African Americans faced **prejudice** in the English colonies. In most colonies

*Slaves brought to the colonies were sold in markets. Merchants and buyers only saw these Africans as property.*

they could not get good jobs, vote, or hold government jobs.

The slave trade continued until the 1800s, and it affected Africa and America. The slave trade provided the colonies with the workers they needed, but it brought suffering to millions of Africans. In Africa it caused families to be torn apart as family members were captured and sent to America. But the slave trade also brought some of West Africa's culture to America. African slaves tried to hold on to their traditions, music, dances, and folk tales. That African culture slowly became part of America's culture.

## Olaudah Equiano 1745–1801(?)

Olaudah Equiano was a slave who became a free man and wrote about his life as a slave. Equiano was born in western Africa. He was kidnapped when he was 11 years old, and he was forced to go on a long march to the coast of Africa.

When Equiano finally arrived at Africa's coast, he saw both the ocean and white people for the first time. He was frightened of both the ocean and the white slave traders who were in charge of his group. Since Equiano only knew his own African language, he was unable to speak to the slave traders. He was forced to board a Dutch slave ship to make the long journey to America. He was so frightened and unhappy that he refused to eat. But food was forced down his throat.

The slave ship went to Barbados in the West Indies. There Equiano was bought by his first master. During his time as a slave, Equiano was bought and sold three times. While he was a slave, his name was changed to Gustavus Vessa. One of his owners allowed him to learn to read and write English. Very few slaves were ever taught to read and write.

Equiano was sold for the last time to a merchant in Philadelphia. While working for the merchant, Equiano earned enough money to buy his own freedom. Equiano settled in England where there was no slavery. Equiano's autobiography was published in 1789. It showed the evils of slavery. It convinced many readers that slavery should end. In his book Equiano described his experiences:

"I had a very unhappy…journey, being in continual fear that the people I was with would murder me. I was now more than a thousand miles from home.… A Dutch ship came into the harbor and they carried me on board. I was exceedingly sea-sick at first.… My master's ship was bound for Barbadoes.… When we came there, I was sold for fifty dollars.…"

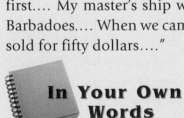

## In Your Own Words

Write a paragraph describing Olaudah Equiano's experiences as a slave and his work to end slavery.

# REVIEW AND APPLY

■ Between A.D. 300 and 1600, Africans built great empires in West Africa.

■ The slave trade involved capturing people in Africa, bringing them to the Americas in slave ships, and selling them as slaves for a large profit.

■ The slave trade lasted almost 400 years, during which time about 10 million Africans were brought to America.

■ The trip to America on slave ships was called the Middle Passage. Many Africans died during this long journey.

■ England, Spain, Portugal, France, and the Netherlands took part in the slave trade.

■ The English and the Spanish used African slaves for plantation work in their colonies.

## VOCABULARY

Find the Meaning ■ **Write the word or phrase that best completes each sentence.**

1. People who believe in the religion of Islam are _____ .
   **Muslims**          **Christians**          **Jews**

2. The money paid to ride in a ship, bus, or plane is the _____ .
   **colony**          **fare**          **mound**

3. The trip to bring slaves from Africa to America was the _____ .
   **First Passage**    **Northwest Passage**  **Middle Passage**

4. Unfair beliefs about another group of people are called _____ .
   **culture**          **contracts**          **prejudice**

5. A person who agreed to work for someone else for a number of years in order to come to America was a(n) _____ .
   **slave**          **indentured servant**          **viceroy**

## COMPREHENSION CHECK

Write the Answer ■ **Write one or more sentences to answer each question.**

1. About how many Africans were brought to America as slaves? _____

   _____

2. How did Mansa Musa help the Empire of Mali? _____

   _____

3. How was African slavery different from European slavery? _____

_____

4. Why did many Africans die during the Middle Passage? _____

_____

5. Why did the English settlers want slaves instead of indentured servants? _____

_____

## CRITICAL THINKING

**Cause and Effect** ■ **A cause is something that makes something else happen. What happens is called the effect.**

*Example*  **Cause:**  **Effect:**

The tornado stuck the town.  Many homes were destroyed.

**Choose a cause or an effect in Group B to complete each sentence in Group A. Write the letter of the correct answer on the blank. Group B has one more answer than you need.**

| Group A | Group B |
|---|---|
| _____ 1. Mali's ruler, Mansa Musa, became a Muslim, so _____ . | A. The population of the West Indies became 90 percent African |
| _____ 2. _____, so they put iron collars and chains on the slaves. | B. Islam became an important religion in West Africa |
| _____ 3. _____, so they brought African slaves to America. | C. The first African Americans in the English colonies were indentured servants |
| _____ 4. _____, so they were free people when their working period ended. | D. African chiefs did not want their captured slaves to escape as they marched to the coast |
| | E. Europeans needed many workers for their colonies in the Americas |

## USING INFORMATION

**Journal Writing** ■ **Africans built three strong empires in West Africa before 1600. Write a paragraph in your journal that tells about one of these early African empires.**

# Chapter 5

# THE ENGLISH SETTLE IN NORTH AMERICA

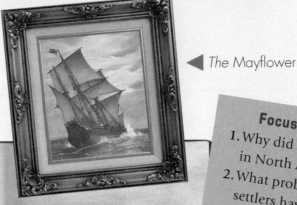

◀ *The Mayflower*

**People**

Queen Elizabeth I • Francis
Drake • King Henry VIII •
John Smith • Pilgrims •
Puritans • Roger Williams •
Anne Hutchinson • William
Penn • James Oglethorpe

**Places**

Roanoke • Jamestown •
Virginia • James River •
Massachusetts • Providence •
Pennsylvania

**New Vocabulary**

religious freedom •
established church • joint
stock company • charter •
representatives •
representative
government • royal
colony •proprietary
colony • proprietor • self-
governing colony • debtors

**Focus on Main Ideas**

1. Why did the English settle
   in North America?
2. What problems did the
   settlers have?
3. How did the New
   England Colonies, the
   Middle Colonies, and
   the Southern Colonies
   get started?

In 1607 England started its first permanent settlement in North America. Slowly more and more English people settled in North America. By the mid-1700s there were 13 English colonies along the Atlantic Ocean.

### England Defeats the Spanish Armada

Spain controlled the seas near North and South America. The English had to weaken Spain's power in the Atlantic Ocean before they could start colonies in North America. Queen Elizabeth I was the ruler who weakened Spain's power.

She encouraged English sea captains to capture Spanish ships near America and steal their cargo of gold, silver, and other products. These English captains were called sea dogs.

The most famous sea dog was Francis Drake. In 1578 Drake captured Spanish ships near South America and stole their gold and silver. Then he sailed through the Strait of Magellan into the Pacific Ocean and back to England. His crew was the second to sail around the world. Drake brought a huge amount of gold to England. Francis Drake became England's hero.

King Philip II of Spain was furious that "sea dogs" were attacking his ships.

*Queen Elizabeth ruled England from 1558 to 1603. During this time England defeated the Spanish and built a stronger nation with colonies in America.*

He decided to attack England with a huge fleet called the Spanish Armada. In 1588, 130 Spanish ships sailed into the waters close to England. England's smaller navy defeated the Spanish Armada. After the defeat more than half of the Spanish ships were destroyed in a storm. As a result Spain no longer controlled the Atlantic Ocean. England could send ships safely to America to start colonies.

## Why Did the English Settle in America?

English settlers came to America for four reasons. First, many came for **religious freedom**. Religious freedom was not allowed in England because all people had to belong to the Church of England. That church began when Queen Elizabeth's father, King Henry VIII, broke away from the Catholic Church and started the Church of England, a Protestant church. Queen Elizabeth made the Church of England the **established church**. At that time this meant that all people in England had to belong to the Church of England and pay taxes to support it. Some people did not want to belong to the Church of England. They decided to follow their own religions in America.

Second, English settlers wanted to become rich. They had heard how the Spanish had become rich from gold and how the French had become rich from the fur trade. The English also hoped to find wealth in America.

Third, people came to America to own land. In England much of the land was used to raise sheep, so it was difficult for people to buy land. Fathers left all their land to their oldest sons when they died. It was almost impossible for other family members to own land. Finally people came to the English colonies to get away from wars in Europe.

## The First English Settlements

England's goal was to control all the land along the Atlantic Ocean from French Canada to Spanish Florida. It would take more than one hundred years to meet this goal.

Roanoke was the first English settlement in North America. The settlement was started in 1587 on an island near present-day North Carolina. John White, the leader at

Roanoke, went back to England for supplies and returned to Roanoke after three years. When he returned all of the settlers were gone. The letters *CRO* had been carved on a tree. To this day no one knows what really happened to the Roanoke settlers.

A lot of money was needed to start a settlement in America. Few people had enough money to pay for the ships and the supplies that were needed. So people were encouraged to buy shares of stock in a **joint stock company**. If the company earned profits from a settlement, the money was shared by all the people who owned stock.

In 1607 Jamestown, Virginia, became the first permanent English settlement in North America. The money for Jamestown came from a joint stock company called the London Company. King James I gave the London Company a **charter**, or a permission paper, to start a colony.

The settlement began in Virginia on the James River with 144 men. They came to America to find gold, but they never found it. The settlers almost starved because they did not want to work or to grow crops. They stayed alive because of food they received from nearby Indians. Their leader, Captain John Smith, forced the men to grow crops. Life at Jamestown was very hard and most of the settlers died. When the settlers learned to grow tobacco in 1612, life began to improve. They sold tobacco to England for a large profit. Each year they grew larger crops of tobacco.

The year 1619 was important in Jamestown for three reasons. In that year the first women from England came to live in the settlement. Also in 1619 Africans were brought to the English colony to work

*The first Africans were brought to the English settlement in Jamestown in 1619. They were considered indentured servants, not slaves, so they were freed after several years.*

as indentured servants. Finally the Virginia House of Burgesses was started. This was the group of **representatives** who wrote laws for the colony. These representatives were chosen by the group of men who were allowed to vote. This was the beginning of **representative government** in the English colonies.

In 1620 a group of people called Pilgrims started a colony in Massachusetts. The Pilgrims came to America for religious freedom. The 102 Pilgrims traveled aboard a small ship called the *Mayflower*. They landed at Cape Cod, Massachusetts. Before leaving their ship, the men signed an agreement called the Mayflower Compact. In this agreement the Pilgrims promised to work together to make laws that would be fair to all. This was the first plan in America for a government in which people would govern themselves.

The Pilgrims spent a month searching for a good place to settle. They chose Plymouth Harbor and started a town there. During the first winter, many Pilgrims died from hunger and disease. Others survived because Indians helped them. Indians taught them how to fish and hunt and grow crops such as corn and squash. The following year the Pilgrims had enough food for the winter. They invited the Indians to join them at a thanksgiving celebration. They thanked God for their good harvest. The American holiday of Thanksgiving began with the first Pilgrim celebration of thanksgiving in 1621.

## The Growth of the English Colonies

Before long more colonies were started. As more settlers came to America, they forced Indians to leave their lands. The settlers and the Indians fought wars against each other over control of land. The Indian population grew smaller as Indians died from wars and European diseases. Some Indian nations disappeared completely.

There were three types of colonies. In a **royal colony** the king controlled the colony and chose the governor who ruled the colony. Each **proprietary colony** had one person or several people who owned the colony. The king gave a **proprietor** a charter to start a colony. The proprietor

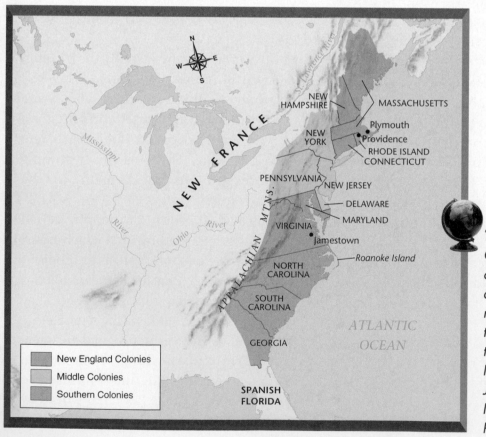

**Thirteen English Colonies** The 13 English colonies developed differently in 3 regions—New England, the Middle Colonies, and the Southern Colonies. In which region is Jamestown located? In which region is Plymouth located?

*The Thanksgiving holiday celebrated in November is a reminder of the Pilgrims' first Thanksgiving. The Pilgrims gave thanks to God and celebrated with the Indians who helped them through their difficult first year.*

chose the governor and controlled the colony. The third type was a **self-governing colony**. In these colonies people voted for their own governor and voted for representatives to make laws for the colony. There were three groups of colonies: The New England Colonies, the Middle Colonies, and the Southern Colonies. Find the names and locations of the 13 colonies on the map on page 46 and the chart on p. 48.

## The New England Colonies

In 1630 about 1,000 people called Puritans started the Massachusetts Bay Colony. They came to America because they were unhappy with the Church of England.

They believed churches should look plainer and church leaders should encourage more Bible study. The Puritans did not allow people to follow other religions in their colony. Only church members were allowed to vote. Puritan leaders controlled the colony's government.

Roger Williams lived in the Massachusetts Bay Colony, but he disagreed with many Puritan ideas. Williams believed all people should have freedom of religion. He said that religion and government should be completely separate from each other. Williams's ideas angered the Puritans, and they forced him to leave Massachusetts.

Williams fled to what is now Rhode Island. He met Indians who helped him.

## The Thirteen English Colonies

| | Name of Colony | Date Started | First Leaders | Reason Started |
|---|---|---|---|---|
| **New England Colonies** | Massachusetts | 1620 (Plymouth), 1630 (Massachusetts Bay Colony) | William Bradford, John Winthrop | for religious freedom |
| | New Hampshire | 1623 | Ferdinando Gorges, John Mason | to earn money from trade and fishing |
| | Rhode Island | 1636 | Roger Williams | for religious freedom |
| | Connecticut | 1636 | Thomas Hooker | for religious freedom and trade |
| **Middle Colonies** | New York | 1624 (Dutch colony), 1664 (English colony) | Peter Minuit (of the Netherlands) | to earn money from trade |
| | New Jersey | 1664 | John Berkeley, George Carteret | to earn money by selling land |
| | Delaware | 1638 | settlers from Sweden | to earn money from trade |
| | Pennsylvania | 1682 | William Penn | for religious freedom for Quakers |
| **Southern Colonies** | Virginia | 1607 | John Smith, John Rolfe | to find gold |
| | Maryland | 1632 | George Calvert (Lord Baltimore) | for religious freedom for Catholics |
| | North Carolina | 1663 | Anthony Cooper, John Colleton, William Berkeley | to earn money from trade and selling land |
| | South Carolina | 1663 | Anthony Cooper, John Colleton, William Berkeley | to earn money from trade and selling land |
| | Georgia | 1732 | James Oglethorpe | new life for debtors |

He bought land from them, and he started the town of Providence. All men were allowed to vote, and Providence became the first American city where all people had religious freedom. In 1644 Rhode Island became a self-governing colony.

Anne Hutchinson was another person who angered the Puritans by talking about different religious ideas. She was forced to leave Massachusetts. She went to Rhode Island and started a new settlement there. Other people moved away from Massachusetts and settled what would become the colonies of New Hampshire and Connecticut.

### The Middle Colonies

The Dutch colony of New Netherlands was south of the New England Colonies.

The English wanted control of the Dutch colony. In 1664 England sent warships to fight for New Netherlands. The Dutch surrendered to the English without fighting. New Netherlands was renamed New York. This area included land which would later become parts of New Jersey, Connecticut, Delaware, and Pennsylvania.

The Pennsylvania colony was started in 1682 as a place where Quakers could have freedom of religion. The Quakers, another group of Protestants, refused to pray in the Church of England. The king gave William Penn, a wealthy Quaker leader, land in America where he could start a colony. Penn paid the Indians for all the land that he took from them. Penn allowed all people to have religious freedom in the colony, so people from many parts of Europe came to Pennsylvania.

## The Southern Colonies

The Virginia colony grew from the original settlement at Jamestown. It was the largest of the Southern Colonies. Maryland was the second colony started in the South. It was started in 1632 by George Calvert, who was also called Lord Baltimore. He started the colony as a place where Catholics would have religious freedom. In 1649 a law called the Toleration Act was passed in Maryland. This law allowed all Christians to have religious freedom in Maryland. Jews were not allowed in the colony.

North Carolina and South Carolina started as a single proprietary colony called Carolana. Later the colony became two royal colonies. In 1732 James Oglethorpe started Georgia, the last of the 13 colonies. Georgia began as a colony for **debtors**. People in England who did not have enough money to pay their debts were sent to jail. Georgia was a place to go to for debtors who had been released from prison. The Georgia colony was north of Spanish Florida. English soldiers stayed in Georgia to stop attacks on the colonies from Spanish Florida.

By 1732 England controlled 13 colonies along the Atlantic Ocean. Each year more and more people from Europe settled in the English colonies.

*This village near Jamestown, Virginia, shows people today what life was like for the Powhatan Indians who lived in the area when the English settlers arrived. There were about 8,500 Indians living in more than 150 villages in the area.*

**49**

# BIOGRAPHY

## William Penn 1644–1718

William Penn started the colony of Pennsylvania in America. As a young man, William Penn began to study at Oxford University. Penn's life at Oxford changed when he became a Quaker. The Quakers believed that all people, both men and women, were equal. They believed that slavery was wrong and that all wars were wrong. They would not bow to another person because they bowed only to God. Quakers said it was important to respect all religions. They refused to pay taxes to the Church of England. Most people in England hated the Quakers because of their ideas. After Penn became a Quaker, he was forced to leave Oxford. The English government passed a law called the Quaker Act. Under this law not more than five Quakers could pray together at one time. William Penn was arrested for praying with a large group of Quakers. He spent many months in jail.

King Charles II had once borrowed a lot of money from William Penn's father. The king had not repaid the money while Penn's father was alive. So after his father died, Penn asked the king to repay the loan. Instead of money Penn asked for land in America. King Charles agreed and gave Penn a charter for Pennsylvania. It was a proprietary colony because William Penn owned it.

In 1682 William Penn went to start the new colony. Penn bought land from Indians and made peace treaties with them. The laws in the new colony gave religious freedom to all people who believed in God. Thousands of people from England, Germany, and the Netherlands moved to Pennsylvania.

William Penn planned the colony's capital, Philadelphia. By the time William Penn died, thousands of people of different religions were living together in peace in Pennsylvania.

## In Your Own Words

Write a paragraph in the journal section of your social studies notebook that tells if you think William Penn should be admired and why.

# REVIEW AND APPLY

- English settlers came to America for religious freedom, to gain wealth, to own land, and to get away from wars in Europe.

- The first permanent English settlement in North America was Jamestown. In 1620 the Pilgrims started a colony in Massachusetts.

- There were three types of English colonies—royal colonies, proprietary colonies, and self-governing colonies.

- The Puritans started the Massachusetts Bay Colony in 1630. Rhode Island, New Hampshire, and Connecticut were started by settlers who left Massachusetts.

- The English captured New Netherlands in 1664 and renamed it New York. Pennsylvania was started as a place where Quakers could have religious freedom.

## VOCABULARY

Writing with Vocabulary Words ■ Use seven or more vocabulary terms below to write a paragraph that tells how the English settled in North America. Write your paragraph in the vocabulary section of your social studies notebook.

| | | |
|---|---|---|
| religious freedom | royal colony | charter |
| joint stock company | established church | representative government |
| debtors | representatives | proprietary colony |

## CRITICAL THINKING

Sequencing ■ Write the numbers 1, 2, 3, 4, 5, and 6 next to these sentences to show the correct order.

_____ The Puritans start the Massachusetts Bay Colony.

_____ William Penn starts the colony of Pennsylvania so that Quakers could have religious freedom.

_____ The first Africans are brought to Jamestown, Virginia, in 1619 as indentured servants.

_____ The English Navy defeats the Spanish Armada.

_____ James Oglethorpe starts the Georgia colony.

_____ In 1607, Jamestown, Virginia, becomes the first permanent English settlement in America.

## COMPREHENSION CHECK

**Reviewing Important Facts** ■ Match each sentence in Group A with the word or phrase from Group B that the sentence explains. You will not use all the words in Group B.

### Group A

_____ 1. Since few people had enough money to start a colony, many colonies were started by this type of business.

_____ 2. This crop brought profit to the English settlement in Jamestown, Virginia.

_____ 3. This was the first representative government in the colonies.

_____ 4. Puritans, Pilgrims, and Roger Williams started colonies in this region.

_____ 5. This was the first plan for self-government in the colonies.

_____ 6. These people lost their land and died from European diseases as the English settled in America.

_____ 7. This colony was once part of New Netherlands.

_____ 8. Lord Baltimore started this colony to give religious freedom to Catholics.

### Group B

A. New York

B. Indians

C. Mayflower Compact

D. joint stock company

E. Virginia House of Burgesses

F. Maryland

G. Georgia

H. New England

I. tobacco

## USING INFORMATION

**Writing an Essay** ■ The English started colonies in America for many different reasons. Choose 2 of the 13 colonies. Explain how and why they were started. Begin the essay with a topic sentence. End your essay with a sentence that summarizes the main idea.

# AMERICAN  GEOGRAPHY

## Movement: People, Products, and Ideas

Movement shows us how people, ideas, and products move from place to place. In Unit 1 you learned how people from Africa, Asia, and Europe moved to the Americas. These people brought ideas, animals, resources, goods, and religions from one part of the world to another. Look at the map below. Each numbered arrow shows a large movement of people from one continent or place to another.

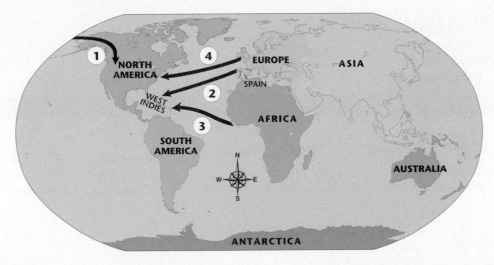

**A.** Write a sentence that explains the movement of people that is represented by each of the four numbered arrows on the map.

1. _____

2. _____

3. _____

4. _____

**B.** Draw arrows on the map above to represent each of the movements of people described below.

1. Movement of Indians from Alaska across North America and South America.

2. Movement of gold from America to Spain.

3. Movement of different religions from Europe to America.

4. The exchange of goods between the Spanish and the Indians.

# Unit 1 Review

Study the time line on this page. You may want to read parts of Unit 1 again. Then use the words or the dates in the box to finish the paragraphs. Write the words or the dates you choose on the correct blanks. The box has one possible answer that you will not use.

**1492**
Christopher Columbus sails west from Spain in search of Asia.

**1539**
Hernando de Soto explores the Southeast.

**1610**
Santa Fe is started as a Spanish mission.

**1682**
La Salle claims Louisiana for France.

1400      1500      1600

**1487**
Dias sails around the southern tip of Africa.

**1513**
Ponce de Léon searches for the Fountain of Youth in Florida.

**1608**
Champlain Starts Quebec in Canada.

**1632**
George Calvert starts Maryland.

| | | |
|---|---|---|
| Iroquois | 1539 | Mexico |
| Aztec | North America | plantations |
| artifacts | Columbus | Middle Passage |
| Asia | astrolabe | religious |
| 1682 | debtors | 1492 |

Thousands of years ago, during the Ice Age, a land bridge connected Asia and Alaska. More than 20,000 years ago, people in Asia crossed the land bridge and walked to _____. Archaeologists have learned about these early Americans by studying _____. In the eastern forest, the _____ formed the Confederation of Five Nations that kept peace for a long time. In Mexico, the _____ built their capital,

54

Tenochtitlan, on an island in a lake. Native Americans did not use the wheel before Europeans came to America. Native Americans and Europeans first met after explorers began to look for a shorter route to _____ . The compass and the _____ made it possible for ships to sail far out in the ocean. The famous explorer, Christopher _____ , tried to reach Asia by sailing west, but instead he reached America. After the explorations of La Salle in _____ , France claimed all the land around the Mississippi River and called it Louisiana.

The Spanish settled in America to find gold and to teach the Catholic religion to Native Americans. Hernan Cortés conquered the Aztec Empire in _____ . Hernando de Soto explored for gold in the Southeast in _____ and reached the Mississippi River. Europeans needed workers for their _____ so they brought Africans to work as slaves. Many Africans did not survive the _____ to America. English settlers came to America for _____ freedom and to get land. In 1732 James Oglethorpe started Georgia as a colony for _____ .

## Looking Ahead to Unit 2

For more than two centuries, Europeans had claimed, explored, conquered, and colonized the Americas. During the 1700s the 13 English colonies grew. For many years, American colonists had been proud to be ruled by England. Each year more and more people came to live in the 13 colonies. Most people enjoyed more freedom in the colonies than they had in Europe. Life would change in the colonies after George III became the new king of England. The colonists grew angry about the changes brought by the new king. As you read Unit 2, you will learn how the 13 English colonies were able to become the new United States of America.

# Unit 2

# FROM COLONIES TO A NATION

**A**mericans in the 13 English colonies were so angry with their king in 1775 that they decided to fight for more freedom. As they prepared to battle, they called themselves Minutemen because they needed only a minute to be ready to fight. They did not have uniforms or enough weapons, but they had a cause that they were willing to die for. By 1781, Americans would defeat the powerful British Army.

As you read Unit 2, you will learn how some Americans created a new, independent nation with a new type of government.

## THINK ABOUT IT

- The first public school laws in the colonies were passed by the Puritans. Why did the Puritans need public schools?

- Americans began to fight in the American Revolution in 1775. Why did they wait until July 4, 1776, to say they were free?

- George Washington led the American Army during the American Revolution. He lost more battles than he won. Why did Americans call Washington a great hero?

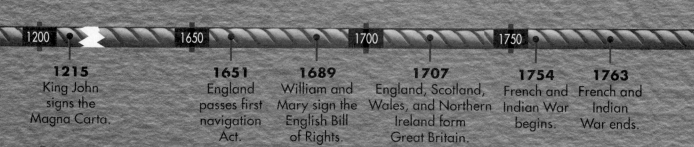

**1200**  **1650**  **1700**  **1750**

**1215**
King John signs the Magna Carta.

**1651**
England passes first navigation Act.

**1689**
William and Mary sign the English Bill of Rights.

**1707**
England, Scotland, Wales, and Northern Ireland form Great Britain.

**1754**
French and Indian War begins.

**1763**
French and Indian War ends.

▲ *Modern patriots play the role of Minutemen.*

**1770**
Five colonists
are killed in
the Boston
Massacre.

**1773**
Sons of Liberty have
the Boston Tea Party.

**1774**
First
Continental
Congress
meets in
Philadelphia.

The American Revolution
begins at Lexington
and Concord.
**1775**

**1775**
Second Continental
Congress meets in
Philadelphia.

**1776**
The Declaration
of Independence
is signed.

**1781**
The British Army
surrenders
at Yorktown.

**1783**
United States
and Great
Britain sign
Treaty of Paris.

**1787**
The
Constitution
is written.

**1788**
The Constitution
is ratified.

**1791**
The Bill
of Rights
is ratified.

1775

1800

57

# LIFE IN THE THIRTEEN COLONIES

◀ Hornbooks were used to teach reading.

### People

Congregationalists •

Eliza Lucas Pinckney •

Jonathan Edwards •

Benjamin Franklin

### Places

New York City • Sweden •

Scotland • Harvard

College • Boston

### New Vocabulary

democracy • cash crops •

manufacturing • planter •

Episcopal Church • indigo •

Great Awakening •

grammar schools • dame

schools • apprentice •

journeyman •

mercantilism • favorable

balance of trade •

Navigation Acts • triangular

trade routes

### Focus on Main Ideas

1. What were some of the differences between New England, the Middle Colonies, and the Southern Colonies?
2. What were the responsibilities of women in the colonies?
3. How did public schools and colleges develop in the colonies?

There were three groups of colonies: the New England Colonies, the Middle Colonies, and the Southern Colonies. The climate, the geography, and the way of life differed in each of these regions.

### Life in the Three Groups of Colonies

The New England Colonies had long, cold winters. The rocky soil made it difficult to grow food. Settlers used the trees from the region's forests for shipbuilding. People in New England used the Atlantic Ocean for fishing, for hunting whales, and for trading.

In New England religion was the center of life. Most of the people were Puritans whose families came from England. Puritans were also called Congregationalists in America. The Puritans believed that God rewarded people who worked hard. In most towns they built meeting houses where they held Sunday services and town meetings. Some of the problems that were discussed at town meetings included how much should the new school master be paid and which roads needed to be repaired. All men who were church members and property owners could speak and vote at these meetings. Town meetings helped build **democracy** in America because they gave a large group of people a voice in their government.

The region to the south of New England, the Middle Colonies, had a milder climate and better soil. The Middle Colonies had settlers who came from many nations in Europe, including Germany, Sweden, France, and Scotland. Most people in the Middle Colonies earned their living through farming. These colonies were called the "breadbasket colonies" because they grew large amounts of wheat and grains as **cash crops**. Farmers used the area's three main rivers to ship their products to Philadelphia and New York City. These busy port cities became the largest cities of the Middle Colonies. Besides trade, **manufacturing** was important, too.

In the Southern Colonies, the climate was warmer than in the other two regions. The warm climate made it possible to grow crops throughout the year. Also there was a larger area of flat land with good soil for farming. In these colonies people grew tobacco and rice on large plantations. These cash crops were sold to other colonies and to England.

Almost everything a **planter**, or plantation owner, and his family needed was made on the plantation. The planter lived in a large house with his family. The owner's wife ran the house and often managed the slaves that worked in the house.

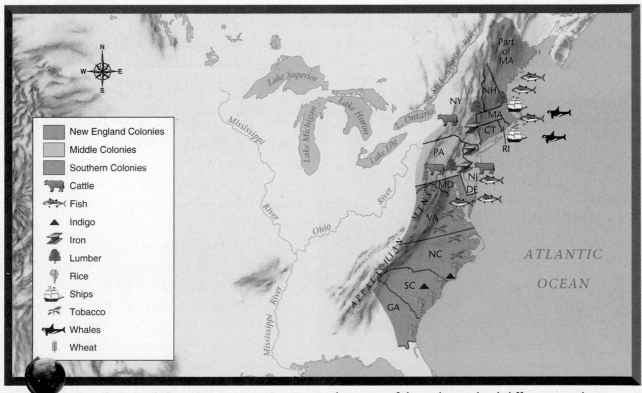

**Products of the Thirteen Colonies** *Each region of the colonies had different products. Use the map key to identify the products. Which region produced cattle?*

Planters depended on African slaves to do most of the field work. Laws called "slave codes" were passed to control the slaves. According to these laws, slaves were the property of their owners and had no rights. Teaching slaves to read and write was against the law. Although there were some African slaves in the Middle Colonies and in New England, most slaves were in the Southern Colonies. By 1775 slaves were one fifth of the population in the 13 colonies.

Unlike the Middle Colonies, most people in the Southern Colonies came from England. And unlike New England, most people belonged to the Church of England, which was called the **Episcopal Church** in America. It was also called the Anglican Church. Laws in Virginia required all people to pay taxes to the Episcopal Church.

Most southerners owned small farms. But the wealthy planters controlled

*Throughout the colonies, skilled workers made products that people needed. This worker makes leather goods the same way they were made back in the time of the colonies.*

businesses, slaves, and governments in the Southern Colonies.

## Family Life, Role of Women, and Social Classes

The family was the most important social group in the colonies. The father was the head of the house, and he expected his family to obey him. Women had few rights in the 13 colonies. A woman could not vote or work in a colonial government. In order to own land, start a business, or sign a contract, a woman had to have permission from her husband or from her father.

All women were expected to do many kinds of work for their families, but wealthy women had servants to help them. Women had to feed their families, so they grew vegetable gardens that provided some of their food. Women cooked meals in large pots over a fire in a fireplace. Pies filled with meat and vegetables were very popular.

Women took care of all children who lived in their homes. Women made soap, candles, and clothing by hand. By working quickly, a woman might make two hundred candles in one day. To make clothing women had to spin thread, weave it into cloth, and sew the cloth into clothing.

Finally most women worked with their husbands on their farms or in their shops and businesses. A few women managed their own plantations. Eliza Lucas Pinckney became famous for managing her father's plantation. She turned **indigo** into an important cash crop in South Carolina.

Social classes were important in the colonies. Yet colonists had more opportunities to move to a higher social class than did people in England. The highest social class was the upper class. The upper class included the wealthy and the well-educated. Ministers, lawyers, southern planters, and rich merchants were part of the upper class. Only upper-class women could afford to wear silk dresses. Upper-class men often wore fancy white wigs. The largest class of people in the colonies was the middle class. Small farmers, shopkeepers, and skilled workers were part of the middle class. Farm workers and servants were in the lower class. Slaves were the lowest level of society and had the least rights.

## Religion and Education

Religion was important throughout the 13 colonies. A religious movement called the **Great Awakening** began during the early 1700s. Jonathan Edwards, a Protestant minister in Massachusetts, was an important leader of this movement. All people were equal before God, Edwards told his followers. Edwards taught that people should not depend on ministers to teach them about God. Instead they could learn about God by reading the Bible by themselves. The Great Awakening helped democracy because it spread the idea that all people are equal.

New England became the leader in the development of public schools because the Puritans believed everyone should be able to read the Bible. In 1647 Massachusetts passed America's first public school law. The law required towns with more than 50 families to hire a teacher for the town's children. Towns with more than 100 families

Jonathan Edwards was an important leader of the Great Awakening. He was from Connecticut, and he became a minister in his grandfather's church in Massachusetts.

had to start **grammar schools** for boys. These grammar schools, the first public schools in America, were small, one-room schools. They were for both rich and poor boys, and tax money supported the schools. Girls often went to **dame schools**, which women ran in their own homes.

There was little public education in the Middle Colonies and in the Southern Colonies. Most schools in the Middle Colonies were private schools that charged fees. In the Southern Colonies, wealthy children were taught at home.

At the age of 12, many middle- and lower-class children received an education by becoming an **apprentice**. An apprentice lived and worked with a master craftsman. A boy could be an apprentice to a printer, shoemaker, glassmaker, silversmith, or

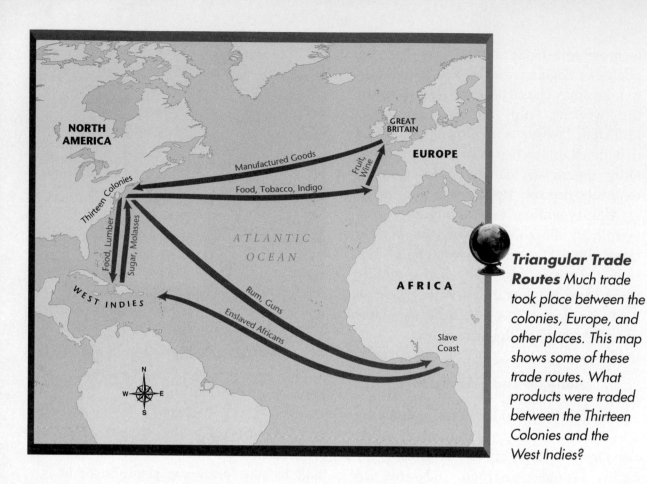

**Triangular Trade Routes** Much trade took place between the colonies, Europe, and other places. This map shows some of these trade routes. What products were traded between the Thirteen Colonies and the West Indies?

Map labels: NORTH AMERICA · GREAT BRITAIN · EUROPE · AFRICA · ATLANTIC OCEAN · Thirteen Colonies · WEST INDIES · Slave Coast · Manufactured Goods · Food, Tobacco, Indigo · Fruit, Wine · Food, Lumber · Sugar, Molasses · Rum, Guns · Enslaved Africans

other craftsman. The craftsman taught reading, writing, and his trade, or business, to the apprentice. After about seven years, the apprentice could work on his own as a **journeyman**. Later, when he was experienced, he was considered a master craftsman who could have his own apprentices.

The first colleges in the colonies were started as schools to train ministers. In 1636 the Puritans started Harvard College, the first college in the colonies.

### Colonial Trade and Cities

Most colonial trade was with other colonies and with England. During the 1600s and the 1700s, Europeans believed in an idea called **mercantilism**. Under mercantilism a nation could be rich only by gaining wealth from rival nations. To get this wealth, a nation needed a **favorable balance of trade**. This means a nation had to sell more products to other countries than it bought from other countries. These products would be sold in exchange for gold and silver. Europeans believed that colonies were needed in order to have a favorable balance of trade. Colonies were a good place to sell products, and they were a good place to get raw materials to make more products.

Beginning in 1651, England passed laws called the **Navigation Acts** to control trade with its colonies. These laws tried to make England richer by forcing the colonies to trade mainly with England. The colonies were not allowed to make products that they could buy from England. All trade had to be done on English ships or on ships that were built in the colonies.

New England, a leader in shipbuilding, sent trading ships to England and to English colonies in all parts of the world. Colonial products, such as lumber and fish, were traded in England for manufactured goods such as furniture and fine clothing. But much trading took place among the 13 colonies. New England merchants shipped fish and lumber to the other colonies. The Southern Colonies sent rice and tobacco to New England. Grain and flour from the Middle Colonies went to the Southern Colonies and to New England.

In order to trade with countries other than England, the colonies developed **triangular trade routes**. To trade with European merchants, the colonial merchants shipped their products to European ports. There they were traded for goods that were not available in England, such as fruits and wine. Next, the fruits and wine were traded in England for manufactured goods. Finally the manufactured goods from England were sold in the colonies.

Another triangular trade route brought African slaves to America. First, colonists traded their products for sugar and molasses in the West Indies. Ships carried sugar and molasses back to the colonies where they were made into rum. In the next step, ships carried rum and guns to Africa. In Africa these were exchanged for slaves.

Then African slaves were shipped to the West Indies or to the colonies.

Trade helped port cities in the colonies grow larger. By 1770 Boston was the busiest port, and Philadelphia was the largest city in the colonies. Cities grew larger each year, but most colonists continued to live on farms and in towns.

By 1760 there were almost 2 million people living in the 13 colonies. About half of the colonists came from European nations other than England. They spoke many languages, belonged to many religions, and earned their livings in many different ways. They thought of themselves as Virginians, New Yorkers, or members of other colonies. Read on to learn how problems with England would help the colonists join together to become Americans.

*Cities such as Philadelphia and Boston became centers of trade. But in the Southern Colonies, ships sailed directly to the plantations.*

# BIOGRAPHY

## Benjamin Franklin 1706–1790

Benjamin Franklin was famous for his work as a printer, a writer, a scientist, an inventor, and a leader in the 13 colonies. People around the world admired him because he could do so many things very well.

Franklin was born in Boston and was the fifteenth child in a family with seventeen children. Because his family had little money, Franklin spent only two years in school. But he educated himself by reading every book he could find.

Franklin became an apprentice in his older brother's printing shop. He enjoyed being a printer, but he did not get along with his brother. So at age 17, he ran away to Philadelphia.

After a few years, Franklin published his own newspaper in Philadelphia. He was the first American to use maps and cartoons in a newspaper. He also published a book each year called *Poor Richard's Almanac*. It was filled with wise sayings like "Early to bed and early to rise, makes a man healthy, wealthy, and wise."

Franklin became famous for his work as an inventor and a scientist. He invented the Franklin stove, which did a good job of warming a cold room because it used less fuel and gave more heat. Scientists around the world admired his experiment that proved that lightning was one form of electricity.

Franklin also contributed to the city of Philadelphia. Franklin started the first hospital, library, and fire department. He also started a school that would later become the University of Pennsylvania.

Later in life Franklin worked hard to help the colonies win their freedom from England. At age 81 he helped write the Constitution, a new set of laws for the United States. He continued to work for Philadelphia and his country until the end of his life at age 84.

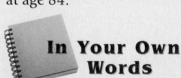

## In Your Own Words

Write a paragraph in the journal section of your social studies notebook that explains the many ways Ben Franklin helped his city and country. Although Franklin did many jobs well, what do you think was his most important work?

# REVIEW AND APPLY

■ Puritans in New England held town meetings so the people could solve problems together.

■ The Middle Colonies had the most diverse population because there were immigrants from many different European nations.

■ Public school education began in New England.

■ Most people in the Southern Colonies owned small farms, but rich plantation owners controlled government and businesses.

■ Colonial women could not vote or work in the government.

■ The triangular trade routes helped the colonies trade with the West Indies, Europe, and Africa.

## VOCABULARY

**Finish the Sentence** ■ **Choose one of the words or phrases from the box to complete each sentence. You will not use all the words in the box.**

1. In a _____ the government is ruled by the people.

2. Crops, like tobacco and indigo, that are grown for profit are called _____ .

3. An _____ was a boy who lived and worked with a master craftsman in order to learn his trade.

4. A _____ owned a large plantation.

5. _____ means to produce goods by machine.

6. The system that helped a nation get rich by gaining wealth from rival nations was called _____ .

7. _____ were laws that forced the colonies to trade mainly with England.

| Navigation Acts |
| planter |
| debtor |
| democracy |
| mercantilism |
| cash crops |
| dame school |
| apprentice |
| manufacturing |

## USING INFORMATION

**Journal Writing** ■ **Write a paragraph in the journal section of your notebook that explains the responsibilities of colonial women.**

## COMPREHENSION CHECK

Choose the Answer ■ Write the letter of the word or phrase that best answers each question.

_____ 1. What right did colonial women **not** have?

    a. to teach
    b. to vote
    c. to cook

_____ 2. Who was a leader of the Great Awakening?

    a. Jonathan Edwards
    b. John Smith
    c. Roger Williams

_____ 3. Which people belonged to the upper class?

    a. farm workers and servants
    b. farmers and shopkeepers
    c. ministers, planters, lawyers, and rich merchants

_____ 4. Which city was the busiest port in the colonies?

    a. Boston
    b. Providence
    c. Jamestown

_____ 5. Where did most people live in the Southern Colonies?

    a. big cities
    b. large plantations
    c. small farms

_____ 6. About how many people lived in the 13 colonies in 1760?

    a. almost 2 thousand
    b. almost 2 million
    c. almost 20 million

## CRITICAL THINKING

Comparing and Contrasting ■ In this chapter, you read about the differences between the New England, Middle, and Southern colonies. Compare and contrast the three regions by completing the chart below. One box is already done for you.

| Region | New England | Middle | Southern |
|---|---|---|---|
| Climate | | | |
| Education | | | |
| The ways people earned a living | shipbuilding, fishing, whale hunting, trade | | |

# AMERICAN GEOGRAPHY

---

## Location: The Thirteen Colonies

Location tells us where a place is. We can use map directions and latitude and longitude to identify the location of a place. We can also identify the location of a place by comparing it to the location of another place. For example, North Carolina could be described as being a southern colony located on the Atlantic Ocean between South Carolina and Virginia. Philadelphia can be described as a city in Pennsylvania on the border with New Jersey.

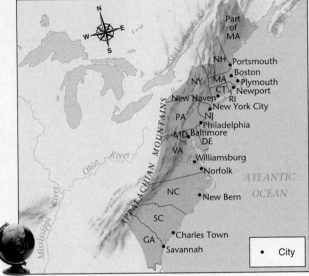

**A. Location of Cities** ■ Study the map and then write about the location of each city. The first one is done for you.

1. Williamsburg, Virginia Williamsburg is on the James River near the Atlantic Ocean. It is in the

   eastern part of the Virginia colony.

2. Boston _____

   _____

3. New York City _____

   _____

**B. Location of the Colonies** ■ Describe the location of each colony.

1. Connecticut _____

   _____

2. New York _____

   _____

3. Georgia _____

   _____

# THE ROAD TO REVOLUTION

◀ *Stamp used to show that tax was paid*

## People

King John • British •
King George III •
George Washington •
Pontiac • Sons of Liberty •
Daughters of Liberty •
Crispus Attucks • Sam
Adams • John Adams •
Patrick Henry • Minutemen

## Places

Wales • Great Britain •
Ohio Valley • Appalachian
Mountains • Montreal •
Lexington • Concord

## New Vocabulary

Magna Carta • Parliament •
frontier • surrendered •
treaty • ally •
proclamation •
representation • taxation •
boycott • Committee of
Correspondence •
Intolerable Acts • militia

### Focus on Main Ideas

1. What events in England led to the development of representative government?
2. What kinds of representative governments did the colonies have?
3. How did the French and Indian War change the relationship between Great Britain and the 13 colonies?
4. Which events between 1763 and 1775 led Americans to fight against Great Britain?

In 1760 Americans in the 13 colonies were proud to be ruled by Great Britain. After all, Great Britain was the world's most powerful nation. As you read this chapter, think about why the colonies were at war with Great Britain only 15 years later.

## Government in England and in the Thirteen Colonies

In order to understand why Americans fought against England, it is neccesary to know how representative government developed in England. In the year 1215, a group of nobles forced King John to sign a paper called the **Magna Carta**. The Magna Carta was important because it was the first set of laws in England to limit the king's power. It did this by allowing nobles to help write the nation's laws. This was the beginning of the lawmaking group called **Parliament**. Members of Parliament worked together to make laws for England. Men who had the right to vote voted for leaders to represent them in Parliament. England had a representative government because of its Parliament.

In 1688 Parliament forced its king, James II, to leave England during the Glorious Revolution. No one was killed during this revolution, and Parliament asked William and Mary to become the new monarchs. In 1689 William and Mary signed a group of laws called the English Bill of Rights. The Bill of Rights said that only Parliament had the power to raise an army or to collect taxes. The Glorious Revolution and the English Bill of Rights were important because they made Parliament more powerful than the king.

England had been an independent country for hundreds of years. In 1536 Henry VIII united the kingdoms of England and Wales. In 1707 the Kingdom of England and Wales was united with the Kingdom of Scotland to form one nation. The new nation was called Great Britain. The people who lived in Great Britain were called the British.

In 1760 King George III became the ruler of Great Britain. Before 1760 Parliament made few laws for its American colonies. Each colonial government made its own laws. Each colony had an assembly with two houses, a lower house and an upper house. Colonists voted for representatives to make laws for them in the lower house. The lower house passed tax laws and controlled the colony's money. The upper house had men who were chosen by the governor of the colony. By 1750 most white men who owned property could vote in the colonies. When he became king, George III decided to take stronger control of the colonies. One reason for this change was the cost of fighting wars against France.

*Nobles in England made King John sign the Magna Carta in 1215. This event was the beginning of representative government in England. Now members of Parliament helped the king write laws. King John's seal is shown above.*

**69**

## The French and Indian War

In Unit 1 you learned how the English and the French first settled in America. The French built a large empire called New France. Canada and Louisiana were parts of New France. Both England and France wanted to rule the land around the Ohio River called the Ohio Valley. French fur traders were the first people from Europe to reach the Ohio Valley. They built forts in the Valley, but few French people settled there.

British settlers began to move west across the Appalachian Mountains into the Ohio Valley. They called the area the **frontier** because it had no cities or towns. Settlers in the frontier cleared the land of trees to start farms. The trees were used to build log cabins and fences. Life on the frontier was difficult. Many settlers died from hunger, disease, and wars with Indians.

The French and the Indians united to attack British settlers in the Ohio Valley. In 1754 the French and Indian War began between the French and the British. Many Indian nations fought alongside the French. They hoped that if the French won, British settlers would no longer be allowed in the Ohio Valley. Only the powerful Iroquois nations fought alongside the British. The Iroquois and the French had been enemies since 1609.

At the start of the war, the British asked George Washington, a 21-year-old soldier from Virginia, to help them fight the French. They told Washington to force the French to leave a fort they had built in western Pennsylvania. Washington and his soldiers were defeated in their early battles with the French. Although Washington lost these battles, he learned how to fight on the frontier. Because Washington showed great courage, he became a war hero in the colonies.

The British captured the French city of Quebec, in 1759. The next year the British captured Montreal and the French **surrendered**. While the French and the British fought in America, they also fought each other in Europe during the Seven Years War. The French lost that war, too.

In 1763 the French and the British signed a peace **treaty** called the Treaty of Paris. The treaty said that France lost all its land in North America except for four small islands. Spain, France's **ally** in the war, gave Florida to Great Britain. Louisiana was split at the Mississippi River. The land east of the river was given to Great Britain. The land west of the river was given to Spain. Great Britain gained more than just the Ohio Valley. It also ruled Canada and all the land along the Atlantic Ocean.

## Problems After the French and Indian War

After the French and Indian War, King George III and the leaders of Parliament angered the people in the American colonies. King George first angered the colonists by writing a **proclamation**, a type of law, that said colonists could not settle in the Ohio Valley. The colonists thought the new law was very unfair. After all, they had fought and died to win the Ohio Valley during the French and Indian War.

The Proclamation of 1763 was written after Pontiac's Rebellion, which occurred earlier that same year. Pontiac, an Ottawa leader, led attacks by a number of Indian nations against British settlements and forts in the Ohio Valley. They destroyed most of the British forts in the area and killed about 2,000 settlers. The fighting stopped at the end of the French and Indian War. The king wrote the proclamation because the British thought it would be expensive and difficult to protect colonists from more Indian attacks.

The colonists were also angry when Parliament began to pass tax laws for the colonies. Money from the colonies would be sent to Great Britain to help pay the debts from the French and Indian War. The chart on this page shows the laws passed by Parliament to tax and control the colonies.

The tax laws angered the colonists. They said Parliament could not tax the colonists because they did not have **representation** in Parliament. "No **taxation** without representation" were the words said throughout the colonies. Representatives from the colonies were not allowed in Parliament. The lawmakers in Parliament believed they had every right to tax the colonies and make laws for them because the colonies belonged to Great Britain.

### The American Colonists Begin to Unite

Rage toward the British began to unite the colonists. They began to work together against Great Britain. Many colonists stopped seeing themselves as British citizens. Instead they began to think of themselves as Americans. Colonists started protest groups called the Sons of Liberty and the Daughters of Liberty. To end unfair tax

## Events Leading to War

| | |
|---|---|
| Proclamation of 1763 | British said colonists could not settle in the Ohio Valley. |
| Sugar Act (1764) | Taxes on sugar and molasses. |
| Stamp Act (1765) | Colonists must buy stamps for all printed material. |
| Quartering Act (1765) | British soldiers must be given food and housing in colonies. |
| Declaratory Act (1767) | Parliament ended the Stamp and Sugar Acts but said it had the right to tax the colonies. |
| Townshend Acts (1767) | Taxes on paint, glass, lead, paper, and tea. |
| Boston Massacre (1770) | A snowball fight leads to British soldiers shooting five Americans. |
| Tea Act (1773) | Tax on tea. |
| Boston Tea Party (1773) | Colonists dump Tea into Boston Harbor. |
| Intolerable Acts (1774) | The British passed laws to punish Boston for the Boston Tea Party. They closed Boston Harbor. |
| First Continental Congress (1774) Lexington and Concord (April 1775) | Delegates from 12 colonies meet and send a letter to King George. The American Revolution begins. |

*Colonists showed their anger at the new tax laws in many ways. Here colonists burn stamps that were used to show that a tax had been paid.*

77

laws, the colonists started a **boycott** against products from Great Britain. When the boycott hurt Britain's trade, Parliament ended some of the tax laws.

Some colonists in Boston used violence to protest. So the British sent soldiers to Boston. On March 5, 1770, a group of American men and boys began throwing rocks and snowballs at a small group of British soldiers. To stop Americans from throwing rocks, British soldiers fired their guns. Five colonists were killed. Crispus Attucks, an African American, was among those killed. The colonists called this the Boston Massacre.

Sam Adams became one of the famous protest leaders in Boston. He started a group called the **Committee of Correspondence**.

*Five colonists, including Crispus Attucks, were killed in the Boston Massacre. The Committee of Correspondence was started to tell other colonists about the Boston Massacre.*

More committees were started in the other colonies. These committees sent information to each other about the Boston Massacre. As people in every colony learned about the Boston Massacre, bitter feelings towards King George grew stronger.

After the British passed the Tea Act in 1773, the Sons of Liberty took action. In New York City and in Philadelphia, they quietly sent tea ships back to Great Britain. But in Boston, Sam Adams planned the Boston Tea Party. One dark night members of the Sons of Liberty put on Indian clothes and boarded the tea ships. They broke open tea chests and threw thousands of pounds of tea into the water.

Back in Great Britain, King George was furious. Parliament passed new laws to punish the people of Boston. The new laws took away self-government from Massachusetts. Boston Harbor was closed until the colonists paid for the tea. More British soldiers were sent to Boston to carry out the laws. The colonists hated these laws so much that they called these laws the **Intolerable Acts**.

## The Colonies Prepare for War

To solve their problems with King George, protest leaders from 12 colonies met in Philadelphia. Georgia did not send its leaders to the meeting of the First Continental Congress in 1774, but that colony agreed to follow the decisions made by the Congress. The best leaders of the colonies were in the Congress. Sam Adams and John Adams came from Massachusetts. Patrick Henry and George Washington were there from Virginia.

The members of the Continental Congress wrote a letter to King George. It said that the colonies were loyal to the king, but laws for the colonies must be made by their own elected representatives. The letter included a list of problems the colonists wanted corrected. The leaders decided that the colonies would boycott British goods until the problems were solved. Each colony would start its own **militia** so the colonies would be prepared if they had to fight the British. Finally they agreed to meet again in May 1775.

## The Shot Heard Round the World

In the months that followed, colonists formed militias. Each colony had militia soldiers who called themselves Minutemen because they needed only one minute to be ready to fight the British. The colonists in Massachusetts began to store weapons in the town of Concord near Boston.

In April 1775 more British soldiers were sent to Massachusetts. The Sons of Liberty learned that the soldiers planned to attack Concord and capture the colonists' weapons. On April 18, 1775, Paul Revere and two other members of the Sons of Liberty rode through the night and warned the people of Concord and Lexington that British soldiers were coming. The next day the Minutemen were ready to fight.

The first battle between the colonists and the British began in Lexington. Eight Minutemen died in that battle. Then the British marched on to Concord where they

*Minutemen would quickly leave their homes, farms, and families to fight the British. The Minutemen are remembered with the statue above in Massachusetts.*

fought the Minutemen again. The British were forced back to Boston.

The fighting at Lexington and Concord has been called "the shot heard round the world." People around the world learned about these famous battles for freedom and representative government. It gave people in other lands the hope that someday they could fight for better governments, too.

Lexington and Concord were the first battles in the American Revolution. When the war began in 1775, Americans were fighting to have the same rights as all British citizens. They wanted self-government in the colonies and representation in Parliament. Read on in Chapter 8 to learn how the American Revolution became a fight for freedom.

# BIOGRAPHY

## Paul Revere 1735–1818

Paul Revere was a famous leader in the American Revolution who helped the United States become a free nation.

Paul Revere was born in Boston. His father was a silversmith, and Revere became a silversmith, too. Revere became a member of the Sons of Liberty. After the Boston Massacre in 1770, Revere made an engraving of the event that became famous.

Revere worked with Sam Adams to plan the Boston Tea Party in 1773. He was one of the men who dumped tea into Boston Harbor. But he is best known for his ride on April 18, 1775, which was made famous by the poem "Paul Revere's Ride," by Henry Wadsworth Longfellow.

Some Americans had learned that the British were planning to attack Concord to capture American weapons. Revere and William Dawes were sent to warn the colonists in Concord and to warn Sam Adams in Lexington. They arrived at Lexington around midnight and warned the colonists that the British would arrive in the morning.

One hour later Revere, Dawes, and Dr. Samuel Prescott began riding to Concord. On the way British soldiers stopped them. Dawes and Prescott escaped, and Prescott reached Concord. The British allowed Revere to return to Lexington the next day without his horse. After walking to Lexington, Revere and Adams escaped to safety. When the British troops from Boston reached Lexington, the Minutemen were ready for them, thanks to Paul Revere.

Revere served in the army in New England during the American Revolution. He also produced gunpowder and cannons for the army. Revere printed the first paper money for the nation.

After the war, Paul Revere continued his work as a silversmith. His silver objects were so popular that Revere became as famous for his work with silver as he was for his famous ride on April 18, 1775.

## In Your Own Words

Write a paragraph in the journal section of your notebook that describes Paul Revere's achievements before, during, and after the American Revolution.

# REVIEW AND APPLY

- In 1215, England's King John signed the Magna Carta, which limited the king's power, and it allowed nobles to start Parliament.

- After the French and Indian War, France lost most of its empire in North America. Great Britain gained Canada and the Ohio Valley.

- After the French and Indian War, the British Parliament passed tax laws for the colonies to help pay for the British war debts. The colonists protested these taxes because the colonists were not represented in the British Parliament.

- The American Revolution started in 1775 with the battles of Lexington and Concord.

## VOCABULARY

**Choose the Meaning** ■ **Write the letter of the word or phrase that best completes each sentence.**

1. The Magna Carta was a paper that limited the power of the _____ .

    a. British king
    b. French king
    c. colonial government

2. Parliament is a _____ .

    a. British colony
    b. British trading group
    c. British lawmaking body

3. Representation means _____ .

    a. making laws for other people
    b. voting for new laws
    c. voting for people to make laws for you

4. A nation that surrenders during a war, _____ .

    a. wins the war
    b. gives up fighting the war
    c. decides to continue fighting the war

5. Taxation is a way for a government to _____ .

    a. raise money
    b. fight a war
    c. start new colonies

6. An ally during a war _____ .

    a. helps your enemy
    b. fights with you against your enemy
    c. is your enemy

7. A militia is a group of citizens that are trained to be _____ .

    a. craftsman
    b. soldiers
    c. farmers

8. The frontier is a region with few _____

    a. Indians
    b. trees
    c. settlers

75

## COMPREHENSION CHECK

Write the Answer ■ Write one or more sentences to answer each question.

1. What were the results of the French and Indian War? _____

_____

_____

2. What changes did King George make in the way the colonies were ruled after the

French and Indian War? _____

_____

3. What was one way the colonists protested against British taxes?

_____

4. What happened at Lexington and Concord in Massachusetts on April 19, 1775?

_____

_____

## CRITICAL THINKING

Distinguishing Relevant Information ■ Imagine you are telling a friend why many colonists decided to protest and fight against Great Britain. Read each sentence below. Decide which sentences are relevant to what you will say. Put a check in front of the relevant sentences. There are 3 relevant sentences.

_____ 1. The British passed the Tea Act in 1773.

_____ 2. George III became the king of England in 1760.

_____ 3. The British would not allow the colonies to have representation in Parliament.

_____ 4. Settlers cleared trees and started farms in the Ohio Valley.

_____ 5. The British closed Boston Harbor after the Boston Tea Party.

## USING INFORMATION

Writing an Opinion ■ Do you think that the colonists were right or wrong for protesting the tax laws made by Parliament? In your notebook, write a paragraph that explains your opinion.

# SOCIAL STUDIES SKILLS

## Comparing Historical Maps

A historical map shows how a region looked during a certain period of history. You can learn how events have changed a region by comparing two maps of the same place that represent different time periods.

The historical map on the left shows North America when the French and Indian War began in 1754. The map on the right shows how European control of North America changed in 1763 as a result of the war.

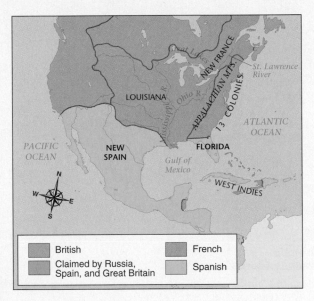

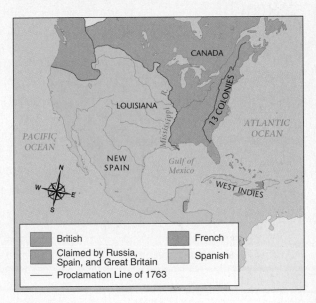

Compare the two maps of North America and write the answer to each question.

1. Which nation ruled Louisiana in 1754? _____

   In 1763? _____

2. Which nation ruled east of the Mississippi River in 1763? _____

3. Which nation ruled Florida in 1754? _____

   In 1763? _____

4. What land did France lose in 1763? _____

5. What land did England control in 1763? _____

6. How did the French and Indian War change Great Britain's control in North America?

   _____

# Chapter 8

# THE AMERICAN REVOLUTION

◄ *The Liberty Bell*

**People**

Thomas Paine • Thomas Jefferson • John Locke • Phillis Wheatley • Marquis de Lafayette • Friedrich von Steuben • Bernardo de Gálvez • Benedict Arnold • General Cornwallis • Joseph Brant • Peter Salem

**Places**

Fort Ticonderoga • Bunker Hill • Trenton • Princeton • Saratoga • Valley Forge • Yorktown

**New Vocabulary**

delegates • commander in chief • blockade • pamphlet • Loyalists • neutral • Patriots • Enlightenment • unalienable rights • pursuit of happiness • traitors • retreat • turning point • morale

**Focus on Main Ideas**

1. What important ideas were in the Declaration of Independence?
2. What were the strengths and the weaknesses of the British and American armies?
3. Who were some important people during the American Revolution? How did they help Americans win the war?

At the start of the American Revolution, the British Army was the strongest in the world. As you read this chapter, think about how Americans were able to defeat the powerful British Army.

## The Second Continental Congress

Soon after the battles of Lexington and Concord, **delegates** from all 13 colonies held the Second Continental Congress. The Congress began in May 1775 in Philadelphia. The Continental Congress decided to form an army with soldiers from all of the colonies. All the delegates agreed that George Washington should be the **commander in chief** of the new Continental Army. Washington had come to the Congress as a delegate. Dressed in his army uniform, Washington looked ready for the difficult job. The Continental Congress also decided to send Benjamin Franklin to France to ask for French help.

While American delegates were working in the Continental Congress, American soldiers had captured British cannons and supplies at Fort Ticonderoga in New York. In June 1775 American troops moved to Breeds Hill and Bunker Hill, two hills near Boston. On these hills American and

British troops fought the Battle of Bunker Hill. The Americans lost the battle, but more than a thousand British soldiers died at Bunker Hill.

Back at the Continental Congress in Philadelphia, the delegates sent a letter to King George called the Olive Branch Petition. It said the colonists wanted peace, and they wanted to be ruled by Great Britain. But the colonists also wanted to have the same rights as British citizens.

A few delegates, one being Patrick Henry, were ready for the colonies to break away from Great Britain and become an independent nation. In one of his famous speeches, Patrick Henry said, "I know not what course others may take, but as for me, give me liberty or give me death!" However most delegates still wanted the colonies to be ruled by Great Britain.

Those feelings changed at the end of 1775. King George refused to read the Olive Branch Petition. Instead British ships were sent to **blockade** American ports.

In January 1776 Thomas Paine convinced many Americans that they should be a free nation. Paine had come to live in America from England. He wrote a **pamphlet** called "Common Sense," which said the colonies should break all ties with Great Britain. Many people in the colonies agreed with "Common Sense."

*In the Battle of Bunker Hill, the Americans had very little gunpowder. They waited until the British came very close before they began to shoot. When they ran out of gunpowder, they used their rifles as clubs. The Americans fought bravely, but they lost the battle.*

*Benjamin Franklin, John Adams, and Thomas Jefferson (shown left to right above) were in the committee of five delegates that wrote the Declaration of Independence.*

Not all colonists agreed with Thomas Paine. About one third of the colonists wanted to remain part of the British Empire. These colonists were called **Loyalists** because they were loyal to King George. Many Loyalists moved to England and Canada during the American Revolution, but thousands stayed and fought for the British. About one third of the colonists wanted to be **neutral** and not fight for either side. One third of the colonists wanted independence; they were called **Patriots**.

## The Declaration of Independence

In June 1776 the delegates at the Congress decided to tell the world that the colonies were an independent nation.

They decided to explain their reasons in a paper called the Declaration of Independence. A committee was given the job of writing the Declaration. They asked Thomas Jefferson, a young delegate from Virginia, to do most of the writing.

Thomas Jefferson used ideas from the **Enlightenment** when he wrote the Declaration. The Enlightenment was a period during the 1600s and 1700s when great thinkers wrote new ideas about government. John Locke was one of the great thinkers of the Enlightenment. He believed that God gave rights that belong to all people and can not be taken away. Locke also believed that people have the right to have a revolution against their government if the government does not protect the rights of the people.

The Declaration of Independence explained that "all men are created equal," and that God gave all people **unalienable rights**. These rights, which can not be taken away, are "life, liberty, and the **pursuit of happiness**." Jefferson used Locke's ideas when he wrote in the Declaration that people can change their government if it tries to take away these rights. The Declaration listed the many ways King George had taken away the rights of the colonists. The Declaration ended by saying the 13 colonies were "free and independent states." Soon Americans began to call their free nation the United States of America.

Jefferson wrote "all men are created equal" at a time when one fifth of the people in the colonies were slaves. Women did not have the right to vote in any of the colonies. Jefferson wanted the Declaration to include sentences that spoke out against slavery.

But when delegates from the Southern Colonies refused to sign the Declaration, those sentences about slavery were removed. All people were not treated equally in America in 1776, but the Declaration set high goals for equal treatment in the future.

On July 4, 1776, the delegates signed and adopted the Declaration of Independence. It took great courage to say the colonies were a free nation. To King George all of the signers were **traitors**. If Americans lost their fight to be free, all of the signers would be punished with death.

## George Washington Becomes Commander in Chief

In July 1776 George Washington went to Boston to take charge of the Continental Army. Washington faced many problems. The Continental Congress could not collect taxes, so there was little money to pay for an army. The soldiers had no uniforms, and they had to buy their own guns. Often the army did not have enough food.

Washington became a hero as commander in chief. He taught the soldiers to work together as an army. Although Washington lost more battles than he won, he refused to give up. He knew when to **retreat** and when to move to another place. Then the army could fight again.

## Comparing the American and British Armies

In 1776 the British were sure they would win the war. They had the strongest army in the world, and they had a large,

Phillis Wheatley, a poet, admired Washington. She published a poem about Washington's greatness. He read the poem, liked it, and later met Phillis Wheatley to thank her.

powerful navy. The Americans lacked supplies, but they knew how to fight in forests and on the frontier. The British soldiers and their leaders did not.

Since Great Britain ruled many colonies around the world, the British Army had soldiers in many far-off places. The British did not have enough soldiers to fight in America. So they hired Hessian soldiers from Germany. The Hessians were paid to fight, and they really did not care which side won. The American soldiers believed in the cause for which they were fighting.

## The Early Years of the War

Soon after the Declaration of Independence was signed, Americans

*On the snowy Christmas Eve of 1776, Washington crossed the icy Delaware River with 2,400 soldiers. The next day they made a surprise attack on a group of Hessian soldiers in Trenton, New Jersey. The Americans captured 900 Hessian soldiers and not one American was killed.*

fought the British in New York. When Washington lost the Battle of Long Island, he retreated to Manhattan. Washington then escaped with his army to New Jersey. Great Britain had won control of New York City and Long Island.

Nathan Hale was a brave American spy at the Battle of Long Island. He was caught by the British and hanged. Just before he died, Hale said, "My only regret is that I have but one life to give for my country."

Washington had two victories at the end of 1776. The first victory was the surprise attack in Trenton after crossing the icy Delaware River. Then the Americans went to nearby Princeton where they won another small battle. These two victories

encouraged the American soldiers to continue fighting.

In September 1777 the British captured Philadelphia. But a few weeks later, in October, Americans won a very important victory in Saratoga, New York. The Americans captured almost 6,000 British prisoners. The Battle of Saratoga became the **turning point** in the war. It proved that the Americans were strong enough to defeat the British. So France decided to send soldiers, ships, and supplies to help the new nation. France's goal was to defeat its old enemy, Great Britain.

Marquis de Lafayette became a French hero during the American Revolution. In 1777 he used his own money to buy a ship, and then he sailed to America with French soldiers. Lafayette fought alongside the Americans until the last battle ended.

## The War After the Battle of Saratoga

After the Battle of Saratoga, Washington led his army to Valley Forge in Pennsylvania. There they spent a long, cold winter. **Morale** was so low that many soldiers left the army to return home. There was not enough food or clothing. Thousands of soldiers wrapped rags around their feet because they did not have shoes to wear. But the men who stayed at Valley Forge that winter became better soldiers, thanks to the work of German General Friedrich von Steuben. Von Steuben drilled the soldiers on how to use weapons, and he taught them the best ways to fight.

After the winter at Valley Forge, more fighting took place in the South and in the West. The British won many battles in the South, but it cost them many lives. In the West, Americans had a victory at Vincennes in the Ohio Valley.

In 1779 Spain started to help the American Army. Bernardo de Gálvez, the Spanish governor of Louisiana, sent gun powder, food, medicine, and money to the American Army. He led a Spanish army that captured British forts and cities along the Gulf of Mexico from Louisiana to Florida.

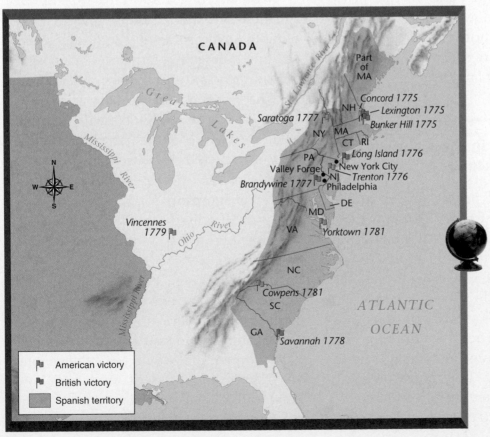

*The American Revolution* Many of the earlier battles of the war took place in New England and the Middle Colonies. Later the British tried to capture the Southern Colonies. Where was the last battle of the war?

One of the best American generals, Benedict Arnold, became a traitor. He wanted to surrender the American fort at West Point, New York, to the British. When Americans learned that Arnold was a traitor, they tried to capture him. But Arnold escaped and became a general in the British Army.

By 1781 General Cornwallis, the leader of the British Army, was losing the war in the South. From August until October, Americans fought Cornwallis at Yorktown, Virginia. With the help of the French Army and the French Navy, the British army was trapped. On October 19, Cornwallis surrendered to Washington. Americans had won their independence!

In 1783 the Americans and the British signed the Treaty of Paris. In this peace treaty, Great Britain recognized the United States as an independent nation. Although Great Britain still ruled Canada, the United States ruled all the land to the east of the Mississippi River.

## Who Fought in the American Revolution?

Many kinds of people fought in the war. Most Indians fought for the British. They hoped that the British would stop Americans from settling on Indian lands. Joseph Brant, a Mohawk leader, helped the British win the Battle of Long Island.

About five thousand African Americans fought for American freedom during the war. Free African Americans and slaves were in the American Army. They fought in every important battle. Peter Salem, a Minuteman, fought the British at Lexington. Later, Salem shot a British commander in the Battle of Bunker Hill. James Armistead, an African American slave, served as a spy for Lafayette. He became a free man after the war.

Large numbers of Irish Americans fought for freedom. Many of these soldiers became generals in the Continental Army.

Jewish Americans fought for American freedom. David Emmanuel became a hero in Georgia. Haym Salomon, a spy for the American Army, was arrested twice by the British. Both times he escaped. He also raised money for the Continental Army.

Thaddeus Kosciusko, a Polish engineer, became good friends with George Washington. Kosciusko's work during the Battle of Saratoga helped Americans win this important battle.

Women were important during the American Revolution, although they were not allowed to be soldiers. While men were fighting, women ran farms and businesses. They served as cooks, nurses, and doctors for the army. Some women worked as spies. George Washington's wife, Martha, spent each winter of the war with the army. She nursed soldiers who were hurt and sewed up the holes in their clothes. Deborah Sampson fought as a soldier. Sampson disguised herself as a man, wore an army uniform, and fought in the Battle of Yorktown.

Americans were proud that they had worked together to win their independence. Early in the war, the Declaration of Independence had said Americans wanted a government that would serve the people. In Chapter 9 you will find out how Americans planned a new government that would protect their rights and freedoms.

# BIOGRAPHY

## Thomas Jefferson 1743–1826

Farmer, lawyer, architect, inventor, governor, president, and writer were all jobs that Thomas Jefferson did well during his long life.

Jefferson was born on his family's farm in Virginia. Jefferson was well educated. He learned several languages and played the violin. He attended college and became a lawyer. Jefferson was elected to the Virginia House of Burgesses in 1769.

Jefferson became a Patriot who spoke out against unfair British laws. He had studied John Locke's ideas about government, and he believed the British were taking away the rights of Americans. So he was glad to be one of Virginia's delegates at the First Continental Congress.

Delegates at the Second Continental Congress asked Jefferson to write the Declaration of Independence. It took two weeks of hard work to write the Declaration. A few men like Benjamin Franklin and John Adams shortened the Declaration after it was finished. The Declaration told why the colonies wanted independence and it explained that governments should get their power from the people.

Jefferson strongly believed that all people should have religious freedom. So during the American Revolution he wrote the "Virginia Statute for Religious Freedom." This law gave religious freedom to all people. During the war Jefferson also served as governor of Virginia.

After the British surrendered, Jefferson helped write the Treaty of Paris. He wrote treaties with other European nations for the United States.

Jefferson was elected the third President of the United States in 1800. He served two terms. In 1817 he started the University of Virginia. Thomas Jefferson and his good friend, John Adams, both died on July 4, 1826. This was exactly fifty years after the Declaration of Independence had been adopted.

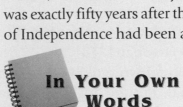
## In Your Own Words

Write a paragraph in the journal section of your social studies notebook that describes Thomas Jefferson's important work. How do you think his work helped American freedom?

# Voices from the Past

## Letters of John and Abigail Adams 1774 – 1776

John Adams was a cousin of Sam Adams and another leader in America's fight for independence. Adams was a delegate from Massachusetts at both the First and Second Continental Congresses. He was away from home for long periods of time during the American Revolution. Abigail Adams, his wife and the mother of their five children, agreed that the colonies should be independent. John and Abigail wrote to each other while he was away from home. Their letters show their love for each other and their support for American independence.

### Letter from Abigail Adams to John
### 19 August, 1774

"The great distance between us makes the time appear very long to me. It seems already a month since you left me. The great anxiety I feel for my country, for you, and for our family renders the day tedious and the night unpleasant.... I want much to hear from you.... The little flock remember Papa, and kindly wish to see him; so does your most affectionate. Abigail Adams"

### Letter from John Adams to Abigail
### 7 October 1774

"I wish I could write to you a dozen letters every day. But the business before me...takes up my time so entirely....

There is a great spirit in the Congress. But our people must be peaceable.... Let them furnish themselves with artillery, arms, and ammunition.... But let them avoid war if possible...."

### Letter from John Adams to Abigail
### 17 June, 1775

"I can now inform you that the Congress have made choice of the modest and virtuous, the amiable, generous, and brave George Washington, Esquire, to be General of the American Army.... I hope the people...will treat the General with all...that politeness and respect, which is due to one of the most important characters in the world...."

### Letter from John Adams to Abigail
### 7 July, 1775

"Your description of the distresses of the worthy inhabitants of Boston and other seaport towns is enough to melt a heart of stone....

It gives me more pleasure than I can express, to learn that you sustain the shocks and terrors of the times. You are really brave, my dear. You are a heroine.... I am forever yours."

..."Remember the ladies
and be more generous
and favorable to them..."

### Letter from Abigail Adams to John
### 9 March, 1776

"You ask what is thought of 'Common Sense.' There is a great deal of good sense delivered in clear, simple, concise, and nervous style."

### Letter from John Adams to Abigail
### 29 March, 1776

"...I am waiting with great impatience for letters from you.... We are taking precautions to defend every place that is in danger, the Carolinas, Virginia, New York, Canada. I can think of nothing but fortifying Boston harbor. I want more cannon than are to be had...."

### Letter from Abigail Adams to John
### 31 March, 1776

"I wish you would ever write me a letter half as long as I write you... I long to hear that you have declared an independency. And, by the way, in the new code of laws which I suppose it will be necessary for you to make, I desire you would remember the ladies and be more generous and favorable to them than your ancestors. Do not put such unlimited power into the hands of the husbands. Remember, all men would be tyrants if they could. If particular care and attention is not paid to the ladies, we are determined to foment a rebellion, and will not hold ourselves bound by any laws in which we have no voice or representation."

### Letter from John Adams to Abigail.
### 3 July, 1776

July, 1776, will be the most memorable...in the history of America. I...believe that it will be celebrated by succeeding generations as the great anniversary festival."

## Write Your Answers

**Write the answer to each question on a separate piece of paper.**

1. In 1774, what did John say the people must do?

2. What did John Adams think of George Washington?

3. What did Abigail think of Thomas Paine's "Common Sense"?

4. What did Abigail tell John to put into the new code of laws?

5. How did John think that July 1776 would be remembered?

# REVIEW AND APPLY

- The Second Continental Congress first met in May 1775. It created a Continental Army and made George Washington commander in chief of the Continental Army.

- When the Declaration of Independence was approved on July 4, 1776, Americans announced their independence from Great Britain.

- The Battle of Saratoga was considered the turning point of the American Revolution because after this American victory, France began to help the Continental Army.

- The Americans won the American Revolution after the British were defeated at the Battle of Yorktown on October 19, 1783.

## VOCABULARY

**Defining and Using Vocabulary** ■ **Use the glossary to find the meaning of each word or phrase listed below. Write each word's definition in your social studies notebook. Then use each word in a sentence.**

blockade                          neutral                        traitor
commander in chief          pamphlet                turning point
delegate                            retreat

## COMPREHENSION CHECK

**Biography Cards** ■ **Complete the index cards by explaining how each person helped the United States win independence.**

Name   _Thomas Jefferson_

How he helped:

Name   _Haym Salomon_

How he helped:

Name   _Thomas Paine_

How he helped:

Name   _George Washington_

How he helped:

| Name _Marquis de Lafayette_ | Name _James Armistead_ |
|---|---|
| How he helped: | How he helped: |

## CRITICAL THINKING

Making Predictions ■ Making predictions means using information that we know in order to think about what probably will happen next.

_Example_  **Fact:**　　　　　　　　　　　　　**Prediction:**
It rained hard for ten days.　　　There will be a flood.

**Read the paragraph below about the end of the American Revolution. Then check two sentences that predict what will happen after the war.**

The American army was defeated in many battles during the American Revolution, but George Washington continued to lead the fight for independence. After seven long years of war, the American army defeated the British at Yorktown. The 13 colonies became one free and independent nation.

_____ 1. The United States would develop a plan for a new government.

_____ 2. Most Americans would want to stay part of Great Britain.

_____ 3. The new nation would give some land back to Great Britain.

_____ 4. Americans would choose a leader for their nation.

5. What do you predict will happen after the American Revolution?

_____

_____

## USING INFORMATION

Writing an Essay ■ There were many battles fought during the American Revolution. Select the battle that you think was the most important to the American victory. Explain why you feel the battle was so important. Start your essay with a topic sentence. End your essay with a sentence that summarizes the main idea. Write your essay in your social studies notebook.

# SOCIAL STUDIES SKILLS

## Interpreting a Line Graph

A line graph uses lines to show how something has changed over a period of time. The line graph below shows how the population in the American colonies changed from 1680 to 1780. A line graph can also show a trend during a period of time. The graph below shows that the trend was for the American population to increase.

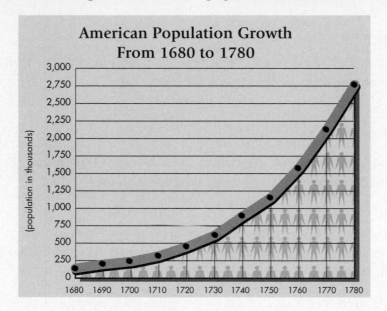

**American Population Growth From 1680 to 1780**

**Study the graph. Then write the answer to each question.**

1. In what year did the colonies have the smallest population? _____

2. Which 40-year period showed the slowest growth? From _____

   to _____

3. Which 30-year period showed the greatest growth? From _____

   to _____

4. When was the population between 500,000 and 1 million? _____

5. When did the population become more than 1 million? _____

6. When did the population become more than 2 million? _____

7. What effect did the American Revolution have on population in the colonies? _____

   _____

# DECLARATION of INDEPENDENCE

When in the course of human events, it becomes necessary for one people to dissolve the political bands which have connected them with another, and to assume among the powers of the earth the separate and equal station to which the laws of nature and of nature's God entitle them, a decent respect to the opinions of mankind requires that they should declare the causes which impel them to the separation.

Sometimes in history, one group of people must become independent from the nation that rules it. The people who are breaking ties must then explain their reasons to the world. That is the purpose of this Declaration of Independence.

We hold these truths to be self-evident: that all men are created equal, that they are endowed by their Creator with certain unalienable rights, that among these are life, liberty, and the pursuit of happiness.

We believe the following things are always true. All people are equal. God gave all people the natural rights of life, liberty, and working for happiness.

That to secure these rights, governments are instituted among men, deriving their just powers from the consent of the governed; that whenever any form of government becomes destructive of these ends, it is the right of the people to alter or to abolish it, and to institute new government, laying its foundation on such principles and organizing its powers in such form as to them shall seem most likely to effect their safety and happiness. Prudence, indeed, will dictate that

governments long established should not be changed for light and transient causes; and accordingly all experience hath shown, that mankind are more disposed to suffer while evils are sufferable, than to right themselves by abolishing the forms to which they are accustomed. But when a long train of abuses and usurpations, pursuing invariably the same object, evinces a design to reduce them under absolute despotism, it is their right, it is their duty, to throw off such government, and to provide new guards for their future security.

Governments are created by people to protect the people's rights. Governments get their power by the consent of the people they rule. People have the right to change or end a government that takes away their natural rights. The people must then start a new government that will protect natural rights. People should never revolt for only a few, unimportant reasons. However, when there is a long history of repeated abuses, then it is the right and the duty of the people to overthrow the ruling government and start a new government that will safeguard the rights of all people.

Such has been the patient sufferance of these colonies; and such is now the necessity which constrains them to alter their former systems of government. The history of the present king of Great Britain is a history of repeated injuries and usurpations, all having in direct object the establishment of an absolute tyranny over these states. To prove this, let facts be submitted to a candid world.

For a long time, the colonies have suffered abuses from the king's government, and so we must change our government. King George, through many unfair actions, has shown that his goals are to take away our rights and to have complete control over the colonies. We want the world to know the following facts about the king's abuses:

He has refused his assent to laws, the most wholesome and necessary for the public good.

The king has refused to approve laws necessary for the good of the colonies.

He has forbidden his governors to pass laws of immediate and pressing importance, unless suspended in their operation till his assent should be obtained, and when so suspended, he has utterly neglected to attend to them.

He has not allowed laws to be passed without his approval. And he has taken a long time to approve those he allows.

He has refused to pass other laws for the accommodation of large districts of people, unless those people would relinquish the right of representation in the legislature, a right inestimable to them and formidable to tyrants only.

He has not allowed all people to have equal representation in the legislatures.

He has called together legislative bodies at places unusual, uncomfortable, and distant from the depository of their public records, for the sole purpose of fatiguing them into compliance with his measures.

He has forced representatives to meet in strange, uncomfortable, and far-off places in order to make them so tired that they would obey his orders.

He has dissolved Representative Houses repeatedly, for opposing with manly firmness his invasions on the rights of the people.

He has shut down colonial legislatures many times when they criticized the king's abuses of the people.

He has refused for a long time, after such dissolutions, to cause others to be elected; whereby the legislative powers, incapable of annihilation, have returned to the people at large for their exercise; the state remaining, in the mean time, exposed to all the dangers of invasion from without, and convulsions within.

After shutting down legislatures, he has taken a long time before holding new elections. The people were in danger because their colonial governments could not make laws to protect them.

He has endeavored to prevent the population of these states; for that purpose obstructing the laws of naturalization of foreigners, refusing to pass others to encourage their migration hither, and raising the conditions of new appropriations of lands.

King George has tried to stop the colonial population from growing by making it difficult for Europeans to come to the colonies. He has made it difficult to buy land in America.

He has obstructed the administration of justice, by refusing his assent to laws for establishing judiciary powers.

He stopped us from carrying out justice by refusing to let us set up courts.

He has made judges dependent on his will alone, for the tenure of their offices, and the amount and payment of their salaries.

Judges depend on the king for their salaries and their jobs, so they make unfair decisions to keep their jobs.

He has erected a multitude of new offices, and sent hither swarms of officers to harass our people, and eat out their substance.

The king sent large numbers of government people to bother us and use up our resources.

He has kept among us, in times of peace, standing armies without the consent of our legislatures.

Even in peaceful times, the king has kept his armies in the colonies without the consent of our legislatures.

He has affected to render the military independent of and superior to the civil power.

He has tried to make the military free from, and more powerful than, our government.

He has combined with others to subject us to a jurisdiction foreign to our constitution, and unacknowledged by our laws; giving his assent to their acts of pretended legislation:

King George has worked with Parliament to give us these unfair laws that we did not help write:

For quartering large bodies of armed troops among us;

They forced us to allow British soldiers to stay in our homes.

For protecting them, by a mock trial, from punishment for any murders which they should commit on the inhabitants of these states;

They protected soldiers who murdered our people by giving them fake trials.

For cutting off our trade with all parts of the world;

They stopped us from trading with other nations.

For imposing taxes on us without our consent;

They made unfair tax laws for us.

For depriving us, in many cases, of the benefits of trial by jury;

They often took away our right to have fair jury trials.

For transporting us beyond seas to be tried for pretended offenses;

They forced some of our people to go to Great Britain for trials for crimes they never committed.

For abolishing the free system of English laws in a neighboring province, establishing therein an arbitrary government, and enlarging its boundaries so as to render it at once an example and fit instrument for introducing the same absolute rule into these colonies;

They took away Quebec's fair government and gave Quebec an unfair government. They can use Quebec as an example of how to bring absolute government to the colonies.

For taking away our charters, abolishing our most valuable laws, and altering fundamentally the forms of our governments;

They took away our charters, they changed our most important laws, and they changed the kind of government we have.

For suspending our own legislatures, and declaring themselves invested with power to legislate for us in all cases whatsoever.

*They have stopped us from meeting in our legislatures. They say they have the power to make all laws for us.*

He has abdicated government here, by declaring us out of his protection and waging war against us.

*King George has given up his power to rule us since he says he cannot protect us and is now fighting a war against us.*

He has plundered our seas, ravaged our coasts, burnt our towns, and destroyed the lives of our people.

*The king has attacked our ships, destroyed our ports, burned our towns, and destroyed our lives.*

He is at this time transporting large armies of foreign mercenaries to complete the works of death, desolation, and tyranny, already begun with circumstances of cruelty and perfidy scarcely paralleled in the most barbarous ages, and totally unworthy the head of a civilized nation.

*He is bringing foreign armies to kill us and destroy the colonies. These soldiers show cruelty that should not be allowed by a modern king.*

He has constrained our fellow citizens taken captive on the high seas to bear arms against their country, to become the executioners of their friends and brethren, or to fall themselves by their hands.

*He has taken Americans off our ships at sea and has forced them to fight against their own people.*

He has excited domestic insurrections amongst us, and has endeavored to bring on the inhabitants of our frontiers, the merciless Indian savages, whose known rule of warfare, is an undistinguished destruction of all ages, sexes and conditions.

*He has told our slaves and servants to fight against us, and he has encouraged the Indians to attack us.*

In every stage of these oppressions we have petitioned for redress in the most humble terms; our repeated petitions have been answered only by repeated injury. A prince whose character is thus marked by every act which may define a tyrant is unfit to be the ruler of a free people.

*We have asked the king to end the unfair treatment of the colonies many times, but each time new abuses were added. A king who acts so unfairly is unfit to rule a free people.*

Nor have we been wanting in attentions to our British brethren. We have warned them from time to time of attempts by their legislature to extend an unwarrantable jurisdiction over us. We have reminded them of the circumstances of our emigration and settlement here. We have appealed to their native justice and magnanimity, and we have conjured them by the ties of our common kindred to disavow these usurpations, which would inevitably interrupt our connections and correspondence. They too have been deaf to the voice of justice and of consanguinity. We must, therefore, acquiesce in the necessity which denounces our separation, and hold them, as we hold the rest of mankind, enemies in war, in peace friends.

*We have hoped the British people would help us end the abuses, so we sent many messages to them. We have told them how Parliament has* mistreated us. The British people have not listened to our messages. Therefore, we must declare that we are a separate nation. We will treat Great Britain as we treat all other nations.

We, therefore, the representatives of the United States of America, in General Congress assembled, appealing to the Supreme Judge of the world for the rectitude of our intentions, do, in the name, and by authority of the good people of these colonies, solemnly publish and declare, that these united colonies are, and of right ought to be, free and independent states; that they are absolved from all allegiance to the British crown, and that all political connection between them and the state of Great Britain is, and ought to be, totally dissolved; and that as free and independent states, they have full power to levy war, conclude peace, contract alliances, establish commerce, and to do all

other acts and things which independent states may of right do.

As representatives of the people of the United States, we declare that these united colonies are one, independent nation. We have completely cut ties to Great Britain. As an independent nation, we have the right to wage war, make peace treaties, have trade with all nations, and do all the things a nation does.

And for the support of this declaration, with a firm reliance on the protection of Divine Providence, we mutually pledge to each other our lives, our fortunes and our sacred honor.

We now trust that God will protect us. We promise to support this Declaration with our lives, our money, and our honor.

John Hancock
(President,
Massachusetts)

### Georgia
Button Gwinnett
Lyman Hall
George Walton

### North Carolina
William Hooper
Joseph Hewes
John Penn

### South Carolina
Edward Rutledge
Thomas Heyward, Jr.
Thomas Lynch, Jr.
Arthur Middleton

### Maryland
Samuel Chase

William Paca
Thomas Stone
Charles Carroll of Carrollton

### Virginia
George Wythe
Richard Henry Lee
Thomas Jefferson
Benjamin Harrison
Thomas Nelson, Jr.
Francis Lightfoot Lee
Carter Braxton

### Pennsylvania
Robert Morris
Benjamin Rush
Benjamin Franklin
John Morton
George Clymer
James Smith

George Taylor
James Wilson
George Ross

### Delaware
Caesar Rodney
George Read
Thomas McKean

### New York
William Floyd
Philip Livingston
Francis Lewis
Lewis Morris

### New Jersey
Richard Stockton
John Witherspoon
Francis Hopkinson
John Hart
Abraham Clark

### New Hampshire
Josiah Bartlett
William Whipple
Matthew Thornton

### Massachusetts
John Adams
Samuel Adams
Robert Treat Paine
Elbridge Gerry

### Rhode Island
Stephen Hopkins
William Ellery

### Connecticut
Roger Sherman
Samuel Huntington
William Williams
Oliver Wolcott

# Chapter 9

# THE NATION'S NEW CONSTITUTION

◀ *Miss Liberty, symbol of the new nation*

**People**

Daniel Shays • James
Madison • Montesquieu •
Federalists •
Antifederalists •
John Jay • Alexander
Hamilton

**Places**

Northwest Territory •
Athens

**New Vocabulary**

central government •
ratified • compromises •
senators • principles •
federalism • federal •
separation of powers •
legislative • executive •
judicial • checks and
balances • flexibility •
amendments

**Focus on Main Ideas**

1. What were some of the problems with the Articles of Confederation?
2. What compromises were used to write the Constitution?
3. What six principles were included in the Constitution?

In 1787 American leaders planned a new kind of government for their new nation. As you read this chapter, think about how our leaders created a government that protects the rights of its people.

## Problems Under the Articles of Confederation

During the American Revolution, the delegates at the Second Continental Congress planned a **central government** for the United States. The laws for this government were called the Articles of Confederation. All 13 states **ratified**, or

voted for, the Articles of Confederation in 1781. Under the new laws, the nation was ruled by Congress. Each state had one vote in Congress. To pass a new law, at least nine states had to vote for it.

The Articles of Confederation helped the nation in a few ways. Under the Articles of Confederation, the United States and Great Britain signed the Treaty of Paris. The new government also passed an important law called the Northwest Ordinance of 1787. This law helped the new nation govern the Northwest Territory, the land between the Ohio and Mississippi rivers and the Great Lakes.

Under the Northwest Ordinance, the Northwest Territory was divided into smaller territories. When each territory had 60,000 people, it could write a constitution. Then it could ask Congress to allow it to become a state.

The Articles of Confederation created a very weak government. The delegates who created it feared that a strong government would take away the rights of the people. The government did not have a president to lead the nation. It also did not have courts to settle problems between states.

The central government was so weak under the Articles of Confederation that the new nation had many problems. Congress could not collect taxes, so the central government had little money. Each state was allowed to print its own money, and money from one state could not be used in another state. Congress could not raise an army, so there was no way to protect the nation.

Shays's Rebellion in 1786 proved that the nation needed a much stronger central government. Many farms and businesses were not able to earn much money after the war. Poor farmers like Daniel Shays of Massachusetts could not pay their state taxes. The courts began taking away their farms. Daniel Shays gathered about one thousand angry farmers and attacked several courthouses. Then he tried to take over buildings where weapons were stored. There was no army to stop Daniel Shays. Finally a group of businesspeople hired their own soldiers to end the fighting. This event showed that the nation needed a strong central government with the power to have an army.

## The Constitutional Convention

In May 1787, 55 delegates met in Philadelphia to correct the problems in the Articles of Confederation. They quickly realized that there were too many problems to correct. They decided to write a new plan of government. They wrote the United States Constitution, the laws that govern our nation today.

The meetings that were held to write the Constitution were called the Constitutional Convention. All delegates agreed that

*Shays's Rebellion proved that the nation needed a stronger government. Daniel Shays had been a captain in the army during the American Revolution.*

George Washington should be president of the Convention. At the age of 81, Benjamin Franklin was the oldest delegate. James Madison of Virginia came to the Convention with more ideas for planning the new government than any other person.

The delegates wanted secrecy during their meetings so they could speak and argue freely. Since they did not want anyone outside the Convention to learn what was said, they kept all doors and windows closed each day. Delegates were not allowed to speak to newspaper reporters.

All of the delegates agreed that the United States should have a representative government. To plan the Constitution, the delegates used ideas that they had learned about earlier governments. The delegates wanted the United States government to be a democracy. They had learned about democracy by studying the government of ancient Athens. All citizens in ancient

Athens could vote and help write new laws. The delegates knew that representative government had first started in England with the Magna Carta and had grown stronger as Parliament gained more power. Finally the delegates had learned Jewish and Christian values about kindness, fairness, and responsibility by studying the Bible.

## Compromises of the Constitution

The delegates to the convention agreed that the new government should have a Congress to make laws. Each state would send representatives to the Congress. But the delegates could not agree on how many representatives each state should have. States with large populations like Virginia wanted more representatives than the smaller states. The small states wanted every state to have the same number of representatives.

The problem was solved because the delegates agreed to the first of several **compromises**. The Great Compromise created a Congress with two parts. One part, the Senate, would have two **senators** from each state. All states would have equal representation in the Senate. The other part, the House of Representatives, would have more representatives from states with larger populations. States with smaller populations would have fewer representatives.

The delegates also made two compromises about slavery. One compromise allowed the slave trade to continue until 1808. After that year Congress could pass laws to end the slave trade. The other compromise, known as the Three-fifths Compromise, solved the problem about how to count slaves for taxes and for representation in Congress.

*During the meeting of the Constitutional Convention, George Washington used this chair and this pen and ink set.*

Delegates from northern states, which did not have a lot of slaves, said that slaves should not be counted for representation since they could not vote. Southern delegates wanted to count slaves because there were many slaves in the South. If slaves were counted, the southern states would have more representatives in Congress. The delegates compromised by allowing three fifths of the number of slaves to be counted as part of each state's population.

## Principles of the Constitution

The Constitution begins with a paragraph called the Preamble. This paragraph states the goals of the Constitution. These goals focus on the weaknesses of the Articles of Confederation. Justice, peace, safety, and freedom are the goals of the nation's government. Then the Constitution explains how the government works. The full text of the Constitution, with explanations, follows this chapter on pages 108–135 in your textbook.

The delegates included six important

principles, or ideas, in the Constitution. They used these six principles to create a government that would be a democracy and a representative government. These principles would protect the rights of the people.

The first principle is that the government gets its power from the people. The first words of the Constitution, "We the people of the United States…," show that it is the American people who decide what the government will do.

The second principle is **federalism**. This means power is shared between the state governments and the **federal**, or central, government. This is shown in the diagram below. For example, both can collect taxes. While power is shared, each government also has certain powers that the other does not. The federal government can print money, but only the state governments can pass education laws.

If power is shared, what happens when federal and state laws disagree? The delegates decided that the Constitution is the nation's highest law. So all federal and state laws must obey the Constitution. Likewise, all federal laws must be obeyed over state laws.

Third, the delegates believed in limited government. This means that the federal government only has the powers that are written in the Constitution.

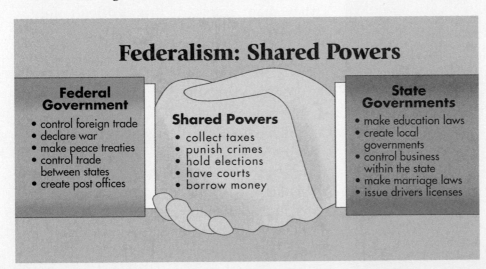

## Federalism: Shared Powers

**Federal Government**
- control foreign trade
- declare war
- make peace treaties
- control trade between states
- create post offices

**Shared Powers**
- collect taxes
- punish crimes
- hold elections
- have courts
- borrow money

**State Governments**
- make education laws
- create local governments
- control business within the state
- make marriage laws
- issue drivers licenses

The fourth principle is the **separation of powers**. This means the powers of the government are divided among three branches of government. Dividing power prevents one part of the government from becoming too powerful. Montesquieu, a well-known French thinker during the Enlightenment, developed the idea of the three branches of government. The **legislative** branch is led by Congress, which makes laws. The **executive** branch carries out the laws passed by Congress. The executive branch is led by the President and the Vice President. The **judicial** branch of the government includes the federal court system. The Supreme Court is the nation's highest court.

The fifth principle uses **checks and balances** to stop one branch of the government from gaining too much power over the other branches. For example, the President has the power to choose judges for federal courts, but the Senate must vote to approve each of these judges.

The sixth principle is **flexibility**. The Constitution must meet the needs of a changing nation. The Elastic Clause of the Constitution allows Congress to pass new laws to carry out its powers. The Constitution also allows new laws called **amendments** to be added to the original Constitution. An amendment can be added if two thirds of the members in both houses of Congress vote for it. Then three fourths of the state governments must vote for it. Twenty-seven amendments have been added to the Constitution.

### Ratifying the Constitution

The delegates at the Constitutional Convention worked hard throughout the long hot summer of 1787. By September they had finished this difficult job. On September 17, 1787, most delegates voted to accept the Constitution. Nine of the thirteen states had to ratify the Constitution in order for it to become the law of the land.

Not all of the delegates were happy with the Constitution. Many delegates feared the federal government would become too strong and would take away the rights of the people. These delegates believed that the new Constitution needed a Bill of Rights similar to the English Bill of Rights. The delegates decided that a Bill

**Separation of Powers**

**Executive**
**The President**
Carry out the laws of Congress
Sign or veto bills
Make foreign treaties
Appoint federal judges

**Legislative**
**Congress**
Pass laws for the nation
Print money and mint coins
Declare war
Create post offices
   and lower courts

**Judicial**
**Federal Courts**
Supreme Court decides if laws
   are unconstitutional
Hear cases in Federal courts
Interpret laws
Settle problems
   between states

of Rights would soon be added to the Constitution.

Before long there were arguments about the Constitution between two groups of people, the Federalists and the Antifederalists. The Federalists supported the Constitution. James Madison, John Jay, and Alexander Hamilton became the most famous Federalists. George Washington and Benjamin Franklin also supported the Constitution. Many Federalists were traders, business owners, or planters. These wealthy people believed a strong central government would protect the nation and its businesses.

The Antifederalists were led by Patrick Henry and Sam Adams. They believed that a strong central government would destroy the rights of the people. They felt state governments needed more power. They were afraid that the President of the United States would act like the king they hated, George III.

By June 1788 nine states had ratified the Constitution. But the Federalists wanted the largest states, New York and Virginia, to ratify it, too. So James Madison and George Washington convinced Virginians to vote for it. In New York, Alexander Hamilton, John Jay, and James Madison wrote many

Some of the new nation's best leaders, including Benjamin Franklin, were at the Constitutional Convention. George Washington was president of the convention. Among the 55 delegates were 8 who had signed the Declaration of Independence and 7 who had been state governors.

*The First Amendment in the Bill of Rights protects the right to free speech and to gather in groups. It is the First Amendment that allows people to tell each other and the government their opinions about issues that are important to them. Without this freedom, there would be no democracy.*

newspaper articles called the "Federalist Papers." These articles explained how the new Constitution would help the nation. Finally New York became the eleventh state to ratify the Constitution.

## The Bill of Rights

The Bill of Rights are laws that protect important rights for every American. These laws, the first ten amendments to the Constitution, were ratified in 1791.

The First Amendment of the Bill of Rights says that the government cannot take away your rights to religious freedom, freedom of speech, or freedom of the press. It says people have the right to gather in groups. The First Amendment says there must be a separation of church and state. This means the government cannot pass laws about religion. Tax money cannot be used to help churches or religious schools. You do not have to belong to a church in order to have the right to vote.

Another amendment says that accused people have the right to a fair, speedy trial. Still another amendment says your property cannot be searched without permission from a judge.

Since 1791 the Constitution and the Bill of Rights have been the laws of the United States. For more than 200 years, those laws have allowed our nation to be a democracy where the rights of all people are respected.

# BIOGRAPHY

## James Madison 1751–1836

James Madison was called the "Great Little Madison" by his friends. Perhaps it was because he weighed less than one hundred pounds and was very short. But it was probably because this man did more to create the Constitution than any other American.

Madison came from Virginia and had written a constitution for that state. When Madison saw the problems that the United States had under the Articles of Confederation, he began to study other types of governments. He believed a strong central government was needed to prevent problems like Shays's Rebellion.

In 1787 Madison became a delegate to the Constitutional Convention. Before going to the Convention, he had written his own plan for a constitution. His plan was known as the Virginia Plan. It included checks and balances, separation of powers, and sharing power between state and federal governments. Most of Madison's ideas became part of the Constitution. To convince delegates to sign the Constitution, Madison made more than one hundred speeches. To get states to ratify the constitution, he wrote the "Federalist Papers" with Alexander Hamilton and John Jay. The "Federalist Papers" were put into a book. It is one of the most important books ever written about government.

After the nation's Constitution was ratified in 1788, Madison wrote the Bill of Rights. His work became the first ten amendments to the Constitution.

Madison kept a journal in which he wrote down everything that was said each day at the Constitutional Convention. Since all meetings were held in secrecy, it is from Madison's journal that we know what happened there.

Madison went on to become the fourth President of the United States. But he is best known as the "Father of the Constitution" because of all he did to create good laws for the United States.

## In Your Own Words

Write a paragraph in the journal section of your social studies notebook that explains why James Madison deserves to be called the "Father of the Constitution."

# REVIEW AND APPLY

- The Articles of Confederation were the first set of laws for the United States.

- The Northwest Ordinance of 1787 divided the Northwest Territory into five territories. These territories became five new states in the United States.

- In May 1787, 55 delegates met in Philadelphia and wrote a new Constitution.

- Antifederalists and federalists argued over the Constitution, which was ratified in 1788.

- Six principles of the Constitution are popular sovereignty, federalism, limited government, separation of powers, checks and balances, and flexibility.

- The first ten amendments of the Constitution are called the Bill of Rights. They protect the individual rights and freedoms of Americans.

## VOCABULARY

**Finish the Sentence ■ Choose one of the words or phrases from the box to complete each sentence. You will not use all the words in the box.**

1. New laws that are added to the Constitution are called

   _____ .

2. A _____ is an important basic belief.

3. Sharing power between the state governments and the

   national government is called _____ .

4. Being able to change in order to meet new conditions is

   called _____ .

5. The _____ branch of government is based in Washington, D.C.

6. To _____ is to approve.

7. The principle that allows the branches of government to limit

   each other's powers is called _____ .

principle
judicial
federal
senator
checks and balances
amendments
flexibility
federalism
ratify
compromise

## USING INFORMATION

**Journal Writing ■ Write a paragraph in your journal that explains why you would have voted for or against the Constitution.**

## COMPREHENSION CHECK

Reviewing Important Facts ■ Match the sentence in Group A with the word or phrase from Group B that the sentence explains. You will not use all the words in Group B.

Group A

_____ 1. The Second Continental Congress created this plan for governing the country.

_____ 2. This law helped the United States govern the land between the Ohio and Mississippi rivers and the Great Lakes.

_____ 3. This plan gave each state two members in the Senate and representation in the House of Representatives based on each state's population.

_____ 4. This is the highest law in the United States.

_____ 5. The President leads this branch of government.

_____ 6. This branch of government passes bills.

Group B

A. Constitution

B. Great Compromise

C. Articles of Confederation

D. executive branch

E. Northwest Ordinance

F. Three-fifths Compromise

G. legislative branch

## CRITICAL THINKING

Categories ■ Read the words in each group. Write a title for each group on the lines above each group. You may use the words in the box for all or part of each title.

| Weaknesses of the Articles of Confederation | Goals of the Constitution |
| Parts of the Constitution | Principles of the Constitution |

1. _____
   no President to lead the nation
   Congress could not raise an army
   Congress could not collect taxes

2. _____
   peace
   freedom
   justice and safety

3. _____
   Preamble
   articles
   amendments

4. _____
   federalism
   flexibility
   checks and balances

# Unit 2 Review

Study the time line on this page. You may want to read parts of Unit 2 again. Then use the words and dates in the box to finish the paragraphs. Write the words and dates you choose on the correct blanks. The box has one possible answer you will not use.

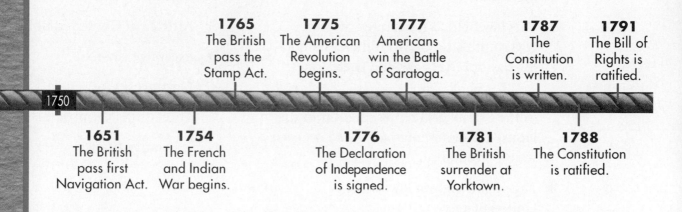

**1765** The British pass the Stamp Act.

**1775** The American Revolution begins.

**1777** Americans win the Battle of Saratoga.

**1787** The Constitution is written.

**1791** The Bill of Rights is ratified.

1750

**1651** The British pass first Navigation Act.

**1754** The French and Indian War begins.

**1776** The Declaration of Independence is signed.

**1781** The British surrender at Yorktown.

**1788** The Constitution is ratified.

| | | |
|---|---|---|
| 1754 | Navigation Acts | Saratoga |
| Harvard College | branches | Great Compromise |
| triangular | American Revolution | July 4, 1776 |
| Great Britain | Treaty of Paris | Stamp Act |
| Yorktown | Philadelphia | Bill of Rights |

Starting in 1651, the British passed _____ to control trade

with the American colonies. The colonies developed _____ trade

routes in order to trade with many nations. Starting in _____ ,

Great Britain and France fought to win control of the Ohio Valley. After France lost

the French and Indian War, _____ ruled all of Canada, the Ohio

Valley, and the colonies along the Atlantic Ocean. To raise money to help pay for the war, Parliament passed new tax laws. One of the new laws passed was the _____, a tax law that required colonists to buy stamps for newspapers, letters, and printed papers. American colonists were angry about the new tax laws.

The _____ began in April 1775 with battles at Lexington and Concord. On _____, Americans used the Declaration of Independence to tell the world the colonies were an independent nation. The turning point of the war was the American victory at the Battle of _____. Finally, in 1781 the British surrendered to George Washington at _____, Virginia. The British and the Americans agreed to peace when they signed the _____ in 1783.

Delegates met in _____ to write the Constitution. To prevent the federal government from becoming too powerful, they divided power between three _____ of government. The _____ solved the problem of representation in Congress. A _____ was added to the Constitution in 1791. The Constitution has governed the United States for more than 200 years.

## Looking Ahead to Unit 3

After the year 1800, the United States grew larger and stronger. The young nation doubled in size with the Louisiana Purchase in 1803. Then in 1812 the United States fought a second war against Great Britain.

During the 1800s, slavery became a bigger problem between the North and the South.

The Missouri Compromise of 1820 prevented a war between North and South. During the 1800s, many people wanted to improve American education, end slavery, and win more rights for women. As you read Unit 3, learn how the 1800s brought growth, change, and problems to the United States.

# THE CONSTITUTION
## of the United States of America

### PREAMBLE

We, the People of the United States, in order to form a more perfect Union, establish justice, insure domestic tranquility, provide for the common defense, promote the general welfare, and secure the blessings of liberty to ourselves and our posterity, do ordain and establish this Constitution for the United States of America.

The preamble is an introduction that states the goals of the Constitution.

We, the people of the United States, want to create a better nation, create a justice system, encourage peace within the nation, defend the nation from enemies, promote the well-being of the people, and protect the freedom of the people now and in future times.

### ARTICLE I. THE LEGISLATIVE BRANCH

**Section 1.** The Congress

All legislative powers herein granted shall be vested in a Congress of the United States, which shall consist of a Senate and House of Representatives.

The power to make laws shall be given to Congress. Congress will have a Senate and a House of Representatives.

**Section 2.** The House of Representatives

The House of Representatives shall be composed of members chosen every second year by the people of the several states, and the electors in each state shall have the qualifications requisite for electors of the most numerous branch of the state legislature.

Members of the House of Representatives shall be elected by voters every two years. Each state decides its own voting requirements, but states must allow all people who vote for members of their state legislatures to vote for members of the House of Representatives.

According to the Fifteenth and Nineteenth Amendments, states cannot take away the right to vote because of race or sex.

No person shall be a Representative who shall not have attained the age of 25 years, and been seven years a citizen of the United States, and who shall not, when elected, be an inhabitant of that state in which he shall be chosen.

To be a member of the House of Representatives, a person must be at least 25 years old, have been an American citizen for at least seven years, and live in the state he or she represents.

Representatives and direct taxes shall be apportioned among the several states which may be included within this Union, according to their respective numbers, which shall be determined by adding to the whole number of free persons, including those bound to service for a term of years, and excluding Indians not taxed, three fifths of all other persons. The actual enumeration shall be made within three years after the first meeting of the Congress of the United States, and within every subsequent term of ten years, in such manner as they shall by law direct. The number of Representatives shall not exceed one for every 30,000, but each state shall have at least one Representative; and until such enumeration shall be made, the state of New Hampshire shall be entitled to choose three, Massachusetts eight, Rhode Island and Providence Plantations one, Connecticut five, New York six, New Jersey four, Pennsylvania eight, Delaware one, Maryland six, Virginia ten, North Carolina five, South Carolina five, and Georgia three.

Representation for each state is based on its population. Every state must have at least one representative. The population of each state must be counted in a census every ten years. The number of representatives from a state can change as the population changes.

The lines in the original Constitution are crossed out because they no longer apply. These lines explain how slaves were to be counted as a result of the Three-Fifths Compromise. The law was overturned by section 2 of the Fourteenth Amendment.

When vacancies happen in the representation from any state, the executive authority thereof shall issue writs of election to fill such vacancies.

When a seat becomes vacant in the House, it must be filled. The state governor must call a special election to fill the seat.

The House of Representatives shall choose their Speaker and other officers; and shall have the sole power of impeachment.

The members of the House must elect a Speaker and other officers. Only the House of Representatives has the power to impeach a member of the federal government.

**Section 3.** The Senate
The Senate of the United States shall be composed of two Senators from each state, chosen by the legislature thereof, for six years; and each Senator shall have one vote.

Each state shall send two senators. Senators serve a six-year term. These senators shall be chosen by the state legislatures.

As part of the Great Compromise, the Framers agreed that all states would have equal representation in the Senate, but representation in the House would be based on population. Since the Seventeenth Amendment was added to the Constitution in 1913, all senators are elected by the voters in every state.

Immediately after they shall be assembled in consequence of the first election, they shall be divided as equally as may be into three classes. The seats of the Senators of the first class shall be vacated at the expiration of the second year, of the second class at the expiration of the fourth year, and of the third class at the expiration of the sixth year, so that one third may be chosen every second year; and if vacancies happen by resignation, or otherwise, during the recess of the legislature of any state, the executive thereof may make temporary appointments until the next meeting of the legislature, which shall then fill such vacancies.

The senators were divided into three groups when they met for the first time in 1789. This was done so that one third of the senator seats would come up for election every two years, while the remaining two thirds of the senators would continue to serve.

The Senate, unlike the House, is a continuing body because only one third of its members are elected at a time.

No person shall be a Senator who shall not have attained the age of thirty years, and been nine years a citizen of the United States, and who shall not, when elected, be an inhabitant of that state for which he shall be chosen.

To be a United States senator, a person must be at least thirty years old, be a citizen for at least nine years, and live in the state he or she represents.

The Vice President of the United States shall be President of the Senate, but shall have no vote, unless they be equally divided.

The Vice President acts as president of the Senate. He or she can vote only to break a tie.

The Senate shall choose their other officers, and also a President *pro tempore*, in the absence of the Vice President, or when he shall exercise the office of President of the United States.

The senators shall elect officers to lead Senate meetings. One of these officers will be a President *pro tempore*, who will lead the Senate when the Vice President cannot attend meetings.

The Senate shall have the sole power to try all impeachments. When sitting for that purpose, they shall be on oath or affirmation. When the President of the United States is tried, the Chief Justice shall preside: and no person shall be convicted without the concurrence of two thirds of the members present.

After the members of the House have voted to impeach a government leader, the impeachment trial can be held only by the Senate. The Chief Justice of the Supreme Court must preside at a trial of the President. A two-thirds vote is needed to convict a leader.

Judgment in cases of impeachment shall not extend further than to removal from office, and disqualification to hold and enjoy any office of honor, trust, or profit, under the United States: but the party convicted shall nevertheless be liable and subject to indictment, trial, judgment, and punishment, according to law.

When a government leader is found guilty by the Senate, that leader is removed from office

and is never allowed to hold another government office. This is the only way a person can be punished by the Senate. However, the guilty leader can be given a regular jury trial and receive punishment from a judge.

Since 1789, only seven people have been found guilty during Senate trials. They were removed from office but never put on trial before a regular court.

## Section 4. Elections

The times, places, and manner of holding elections for Senators and Representatives, shall be prescribed in each state by the legislature thereof; but the Congress may at any time by law make or alter such regulations, except as to the places of choosing Senators.

State legislatures shall decide the places, times, and ways to hold elections for senators and representatives. Congress can make laws to change state decisions on the times and ways to hold elections. It cannot change state decisions on the places for holding elections.

All states hold elections for members of Congress on the first Tuesday after the first Monday in November of even-numbered years.

The Congress shall assemble at least once in every year, and such meeting shall be on the first Monday in December, unless they shall by law appoint a different day.

Congress must meet at least once a year.

## Section 5. Meetings of Congress

Each House shall be the judge of the elections, returns, and qualifications of its own members, and a majority of each shall constitute a quorum to do business; but a smaller number may adjourn from day to day, and may be authorized to compel the attendance of absent members, in such manner, and under such penalties as each House may provide.

Each house decides whether its members meet the qualifications that were stated in Sections 2 and 3 and whether they were legally elected. A quorum, or majority, of members must be present for each house to do business. Each house can decide on punishment for members who miss meetings.

Meetings are often held without a quorum, but a quorum is always needed when voting on a bill.

Each House may determine the rules of its proceedings, punish its members for disorderly behavior, and, with the concurrence of two thirds, expel a member.

Each house makes its own rules for running meetings and deciding how members who disobey rules should be punished. A house can expel one of its members with a two-thirds vote.

Each house has different rules for debates. These rules allow the Senate to have long debates and filibusters, while the House limits debating time.

Each House shall keep a journal of its proceedings, and from time to time publish the same, excepting such parts as may in their judgment require secrecy; and the yeas and nays of the members of either House on any question, shall, at the desire of one fifth of those present, be entered on the journal.

Each house shall publish a journal that tells what happened at each session. Secret information that affects the nation's security may not be published. Voting records on bills are published when one fifth of the members present vote for publication.

Congress's journal, *The Congressional Record*, can be found in public libraries.

Neither House, during the session of Congress, shall, without the consent of the other, adjourn for more than three days, nor to any other place than that in which the two Houses shall be sitting.

Both houses must agree on when to end a session for more than three days. Each house must always meet in the same place.

## Section 6. Salaries and Rules

The Senators and Representatives shall receive a compensation for their services, to be ascertained by law, and paid out of the Treasury of the United States. They shall in all cases, except treason, felony, and breach of the peace, be privileged from arrest during their attendance at the session of their respective Houses, and in going to and returning from the same; and for any speech or debate in either House, they shall not be questioned in any other place.

Members of Congress shall be paid salaries that are decided in laws passed by Congress. Salaries are paid from the nation's treasury. Members cannot be arrested while going to and from their work in Congress unless they commit serious crimes. They cannot be arrested for anything they say or write as part of their work during a session.

No Senator or Representative shall, during the time for which he was elected, be appointed to any civil office under the authority of the United States, which shall have been created, or the emoluments whereof shall have been increased during such time; and no person holding any office under the United States, shall be a member of either House during his continuance in office.

Members of Congress cannot be appointed to government jobs that were created or given a higher salary while they were in office. People cannot serve in Congress while they hold a government job. This clause helps to keep a separation of powers.

## Section 7. Bills

All bills for raising revenue shall originate in the House of Representatives; but the Senate may propose or concur with amendments as on other bills.

All tax bills must start in the House of Representatives. After the bills are passed by the House, they are sent to the Senate. The Senate can approve or amend them.

Every bill which shall have passed the House of Representatives and the Senate, shall, before it become a law, be presented to the President of the United States; if he approve he shall sign it, but if not he shall return it, with his objections, to that House in which it shall have originated, who shall enter the objections at large on their journal, and proceed to reconsider it. If after such reconsideration two thirds of that House shall agree to pass the bill, it shall be sent, together with the objections, to the other House, by which it shall likewise be reconsidered, and if approved by two thirds of that House, it shall become a law. But in all such cases the votes of both Houses shall be determined by yeas and nays, and the names of the persons voting for and against the bill shall be entered on the journal of each House respectively. If any bill shall not be returned by the President within ten days (Sundays excepted) after it shall have been presented to him, the same shall be a law, in like manner as if he had signed it, unless the Congress by their adjournment prevent its return, in which case it shall not be a law.

Every bill that is passed by the House and Senate must then be read by the President. A bill becomes a law if the President signs it within ten days, not counting Sundays. If the President does not approve of the bill, he can veto it by returning the bill unsigned to the house that introduced it. Congress can override the President's veto if two thirds of the members of both houses vote for the bill. Congress's journal must show how the members voted. A bill also becomes a law if the President holds it for ten days, without counting Sundays, and does not sign it. If Congress adjourns and the President holds a bill without signing it for ten days, not counting Sundays, the bill cannot become a law. This last method of defeating a bill is called a pocket veto.

Every order, resolution, or vote, to which the concurrence of the Senate and House of Representatives may be necessary (except on a question of adjournment), shall be presented to the President of the United States; and before the same shall take effect, shall be approved by him, or being disapproved by him, shall be repassed by two thirds of the Senate and House of Representatives, according to the rules and limitations prescribed in the case of a bill.

Every order and joint resolution that is passed by both the Senate and the House needs the President's approval. The President must approve or veto resolutions just as he does bills.

## Section 8. Powers of Congress
The Congress shall have power:

Congress shall have these powers:

To lay and collect taxes, duties, imposts, and excises, to pay the debts and provide for the common defense and general welfare of the United States; but all duties, imposts, and excises shall be uniform throughout the United States;

To collect different kinds of taxes in order to pay for the nation's government and defense; Federal taxes must be the same for every part of the nation.

To borrow money on the credit of the United States;

To borrow money;

The government borrows money by selling bonds. It must repay borrowed money.

To regulate commerce with foreign nations, and among the several states, and with the Indian tribes;

To control commerce with foreign nations, between the states of the nation, and with the Indian tribes;

*Commerce* means trade and business. This commerce clause allows Congress to pass all laws necessary for helping business between states. It also allows Congress to pass laws that control transportation between states.

To establish a uniform rule of naturalization, and uniform laws on the subject of bankruptcies throughout the United States;

To make laws on how people can become citizens; to pass laws about bankruptcy, or losing all of one's money, for the entire nation;

To coin money, regulate the value thereof, and of foreign coin, and fix the standard of weights and measures;

To print and coin money and decide how much that money is worth; to decide how much foreign money is worth in the United States; to set standards for weights and measures;

To provide for the punishment of counterfeiting the securities and current coin of the United States;

To make laws about punishing people who produce counterfeit money, stamps, and government bonds;

To establish post offices and post roads;

To set up post offices and create routes for delivering mail;

To promote the progress of science and useful arts, by securing for limited times to authors and inventors the exclusive right to their respective writings and discoveries;

To promote art and science in the nation by issuing copyrights and patents;

To constitute tribunals inferior to the Supreme Court;

To create a system of lower federal courts; The Framers planned the highest court, the Supreme Court, but gave to Congress the job planning all lower courts.

To define and punish piracies and felonies committed on the high seas, and offenses against the law of nations;

To punish crimes committed on the seas and against other nations;

To declare war, grant letters of marque and reprisal, and make rules concerning captures on land and water;

To declare war and issue letters of marque and reprisal; The President can send troops to fight in any part of the world, but only Congress can declare war. Letters of marque and reprisal were documents issued to allow private ships to attack enemy ships. Since the Civil War, the United States has obeyed an international law that does not allow the use of letters of marque and reprisal.

To raise and support armies; but no appropriation of money to that use shall be for a longer term than two years;

To create and pay for an army; Congress can provide enough money to support the army for two years at a time;

This clause keeps the army under civilian control and limits its power. Since the army depends on Congress for money, it cannot become so powerful that it will take control of the government.

To provide and maintain a navy;

To provide and take care of a navy;

To make rules for the government and regulation of the land and naval forces;

To make rules for controlling the army and navy; In 1950, Congress used this power to pass military laws called the Uniform Code of Military Justice. Since then, amendments have been added to that law.

To provide for calling forth the militia to execute the laws of the Union, suppress insurrections and repel invasions;

To call the militia, or National Guard, into action in order to carry out the nation's laws, put down riots and revolts, and fight against invading enemies;

To provide for organizing, arming, and disciplining the militia, and for governing such part of them as may be employed in the service of the United States, reserving to the states respectively, the appointment of the officers, and the authority of training the militia according to the discipline prescribed by Congress;

To make rules for organizing, controlling, and arming the state militia; states can appoint officers for the Guard, but all soldiers must be trained according to the laws of Congress; Since the National Defense Act was passed in 1916, federal money has been used to help pay for the National Guard. The President can call on the National Guard to help during an emergency or to fight during a war.

To exercise exclusive legislation, in all cases whatsoever, over such district (not exceeding ten miles square) as may, by cession of particular states, and the acceptance of Congress, become the seat of the government of the United States, and to exercise like authority over all places purchased by the consent of the legislature of the state in which the same shall be, for the erection of forts, magazines, arsenals, dockyards, and other needful buildings. And,

To make all laws for the District of Columbia, where the nation's capital is located; to make laws for land owned by the federal government; This land includes national parks, forests, and post offices.

To make all laws which shall be necessary and proper for carrying into execution the foregoing powers, and all other powers vested by this Constitution in the government of the United States, or in any department or officer thereof.

To make all necessary laws so Congress can carry out the powers listed in the Constitution. This clause is called the elastic clause because it allows Congress to write laws that are needed for a changing nation.

**Section 9.** Powers Not Given to Congress

The migration or importation of such persons as any of the states now existing shall think proper to admit, shall not be prohibited by the Congress prior to the year 1808; but a tax or duty may be imposed on such importation, not exceeding ten dollars for each person.

Congress could not make laws to stop the slave trade until the year 1808. This clause was one of the compromises made by the Framers. In 1808, Congress passed a law that stopped the nation from importing slaves from Africa.

The privilege of the writ of *habeas corpus* shall not be suspended, unless when in cases of rebellion or invasion the public safety may require it.

Congress cannot take away the right of *habeas corpus* except if there is a revolution or war.

The writ of habeas corpus is a legal order that says a police officer or sheriff must appear before a judge with a person who is being held in jail. The judge decides whether the accused person is being held legally, and if not, the person must be released. The writ of habeas corpus protects people from being kept in jail without a fair trial.

No bill of attainder or *ex post facto* law shall be passed.

Congress cannot pass a bill of attainder or an *ex post facto* law.

This clause protects a person from being punished without a trial and from being punished for something that was made illegal after he or she did it.

No capitation, ~~or other direct tax~~, shall be laid, unless in proportion to the census or enumeration herein before directed to be taken.

Congress cannot collect a tax on each person unless the tax is based on state populations in the last census.

This clause was changed by the Sixteenth Amendment in 1913. That amendment allows Congress to collect a direct tax on people's income.

No tax or duty shall be laid on articles exported from any state.

Congress cannot tax goods that are exported from one state to another.

No preference shall be given by any regulation of commerce or revenue to the ports of one state over those of another: nor shall vessels bound to, or from, one state be obliged to enter, clear, or pay duties in another.

Congress cannot favor any state when making laws to control trade between states. Ships shall not be taxed when they go from one state to another.

No money shall be drawn from the treasury, but in consequence of appropriations made by law; and a regular statement and account of the receipts and expenditures of all public money shall be published from time to time.

Federal money can only be spent to pay for legislation passed by Congress. It must publish records that show how money is spent.

The power of Congress to spend money is very important. The President can plan programs and policies, but only Congress can provide the money to pay for them.

No title of nobility shall be granted by the United States; and no person holding any office of profit or trust under them, shall, without the consent of the Congress, accept of any present, emolument, office, or title, of any kind whatever, from any king, prince, or foreign state.

Congress is not allowed to give titles of nobility, such as prince, king, or duke, to any person. Members of the government cannot accept gifts or titles from foreign nations without permission from Congress.

This clause is based on the idea from the Declaration of Independence that all people are equal. The Framers did not want the nation to have a noble class of titled people who were more powerful and important than the rest of the population.

## Section 10. Powers Not Given to the States

No state shall enter into any treaty, alliance, or confederation; grant letters of marque and reprisal; coin money; emit bills of credit; make any thing but gold and silver coin a tender in payment of debts; pass any bill of attainder, *ex post facto* law, or law impairing the obligation of contracts, or grant any title of nobility.

States shall not have the power to make treaties and alliances with foreign nations or to coin money. These powers belong to the federal government. Neither state nor federal governments have the power to pass bills of attainder and *ex post facto* laws or to grant titles of nobility.

No state shall, without the consent of the Congress, lay any imposts or duties on imports or exports, except what may be absolutely necessary for executing its inspection laws: and the net produce of all duties and imposts, laid by any state on imports or exports, shall be for the use of the Treasury of the United States; and all such laws shall be subject to the revision and control of the Congress.

States are not allowed to tax imported or exported goods without permission from Congress. They may charge a small fee for the inspection of goods that enter the state. If Congress does permit states to tax goods, the tax money must belong to the United States Treasury. These laws can be changed by Congress.

No state shall, without the consent of Congress, lay any duty of tonnage, keep troops, or ships of war in time of peace, enter into any agreement or compact with another state, or with a foreign power, or engage in war, unless actually invaded, or in such imminent danger as will not admit of delay.

States cannot tax goods on ships. They cannot have their own army and navy, but they can have soldiers in the National Guard. States cannot make treaties or declare war against other nations unless the state is invaded.

Our system of federalism gives all powers of foreign policy and national defense to the federal government.

## ARTICLE II. THE EXECUTIVE BRANCH

### Section 1. President and Vice President

The executive power shall be vested in a President of the United States of America. He shall hold his office during the term of four years, and, together with the Vice President, chosen for the same term, be elected, as follows:

The executive power is given to a President of the United States. The President and the Vice President shall serve four-year terms and be elected as follows:

Each state shall appoint, in such manner as the legislature thereof may direct, a number of electors equal to the whole number of Senators and Representatives to which the state may be entitled in the Congress: but no Senator or Representative, or person holding an office of trust or profit under the United States, shall be appointed an elector.

Each state shall choose a group of people called electors to elect the President. The number of electors from a state must equal the number of senators and representatives from that state. Members of Congress and other government officials cannot be electors.

The electors shall meet in their respective states, and vote by ballot for two persons, of whom one at least shall not be an inhabitant of the same state with themselves. And they shall make a list of all the persons voted for, and of the number of votes for each; which list they shall sign and certify, and transmit sealed to the seat of the government of the

United States, directed to the President of the Senate. The President of the Senate shall, in the presence of the Senate and House of Representatives, open all the certificates, and the votes shall then be counted. The person having the greatest number of votes shall be the President, if such number be a majority of the whole number of electors appointed; and if there be more than one who have such majority, and have an equal number of votes, then the House of Representatives shall immediately choose by ballot one of them for President; and if no person have a majority, then from the five highest on the list the said House shall in like manner choose the President. But in choosing the President, the votes shall be taken by states, the representation from each state having one vote; a quorum for this purpose shall consist of a member or members from two thirds of the states, and a majority of all the states shall be necessary to a choice. In every case, after the choice of the President, the person having the greatest number of votes of the electors shall be the Vice President. But if there should remain two or more who have equal votes, the Senate shall choose from them by ballot the Vice President.

This clause, or paragraph, explains how to elect the President and Vice President. It was changed by the Twelfth Amendment, in 1804.

The Congress may determine the time of choosing the electors, and the day on which they shall give their votes; which day shall be the same throughout the United States.

Congress sets one date for choosing electors and sets another date for electors to vote for President. The dates must be the same for the entire nation.

Electors are chosen every fourth year on Election Day, which is the first Tuesday after the first Monday in November.

No person except a natural-born citizen, or a citizen of the United States, at the time of the adoption of this Constitution, shall be eligible to the office of President; neither shall any person be eligible to that office who shall not have attained the age of 35 years, and been 14 years a resident within the United States.

To be President, a person must be a citizen who was born in the United States, be at least 35 years old, and live in the nation for at least 14 years.

In case of the removal of the President from office, or of his death, resignation, or inability to discharge the powers and duties of the said office, the same shall devolve on the Vice President, and the Congress may by law provide for the case of removal, death, resignation, or inability, both of the President and Vice President, declaring what officer shall then act as President, and such officer shall act accordingly until the disability be removed, or a President shall be elected.

The Vice President shall become the President if the nation's President dies, resigns, or is unable to work. Congress must decide who becomes President if the nation does not have a Vice President.

The Twenty-fifth Amendment tells when the Vice President becomes the President and how another person must then be chosen to be the new Vice President.

The President shall, at stated times, receive for his services a compensation, which shall neither be increased nor diminished during the period for which he shall have been elected, and he shall not receive within that period any other emolument from the United States, or any of them.

The President shall receive a salary. The amount will be decided by Congress, and it cannot be changed while the President is in office. A President cannot receive money from any state or from any other part of the federal government while in office.

Before he enter on the execution of his office, he shall take the following oath or affirmation:

"I do solemnly swear (or affirm) that I will faithfully execute the office of President of the United States, and will to the best of my ability, preserve, protect, and defend the Constitution of the United States."

On the day a President takes office, he must take the Presidential Oath. With this oath, the new President swears to carry out the duties of the presidency and to protect and defend the United States Constitution.

## Section 2. President's Powers

The President shall be Commander in Chief of the Army and Navy of the United States, and of the militia of the several states, when called into the actual service of the United States; he may require the opinion, in writing, of the principal officer in each of the executive departments, upon any subject relating to the duties of their respective offices, and he shall have power to grant reprieves and pardons for offenses against the United States, except in cases of impeachment.

The President shall be the commander in chief of the Army, Navy, and National Guard. He may order the leaders of executive departments to report on their work. The President has the power to grant pardons for federal crimes. Pardons cannot be granted to a person who has been impeached.

This clause puts the military under civilian control. The clause also allows the President to create a cabinet with executive department leaders.

He shall have power, by and with the advice and consent of the Senate, to make treaties,

provided two thirds of the Senators present concur; and he shall nominate, and by and with the advice and consent of the Senate, shall appoint ambassadors, other public ministers and consuls, judges of the Supreme Court, and all other officers of the United States, whose appointments are not herein otherwise provided for, and which shall be established by law: but the Congress may by law vest the appointment of such inferior officers, as they think proper, in the President alone, in the courts of law, or in the heads of departments.

The President can make treaties with foreign nations, but the treaties cannot be used unless two thirds of the senators vote for them. The President appoints ambassadors to foreign nations and judges to the Supreme Court. These appointments must receive a majority of votes in the Senate. The President can appoint people to less-important government offices. Senate approval is not needed for less-important positions.

This clause gives the President the power to make foreign policy. The Senate checks the President's power of making appointments.

The President shall have power to fill up all vacancies that may happen during the recess of the Senate, by granting commissions which shall expire at the end of their next session.

The President can appoint people to government jobs when the Senate is not in session. These jobs will be temporary, since the appointments were not approved by the Senate.

## Section 3. Other Powers

He shall from time to time give to the Congress information of the state of the Union, and recommend to their consideration such measures as he shall judge necessary and expedient; he may, on extraordinary occasions, convene both Houses, or either of them, and in case of disagreement between them, with respect to the time of adjournment, he may adjourn them to such time as he shall think proper; he shall receive ambassadors and other public ministers; he shall take care that the laws be faithfully executed, and shall commission all the officers of the United States.

The President shall deliver a State of the Union address to both houses of Congress. When necessary, he shall recommend to Congress new laws that the nation needs. To deal with emergencies and serious problems, the President may call on Congress to meet in special sessions after it has adjourned. If the two houses cannot agree on when to adjourn, then the President shall decide when Congress shall adjourn. The President shall meet with ambassadors and leaders from other nations. The President must make sure the laws of Congress are carried out properly. The President gives federal officers the power to have their jobs and to do their responsibilities.

Planning the nation's budget is one of the President's major responsibilities. After the President prepares the budget, it must be passed by Congress. Congress checks the President's power because it can vote against the budget or not provide the money the President wants for new programs. Very few special sessions of Congress are called since Congress now meets for most of the year.

## Section 4. Impeachment

The President, Vice President, and all civil officers of the United States, shall be removed from office on impeachment for, and conviction of, treason, bribery, or other high crimes and misdemeanors.

The President, Vice President, and all officers not in the military can be removed from office through impeachment. A President and other officials can be impeached for treason, or giving help to enemy nations, for bribery, and for committing crimes.

Andrew Johnson was the only President to be impeached. The Senate lacked one vote for the required two-thirds vote that was needed to find him guilty.

## ARTICLE III. THE JUDICIAL BRANCH

### Section 1. Judges

The judicial power of the United States, shall be vested in one Supreme Court, and in such inferior courts as the Congress may from time to time ordain and establish. The judges, both of the Supreme and inferior courts, shall hold their offices during good behavior, and shall, at stated times, receive for their services, a compensation, which shall not be diminished during their continuance in office.

Judicial power is given to the Supreme Court and to lower courts that are set up by Congress. Judges of the Supreme Court and the lower federal courts are appointed for lifetime terms, unless they are impeached for wrongdoing. Judges shall be paid salaries that cannot be lowered while they are in office.

The Framers wanted the courts to be separate from the other branches so that judges would not be pressured by Congress or the President to make unfair decisions.

### Section 2. Federal Courts

The judicial power shall extend to all cases, in law and equity, arising under this Constitution, the laws of the United States, and treaties made, or which shall be made, under their authority; to all cases affecting ambassadors, other public ministers and consuls; to all cases of admiralty and maritime jurisdiction; to controversies to which the United States shall be a party; to controversies between two or more states, between a state and citizens of another state; between citizens of different states; between citizens of the same state claiming lands under grants of different states, and between a state, or

~~the citizens thereof, and foreign states, citizens or subjects.~~

Federal courts have the power to hear many different kinds of cases. They can hear all cases that deal with the Constitution, the laws of Congress, ambassadors, ships at sea, the actions of government leaders, problems between two states, and problems between citizens and their state.

The Eleventh Amendment, in 1795, changed this clause slightly. Only state governments can deal with problems between a state and citizens of another state or nation.

This clause gives the Supreme Court the power of judicial review, which is the right to overturn any law that is found unconstitutional. Judicial review is one of the most important powers of the Supreme Court. For example, the Supreme Court used this power to overturn state segregation laws.

In all cases affecting ambassadors, other public ministers and consuls, and those in which a state shall be party, the Supreme Court shall have original jurisdiction. In all the other cases before mentioned, the Supreme Court shall have appellate jurisdiction, both as to law and fact, with such exceptions, and under such regulations, as the Congress shall make.

The Supreme Court has two kinds of jurisdiction, or power, to hear cases. It has original jurisdiction, which is the power to hear cases the first time they go to court; it has appellate jurisdiction, which is the power to hear cases that were decided in a lower court and appealed to the Supreme Court. The Supreme Court has original jurisdiction in cases that involve states or ambassadors. These cases are presented directly to the Supreme Court. Most cases that are heard by the Supreme Court have appellate jurisdiction. Congress can make rules about appealing cases to the Supreme Court.

The trial of all crimes, except in cases of impeachment, shall be by jury; and such trial shall be held in the state where the said crimes shall have been committed; but when not committed within any state, the trial shall be at such place or places as the Congress may by law have directed.

All cases dealing with federal crimes shall be decided by a jury trial in a federal court in the state where the crime was committed.

The right to a jury trial is one of the most important constitutional rights. It began with the Magna Carta in 1215. The Fifth and Sixth Amendments guarantee the rights of accused people.

## Section 3. Treason

Treason against the United States, shall consist only in levying war against them, or in adhering to their enemies, giving them aid and comfort. No person shall be convicted of treason unless on the testimony of two witnesses to the same overt act, or on confession in open court.

A person commits treason against the United States by making war against the nation or by helping the enemies of the nation. A person can be convicted of treason only if two people state before a judge that they witnessed the same act of treason, or if the person confesses to the crime in an open court.

The Congress shall have power to declare the punishment of treason, but no attainder of treason shall work corruption of blood, or forfeiture except during the life of the person attainted.

Congress has the power to make laws for the punishment of treason. Only the person who committed treason, and not the person's family, can be punished.

120

# ARTICLE IV. RELATIONS BETWEEN STATES

## Section 1. Laws

Full faith and credit shall be given in each state to the public acts, records, and judicial proceedings of every other state. And the Congress may by general laws prescribe the manner in which such acts, records, and proceedings shall be proved, and the effect thereof.

Every state must respect the laws, records, and court decisions of every other state.

For example, every state has its own marriage laws. A marriage that takes place in one state is accepted in every other state.

## Section 2. Citizens

The citizens of each state shall be entitled to all privileges and immunities of citizens in the several states.

When citizens visit another state, they must be given the same rights as the people of that state. States cannot treat citizens of other states unfairly.

A person charged in any state with treason, felony, or other crimes, who shall flee from justice, and be found in another state, shall, on demand of the executive authority of the state from which he fled, be delivered up, to be removed to the state having jurisdiction of the crime.

If a person charged with a crime escapes to another state, that person must be found and returned to the state he or she ran away from.

Returning an accused person to the state or nation where the crime took place is called extradition.

No person held to service or labor in one state, under the laws thereof, escaping into another, shall, in consequence of any laws or regulation therein, be discharged from such ser vice or labor, but shall be delivered up on claim of the party to whom such service or labor may be due.

This clause is about returning runaway slaves. This clause was overturned in 1865 by the Thirteenth Amendment, which ended slavery.

## Section 3. States and Territories

New states may be admitted by the Congress into this Union; but no new state shall be formed or erected within the jurisdiction of any other state; nor any state be formed by the junction of two or more states, or parts of states, without the consent of the legislatures of the states concerned, as well as of the Congress.

Congress has the power to admit new states to the Union. New states cannot be created by dividing one state or by joining two or more states, or parts of states, unless the states and Congress agree.

Since 1787, 37 states have become part of the United States. They were all admitted to the Union by Congress. Five of them—Vermont, Kentucky, Tennessee, Maine, and West Virginia— were formed from older states, with their consent.

The Congress shall have power to dispose of and make all needful rules and regulations respecting the territory or other property belonging to the United States; and nothing in this Constitution shall be so construed as to prejudice any claims of the United States, or of any particular state.

Congress shall make rules for selling and controlling federal property and territory.

## Section 4. Protecting the States

The United States shall guarantee to every state in this Union a republican form of government, and shall protect each of them against invasion; and on application of the legislature, or of the executive (when the legislature cannot be convened) against domestic violence.

The United States guarantees that every state shall have a representative government. The federal government shall protect states from enemy invasions. If fighting and violence start in a state, the state legislature or governor can request help from the federal government.

## ARTICLE V. ADDING AMENDMENTS

The Congress, whenever two thirds of both Houses shall deem it necessary, shall propose amendments to this Constitution, or, on the application of the legislatures of two thirds of the several states, shall call a convention for proposing amendments, which, in either case, shall be valid to all intents and purposes, as part of this Constitution, when ratified by the legislatures of three fourths of the several states, or by conventions in three fourths thereof, as the one or the other mode of ratification may be proposed by the Congress; provided that no amendment which may be made prior to the year 1808 shall in any manner affect the first and fourth clauses in the ninth section of the first article; and that no state, without its consent, shall be deprived of its equal suffrage in the Senate.

Amendments can be added to change the Constitution. The process to add amendments begins by proposing the new amendment. A proposal is made by a two-thirds vote for an amendment in both the Senate and House. One can also be made by two thirds of the state legislatures voting to have a national convention to propose an amendment. There are two ratification methods. Three fourths of the state legislatures must vote for the amendment, or three fourths of the state conventions must ratify it. Congress has the power to decide which method should be used for ratification.

Because the Framers made it difficult to add amendments, only 27 have been added to the Constitution. The Twenty-first Amendment was the only one ratified by state conventions. Amendments have allowed the Constitution to be a flexible document.

## ARTICLE VI. THE SUPREME LAW OF THE LAND

All debts contracted and engagements entered into, before the adoption of this Constitution, shall be as valid against the United States, under this Constitution, as under the Confederation.

The United States government must repay debts on money that was borrowed before the Constitution was adopted.

The United States borrowed large amounts of money for the American Revolution and during the years after the war. The Framers wanted the money repaid so that people and other nations would trust the government of the new nation.

This Constitution, and the laws of the United States which shall be made in pursuance thereof; and all treaties made, or which shall be made, under the authority of the United States, shall be the supreme law of the land; and the judges, in every state, shall be bound thereby, anything in the constitution or laws of any state to the contrary notwithstanding.

The Constitution, the laws of Congress, and all treaties are the highest laws of the nation. State judges must understand that the United States Constitution is supreme over state laws.

This clause is called the Supremacy Clause. All state and local laws must agree with the Constitution. The Supreme Court can overturn laws that do not agree with the Constitution.

The Senators and Representatives before mentioned, and the members of the several state legislatures, and all executive and judicial officers, both of the United States and of the several states, shall be bound, by oath or affirmation, to support this Constitution; but no religious test shall ever be required as a qualification to any office or public trust under the United States.

All members of Congress, members of state legislatures, and all executive and judicial branch workers must take an oath and promise to obey the United States Constitution. There can be no religious requirements for people who apply for government jobs.

This clause shows the supremacy of the Constitution. Leaders of state and local governments must promise to obey the United States Constitution and to accept it as the highest law of the nation.

## ARTICLE VII. RATIFICATION

The ratification of the conventions of nine states, shall be sufficient for the establishment of this Constitution between the states so ratifying the same.

The Constitution will become the nation's law when nine states ratify it. Each state will hold a convention to vote on ratification.

Done in convention by the unanimous consent of the states present the 17th day of September in the year of our Lord 1787 and of the independence of the United States of America the 12th. IN WITNESS whereof we have hereunto subscribed our names,

The Constitution was signed by delegates from all 12 states at the Convention. It was signed on September 17, 1787. The nation became independent 12 years before the Constitution was written. Here are the names of the states and their delegates who signed:

### George Washington
President and deputy from Virginia
attest: William Jackson, Secretary

**New Hampshire**
John Langdon
Nicholas Gilman

**Massachusetts**
Nathaniel Gorham
Rufus King

**Connecticut**
William Samuel Johnson
Roger Sherman

**New York**
Alexander Hamilton

**New Jersey**
William Livingston
David Brearley
William Paterson
Jonathan Dayton

**Pennsylvania**
Benjamin Franklin
Thomas Mifflin
Robert Morris
George Clymer
Thomas FitzSimons
Jared Ingersoll
James Wilson
Gouverneur Morris

**Delaware**
George Read
Gunning Bedford, Jr.
John Dickinson
Richard Bassett
Jacob Broom

**Maryland**
James McHenry
Daniel of St. Thomas Jenifer
Daniel Carroll

**Virginia**
John Blair
James Madison, Jr.

### North Carolina
William Blount
Richard Dobbs Spaight
Hugh Williamson

### South Carolina
John Rutledge
Charles Cotesworth Pinckney
Charles Pinckney
Pierce Butler

### Georgia
William Few
Abraham Baldwin

The Constitution was ratified in 1788. Under the laws of this Constitution, Congress met for the first time in 1789. George Washington became the nation's first President in that same year.

---

## AMENDMENTS

The first ten amendments are called the Bill of Rights. They were ratified on December 15, 1791. The other amendments were ratified in the years shown in parentheses.

**AMENDMENT I.** Freedom of Religion, Speech, Press, Assembly, and Petition

Congress shall make no law respecting an establishment of religion, or prohibiting the free exercise thereof; or abridging the freedom of speech, or of the press; or the right of the people peaceably to assemble, and to petition the government for a redress of grievances.

Congress cannot make laws to establish a religion for the nation. It cannot stop people from having freedom of religion. Congress cannot pass laws that take away freedom of speech, freedom of the press, or the right to assemble peacefully in groups. It cannot stop people from asking government leaders to correct something that the people think is wrong.

At the time the Bill of Rights was written, the United States was one of the first nations to allow freedom of religion. The separation of church and state clause in the First Amendment requires that religion be completely separate from the government. This differed from British law, which allowed an official religion that was supported with government money.

Americans use their First Amendment rights when they form groups that work for causes and when they write letters to government leaders. People are not allowed to use their rights to hurt others.

**AMENDMENT II.** The Right to Bear Arms

A well regulated militia, being necessary to the security of a free state, the right of the people to keep and bear arms shall not be infringed.

Every state needs a well-armed militia to protect the people. The federal government cannot take away the right of the people to have guns.

State governments can pass laws to control the ownership of guns. The Second Amendment has been used to prevent Congress from passing gun-control laws.

**AMENDMENT III.** The Housing of Soldiers

No soldier shall, in time of peace, be quartered in any house, without the consent of the owner, nor in time of war, but in a manner to be prescribed by law.

People cannot be forced to have soldiers eat and sleep in their homes in peaceful times. In order for soldiers to stay in civilian homes during a war, Congress must pass a special law.

**AMENDMENT IV.** Search and Arrest

The right of the people to be secure in their persons, houses, papers, and effects, against unreasonable searches and seizures, shall not be violated, and no warrants shall issue, but upon probable cause, supported by oath or affirmation, and particularly describing the place to be searched, and the persons or things to be seized.

People have the right to be safe from police searches and arrests in their homes. Police are not allowed to search people or their homes, arrest people, or seize evidence without a court order or warrant from a judge. A judge can only issue a warrant for very good reasons. Evidence that is taken without a warrant cannot be used to convict a person.

## AMENDMENT V. The Rights of Accused Persons

No person shall be held to answer for a capital, or otherwise infamous crime, unless on a presentment or indictment of a grand jury, except in cases arising in the land or naval forces, or in the militia, when in actual service, in time of war or public danger; nor shall any person be subject for the same offenses to be twice put in jeopardy of life or limb; nor shall be compelled in any criminal case to be a witness against himself, nor be deprived of life, liberty, or property, without due process of law; nor shall private property be taken for public use without just compensation.

A person can stand trial for a capital crime or other serious crime only after being accused of the crime by a grand jury. A capital crime is a crime that can be punished with the death penalty. Once a jury decides that a person is not guilty, that person cannot be tried again for the same crime in the same court. This is known as double jeopardy. Accused people cannot be forced to speak or provide evidence against themselves. Every accused person has the right to due process. This means they must receive fair treatment according to the law. The government must pay a fair price to people when it takes private property for government use.

## AMENDMENT VI. The Right to a Fair Trial

In all criminal prosecutions, the accused shall enjoy the right to a speedy and public trial, by an impartial jury of the state and district wherein the crime shall have been committed, which district shall have been previously ascertained by law, and to be informed of the nature and cause of the accusation; to be confronted with the witnesses against him; to have compulsory process for obtaining witnesses in his favor; and to have the assistance of counsel for his defense.

Every accused person has the right to a speedy trial. The accused must be given a public trial by a fair jury. Accused people must be told what crimes they have been charged with. At the trial, they have the right to question witnesses who present evidence against them. Accused people can have their own witnesses with evidence to support their case. An accused person has the right to be defended in court by a lawyer.

The Framers believed in the importance of a speedy trial. They had seen how accused people in Great Britain were sometimes held in jail for a long time without a trial. Accused people have the right to a jury trial only when they say that they are innocent of the crime. A person who pleads guilty to a crime is sentenced by a judge and does not stand trial. The Sixth Amendment also gives accused people the right to a defense lawyer. In the 1963 case *Gideon* v. *Wainwright*, the Supreme Court decided that a person cannot receive a fair trial without a defense lawyer. Because of that decision, states must provide lawyers to all people who cannot pay for their own defense.

## AMENDMENT VII. Civil Cases

In suits at common law, where the value in controversy shall exceed twenty dollars, the right of trial by jury shall be preserved, and no fact tried by a jury, shall be otherwise re-examined in any court of the United States, than according to the rules of the common law.

This amendment guarantees the right to a jury trial in civil cases that involve at least twenty dollars.

Civil cases are about problems between people, such as money, property, and divorce. Although the Seventh Amendment applies to federal courts, most states also allow jury trials for civil cases.

## AMENDMENT VIII. Bail and Punishment

Excessive bail shall not be required, nor excessive fines imposed, nor cruel and unusual punishments inflicted.

Courts cannot ask accused people to pay unfair amounts of bail money. People cannot be punished with fines that are too high. A person who is found guilty should not be given a cruel or unfair punishment for the kind of crime committed.

Bail is money that a judge orders an accused person to give to the court. Bail money is held by the court until the trial, and then returned when the accused person goes on trial. Since bail money is used to guarantee that the accused person will not run away, the money is not returned if the accused does not come to the trial. If an accused person cannot pay bail, that person must wait in jail until the trial begins. The Framers did not want the amount of bail to be so high that accused people would be forced to wait in jail for their trials.

## AMENDMENT IX. Other Rights

The enumeration in the Constitution, of certain rights, shall not be construed to deny or disparage others retained by the people.

The Constitution explains certain rights that the government must protect. The people have many other important rights that are not listed in the Constitution, and those rights must be protected by the government.

## AMENDMENT X. Powers Belonging to States

The powers not delegated to the United States by the Constitution, nor prohibited by it to the states, are reserved to the states respectively, or to the people.

All of the powers that the Constitution did not give to the federal government and did not keep from the states belong to state governments and to their people.

When the Constitution was written, many people feared that the federal government would have too much power over the states. The Tenth Amendment showed that federalism allows both a strong federal government and separate state governments with many powers of their own.

## AMENDMENT XI. Cases Against States (1795)

The judicial power of the United States shall not be construed to extend to any suit in law or equity, commenced or prosecuted against one of the United States by citizens of any state, or by citizens or subjects of any foreign state.

A state cannot be sued in a federal court by a citizen from another state or from a foreign nation.

## AMENDMENT XII. Election of the President and Vice President (1804)

The electors shall meet in their respective states and vote by ballot for President and Vice President, one of whom, at least, shall not be an inhabitant of the same state with themselves; they shall name in their ballots the person voted for as President, and in distinct ballots the person voted for as Vice President, and they shall make distinct lists of all persons voted for as President, and of all persons voted for as Vice President, and of the number of votes for each, which lists they shall sign and certify, and transmit sealed to the seat of the government of the United States, directed to the President of the Senate; the President of the Senate shall, in the presence of the Senate and House of Representatives, open all the certificates and the votes shall then be counted. The person having the greatest number of votes for President shall be the President, if such number be a majority of the whole number of electors appointed; and if no person have such majority, then from the persons having the highest numbers, not exceeding three on the list of those voted for as President, the House of Representatives shall choose immediately, by ballot, the President. But in choosing the President, the votes shall be taken by states, the representation from each state having one vote; a quorum for this purpose shall consist of a member or members from two-thirds of the states, and a majority of all the states shall be necessary to a choice. And if the House of Representatives shall not choose a President whenever the right of choice shall devolve upon them, before the fourth day of March next following, then the Vice President shall act as President, as in the case of the death or other constitutional disability of the President. The person having the greatest number of votes as Vice President, shall be the Vice President, if such number be a majority of the whole number of electors appointed, and if no person have a majority, then from the two highest numbers on the list, the Senate shall choose the Vice President; a quorum for the purpose shall consist of two-thirds of the whole number of Senators, and a majority of the whole number shall be necessary to a choice. But no person constitutionally ineligible to the office of President shall be eligible to that of Vice President of the United States.

To elect a President, electors shall meet in their own states and cast one ballot for a presidential candidate and another ballot for a vice-presidential candidate. When all electors have voted, the ballots are sent to the president of the United States Senate. The president of the Senate shall count the votes for each candidate in front of both houses of Congress. The presidential candidate with the greatest number of votes shall be

President. The winning candidate must receive more than half of the electoral votes. If none of the candidates receive a majority of votes, then the House of Representatives must choose one of the candidates to be President. Each state is allowed only one vote when electing the President. At least two thirds of the states must cast votes. To be elected, a candidate must receive a majority of votes in the House. If the House does not choose a President by March 4, the Vice President shall act as President. (The date of March 4 was later changed to January 20 in the Twentieth Amendment.) The vice-presidential candidate with the greatest number of electoral votes shall be the Vice President. If none of the candidates receive a majority of votes, then the Senate shall choose the Vice President. Two thirds of the senators must vote. The candidate who receives a majority of votes shall be Vice President. The Vice President must meet the same constitutional requirements of age, residency, and citizenship as the President.

The Twelfth Amendment overturned the procedures for electing a President that were listed in Article 2, Section 1, Clause 3. Much of the presidential election process is not included in the Constitution. Thomas Jefferson and John Quincy Adams were the only presidents that were chosen by the House of Representatives.

## AMENDMENT XIII. Slavery (1865)

Section 1. Neither slavery nor involuntary servitude, except as a punishment for a crime whereof the party shall have been duly convicted, shall exist within the United States, or any place subject to their jurisdiction.

Section 2. Congress shall have power to enforce this article by appropriate legislation.

This amendment ended slavery. It said that slavery shall not exist in the United States or in territories ruled by this nation. Forced labor can be used only as a punishment for crime.

127

Congress shall have the power to make laws to carry out this amendment.

**AMENDMENT XIV. Rights of Citizens (1868)**

Section 1. All persons born or naturalized in the United States, and subject to the jurisdiction thereof, are citizens of the United States and of the state wherein they reside. No state shall make or enforce any law which shall abridge the privileges or immunities of citizens of the United States; nor shall any state deprive any person of life, liberty, or property, without due process of law; nor deny to any person within its jurisdiction the equal protection of the laws.

All people who are born or naturalized in the United States are citizens of both the nation and the state where they live. A naturalized citizen is a person who was born in a different nation, moved to the United States, and went through a legal process to become a citizen. States cannot make laws that take away the rights of citizens. States must give all people the right to due process. They cannot punish people by taking away their life, freedom, or property without due process. Every person in a state must be given equal protection by the laws.

The first sentence in this amendment gave citizenship to African Americans. The Fifth Amendment guaranteed due process to people accused of crimes by the federal government. The Fourteenth Amendment guarantees that state governments will also allow due process to all people. Many civil rights laws that have been passed by Congress are based on the Fourteenth Amendment. The equal protection clause was used by the Supreme Court when it ruled on the *Brown v. Topeka Board of Education* case. The Supreme Court decided that separate schools for African American children and white children did not allow equal protection. That decision and the Fourteenth Amendment were used to overturn state segregation laws across the nation.

Section 2. Representatives shall be apportioned among the several states according to their respective numbers, counting the whole number of persons in each state, excluding Indians not taxed. But when the right to vote at any election for the choice of electors for President and Vice President of the United States, representatives in Congress, the executive and judicial officers of a state, or the members of the legislature thereof, is denied to any of the male inhabitants of such state, being 21 years of age, and citizens of the United States, or in anyway abridged, except for participation in rebellion or other crime, the basis of representation therein shall be reduced in the proportion which the number of such male citizens shall bear to the whole number of male citizens 21 years of age in such state.

The number of members from each state in the House of Representatives depends on the state's population. This clause overturned the Three-Fifths Compromise that was used in Article 1. This clause says that everyone is counted in the census except Indians, who are not taxed. States cannot take away the right to vote in state or federal elections unless a person has committed a serious crime. States that unfairly take away the right to vote will have fewer representatives in Congress. States must allow all men who are over the age of 21 to vote.

This amendment says states that take away voting rights can be punished by losing some of their representatives in Congress, but this punishment has never been used. Voting rights were given to women in the Nineteenth Amendment and to people as young as eighteen in the Twenty-sixth Amendment.

Section 3. No person shall be a Senator or Representative in Congress, or elector of President and Vice President, or hold any office, civil or military, under the United States, or under any state, who, having previously taken an oath, as a member of Congress, or as an officer of the United States, or as a member of any state legislature, or as an executive or judicial officer of any state, to support the Constitution of the United States, shall have engaged in insurrection or rebellion against the same, or given aid or comfort to the enemies thereof. But Congress may, by a vote of two-thirds of each house, remove such disability.

This section was added to punish people who had been Confederate leaders during the Civil War. It says that they cannot hold office in the federal government. Congress can vote to remove this penalty.

In 1898, Congress removed this punishment for Confederate leaders.

Section 4. The validity of the public debt of the United States, authorized by law, including debts incurred for payment of pensions and bounties for services in suppressing insurrection or rebellion, shall not be questioned. But neither the United States nor any state shall assume or pay any debt or obligation incurred in aid of insurrection or rebellion against the United States, or any claim for the loss or emancipation of any slave; but all such debts, obligations and claims shall be held illegal and void.

The United States is required by law to pay its debts on money borrowed for the Civil War. Neither the United States government nor the state governments are allowed to pay the war debts of the Confederate States. People who once owned slaves will not be paid for the loss of their slaves.

Section 5. The Congress shall have power to enforce, by appropriate legislation. the provisions of this article.

Congress shall have the power to make the laws that are needed to carry out this amendment.

**AMENDMENT XV.** Right to Vote (1870)

Section 1. The right of citizens of the United States to vote shall not be denied or abridged by the United States or by any state on account of race, color, or previous condition of servitude.

Citizens cannot be prevented from voting because of race, color, or because they have been slaves.

Section 2. The Congress shall have power to enforce this article by appropriate legislation.

Congress shall have the power to make laws to enforce this amendment.

The Fifteenth Amendment could only be carried out by laws of Congress. Many states passed laws that made it difficult for African Americans to vote. Martin Luther King, Jr., worked hard to win fair voting laws. His work influenced Congress, and in 1965 the Voting Rights Act was passed.

**AMENDMENT XVI.** Income Tax (1913)

The Congress shall have power to lay and collect taxes on incomes, from whatever source derived, without apportionment among the several states, and without regard to any census or enumeration.

Congress shall have the power to collect taxes on income. The amount of tax money collected does not depend on state populations.

Almost half of the money in the federal budget now comes from personal income taxes.

**AMENDMENT XVII.** Election of Senators (1913)

The Senate of the United States shall be composed of two Senators from each state, elected by the people thereof, for six years; and each Senator shall have one vote. The electors in each state shall have the qualifications requisite for electors of the most numerous branch of the state legislatures.

When vacancies happen in the representation of any state in the Senate, the executive authority of such state shall issue writs of election to fill such vacancies: *Provided*, That the legislature of any state may empower the executive thereof to make temporary appointments until the people fill the vacancies by election as the legislature may direct.

This amendment shall not be so construed as to effect the election or term of any Senator chosen before it becomes valid as part of the Constitution.

The United States Senate shall have two senators from each state. They shall be elected by the people of their states to serve six-year terms. Each senator shall have one vote. When there is a vacant seat in the Senate because a senator can no longer represent the state, the governor of that state shall call an election for a new senator. The state legislature can allow the governor to appoint a temporary senator, who will serve until the election takes place.

This amendment overturned the method of choosing senators that was discussed in Article 1, Section 3, Clauses 1 and 2, of the Constitution. Article 1 required that senators be elected by state legislatures. This amendment allows senators to be elected directly by the people in the same way that members of the House of Representatives are chosen. The amendment gives people a greater voice in government since they can choose their own representatives for both houses of Congress.

## ~~AMENDMENT XVIII.~~ Prohibition of Liquor (1919)

~~Section 1. After one year from the ratification of this article the manufacture, sale, or transportation of intoxicating liquors within, the importation thereof into, or the exportation thereof from the United States and all territory subject to the jurisdiction thereof for beverage~~ ~~purposes is hereby prohibited.~~

One year after this amendment is ratified, liquor cannot be manufactured, sold, imported, or exported in the United States.

~~Section 2. The Congress and the several states shall have concurrent power to enforce this article by appropriate legislation.~~

Congress and the states have the power to make laws to enforce this amendment.

~~Section 3. This article shall be inoperative unless it shall have been ratified as an amendment to the Constitution by the legislatures of the several states, as provided in the Constitution, within seven years from the date of the submission hereof to the states by the Congress.~~

This amendment must be ratified within seven years or it cannot be part of the Constitution.

This amendment was repealed in 1933 by the Twenty-first Amendment. The laws against liquor were called Prohibition Laws. During the time known as Prohibition, a great deal of liquor was manufactured and sold illegally.

## AMENDMENT XIX. Woman Suffrage (1920)

The right of citizens of the United States to vote shall not be denied or abridged by the United States or by any state on account of sex.

Citizens of the United States shall not be prevented from voting because of their sex.

Congress shall have power to enforce this article by appropriate legislation.

Congress shall have the power to pass laws to carry out this amendment.

Wyoming was the first state to give women the right to vote in state elections. Later, other states gave this right to women. But women in all states wanted to vote in national elections, so they worked for the woman suffrage amendment. From 1878 to 1918, an amendment on woman suffrage was proposed and defeated each year in Congress. Finally, the House approved the amendment in 1918, and the Senate did so in 1919. When it was ratified in 1920, woman had the right to vote in local, state, and national elections.

## AMENDMENT XX. Lame Duck Amendment (1933)

Section 1. The terms of the President and Vice President shall end at noon on the 20th day of January, and the terms of Senators and Representatives at noon on the third day of January, of the years in which such terms would have ended if this article had not been ratified; and the terms of their successors shall then begin.

The term of office of the President and Vice President shall end on January 20 at noon. The term of office for senators and representatives of Congress shall end on January 3 at noon. The new President and Vice President will take office on January 20. New members of Congress will take office on January 3.

Members of Congress who were defeated in the November elections are considered to have less power from that time until the new members are sworn in. These defeated members are called lame ducks. This amendment shortened the length of time a Lame Duck could remain in office.

Until this amendment, newly elected members did not begin work until March 4. This was so because when the Constitution was written, it took a long time for mail to reach the members and inform them of their new job. Then it took a while for them to travel to the capital to begin their work.

Section 2. The Congress shall assemble at least once in every year, and such meeting shall begin at noon on the third day of January, unless they shall by law appoint a different day.

Congress shall meet at least once each year.

The meetings shall begin on January 3 at noon.

Section 3. If, at the time fixed for the beginning of the term of the President, the President elect shall have died, the Vice President elect shall become President. If a President shall not have been chosen before the time fixed for the beginning of his term, or if the President elect shall have failed to qualify, then the Vice President elect shall act as President until a President shall have qualified; and the Congress may by law provide for the case wherein neither a President elect nor a Vice President elect shall have qualified, declaring who shall then act as President, or the manner in which one who is to act shall be selected, and such person shall act accordingly until a President or Vice President shall have qualified.

If the President elect dies, the Vice President elect shall become the new President. If a new President has not been chosen before the time the new term is to begin, the Vice President elect will act as President. Congress can pass laws to decide who will be a temporary President if the nation does not have a President elect or a Vice President elect.

This section discusses problems that have never happened in the history of the United States.

Section 4. The Congress may by law provide for the case of the death of any of the persons from whom the House of Representatives may choose a President whenever the right of choice shall have devolved upon them, and for the case of the death of any of the persons from whom the Senate may choose a Vice President whenever the right of choice shall have devolved upon them.

The Twelfth Amendment required the House of Representatives to choose a President if none of the presidential candidates received a majority of electoral votes. If one of the three presidential candidates dies, Congress can pass a law on how to choose a President. This also applied to the Vice President.

This situation has never occurred, and Congress has never had to pass this type of law.

Section 5. Sections 1 and 2 shall take effect on the 15th day of October following the ratification of this article.

After this amendment is ratified, Sections 1 and 2 will take effect on October 15.

Section 6. This article shall be inoperative unless it shall have been ratified as an amendment to the Constitution by the legislatures of three-fourths of the several states within seven years from the date of its submission.

This amendment must be ratified within seven years by three fourths of the state legislatures.

## AMENDMENT XXI. Repeal of the Eighteenth Amendment (1933)

Section 1. The Eighteenth article of amendment to the Constitution of the United States is hereby repealed.

The Eighteenth Amendment on prohibition is no longer a law of the United States.

Section 2. The transportation or importation into any state, territory, or possession of the United States for delivery or use therein of intoxicating liquors, in violation of the laws thereof, is hereby prohibited.

States can make their own laws about selling, transporting, or prohibiting liquor. It is a federal crime to disobey a state's liquor laws.

Section 3. This article shall be inoperative unless it shall have been ratified as an

amendment to the Constitution by conventions in the several states, as provided in the Constitution, within seven years from the date of the submission hereof to the states by the Congress.

To become an amendment, this law must be ratified by state conventions within seven years.

The Twenty-first Amendment was the only amendment ratified by state conventions. Although Americans drank less liquor during the years the Prohibition Amendment was in effect, the amendment encouraged people to break the law in order to buy, sell, and manufacture liquor.

## AMENDMENT XXII. Terms of the Presidency (1951)

Section 1. No person shall be elected to the office of the President more than twice, and no person who has held the office of President, or acted as President, for more than two years of a term to which some other person was elected President shall be elected to the office of the President more than once. But this article shall not apply to any person holding the office of President when this article was proposed by the Congress, and shall not prevent any person who may be holding the office of President, or acting as President, during the term within which this article becomes operative from holding the office of President or acting as President during the remainder of such term.

No person shall be elected to more than two terms of presidential office. A President who serves two years of another President's elected term can be elected to two more terms. A President shall not serve for more than ten years.

Section 2. This article shall be inoperative unless it shall have been ratified as an amendment to the Constitution by the legislatures of three fourths of the several States within seven years from the date of its submission to the States by Congress.

This amendment cannot be part of the Constitution unless it is ratified by three fourths of the state legislatures within seven years.

George Washington served only two terms of office. This tradition was followed by every President until Franklin D. Roosevelt was elected to four terms. Many Americans felt a President could become too powerful if he remained in office for more than ten years. So this amendment was added to the Constitution.

## AMENDMENT XXIII. Voting in the District of Columbia (1961)

Section 1. The district constituting the seat of government of the United States shall appoint in such manner as the Congress may direct: A number of electors of President and Vice President equal to the whole number of Senators and Representatives in Congress to which the district would be entitled if it were a state, but in no event more than the least populous state; they shall be in addition to those appointed by the states, but they shall be considered, for the purposes of the election of the President and Vice President, to be electors appointed by a state; and they shall meet in the district and perform such duties as provided by the Twelfth article of amendment.

The people of the District of Columbia, as residents of the nation's capital and seat of government, shall vote for electors in presidential elections. The number of electors is to be the same as if the District of Columbia were a state. It cannot have more electors than the state with the smallest population. The electors shall help elect a President by following the rules of the Twelfth Amendment.

Section 2. The Congress shall have power to enforce this article by appropriate legislation.

Congress has the power to make laws to enforce this amendment.

Until 1961, citizens of Washington, D.C., could not vote in presidential elections. The District of Columbia is an area that is located between Maryland and Virginia. Since it is not a state, its citizens were not allowed to vote for President.

## AMENDMENT XXIV. Poll Taxes (1964)

Section 1. The right of citizens of the United States to vote in any primary or other election for President or Vice President, for electors for President or Vice President, or for Senator or Representative in Congress, shall not be denied or abridged by the United States or any state by reason of failure to pay any poll tax or other tax.

It is the right of every citizen to vote in primary elections and presidential elections. Every citizen has the right to vote for senators and representatives in Congress. The federal and state governments cannot take away these rights because a person does not pay a poll tax or other kind of tax.

Section 2. The Congress shall have the power to enforce this article by appropriate legislation.

Congress has the power to make laws to enforce this amendment.

After 1889, eleven southern states had poll taxes. The poll-tax laws were used to prevent African Americans from voting. The Twenty-fourth Amendment said poll taxes could not be used to take away voting rights in federal elections. The amendment did not prevent states from having poll taxes for state and local elections. In 1966, the Supreme Court ruled that poll taxes were against the Equal Protection Clause of the Fourteenth Amendment. All poll taxes were declared unconstitutional, and they could no longer be used to stop people from voting.

## AMENDMENT XXV. Presidential Succession (1967)

Section 1. In case of the removal of the President from office or his death or resignation, the Vice President shall become President.

*The Vice President shall become President if the President dies, resigns, or is removed from office.*

Section 2. Whenever there is a vacancy in the office of the Vice President, the President shall nominate a Vice President who shall take office upon confirmation by a majority vote of both houses of Congress.

*Since the nation must have a Vice President, this office must be filled if it becomes vacant. The President shall nominate a person for Vice President. If a majority of senators and representatives vote for the nominated person, that person becomes the new Vice President.*

*Checks and balances are used since the House and Senate can check the President's choice for Vice President.*

Section 3. Whenever the President transmits to the president *pro tempore* of the Senate and the Speaker of the House of Representatives his written declaration that he is unable to discharge the powers and duties of his office, and until he transmits to them a written declaration to the contrary, such powers and duties shall be discharged by the Vice President as Acting President.

*If a President is unable to carry out his duties, he must write and tell the president pro tempore of the Senate and the Speaker of the House. Then the Vice President must be acting President until the President is able to work again.*

*In 1985, Vice President George Bush acted as President while Ronald Reagan had surgery.*

Section 4. Whenever the Vice President and a majority of either the principal officers of the executive departments or of such other body as Congress may by law provide, transmit to the President pro tempore of the Senate and the Speaker of the House of Representatives their written declaration that the President is unable to discharge the powers and duties of his office, the Vice President shall immediately assume the powers and duties of the office as Acting President.

Thereafter, when the President transmits to the President pro tempore of the Senate and the Speaker of the House of Representatives his written declaration that no inability exists, he shall resume the powers and duties of his office unless the Vice President and a majority of either the principal officers of the executive department or of such other body as Congress may by law provide, transmit within four days to the President pro tempore of the Senate and the Speaker of the House of Representatives their written declaration that the President is unable to discharge the powers and duties of his office. Thereupon Congress shall decide the issue, assembling within 48 hours for that purpose if not in session. If the Congress, within 21 days after receipt of the latter written declaration, or, if Congress is not in session, within 21 days after Congress is required to assemble, determines by two-thirds vote of both houses that the President is unable to discharge the powers and duties of his office, the Vice President shall continue to discharge the same as Acting President; otherwise, the President shall resume the powers and duties of his office.

*If the Vice President and a majority of cabinet leaders or Congress feels that the President is unable to carry out his duties, then they must tell this in writing to the president pro tempore of the Senate and the Speaker of the House. Then the Vice President shall be acting President. Then, if the President writes that he is again able to carry out his duties, he will do so. However, the Vice*

President and a majority of cabinet leaders can write declaring the President still unfit. Both houses must vote on the President's condition within 21 days. The Vice President will remain acting President if two thirds of the members of both houses vote for the Vice President. If there are not enough votes for the Vice President, the President can start to work again.

This amendment was added to make clear just what steps would be followed to decide whether the President is unable to carry out his duties. This was not made clear in Article 2, Section 1, Clause 6.

**AMENDMENT XXVI.** Voting Age of 18 (1971)

Section 1. The right of citizens of the United States, who are 18 years of age or older, to vote shall not be denied or abridged by the United States or by any state on account of age.

All citizens who are at least 18 years of age shall be allowed to vote in state and federal elections.

Section 2. The Congress shall have power to enforce this article by appropriate legislation.

Congress shall have the power to pass laws to enforce this amendment.

The Constitution in 1787 gave the right to vote to white men. After the Civil War, the right to vote was given to African Americans. Then woman suffrage became law with the Nineteenth Amendment. Voting rights were given to the people of Washington, D.C., in 1961. Finally in 1971, the right to vote was given to 18-year-olds.

**AMENDMENT XXVII.** Congressional Pay (1992)

No law varying the compensation for the services of the Senators and Representatives shall take effect, until an election of Representatives shall have intervened.

Salary increases given to members of Congress will not take effect until after the next congressional election. This amendment prevents the members of Congress in session from giving themselves higher pay.

This amendment was originally introduced in 1789, but was not ratified for the Constitution by the necessary three fourths of the states until 1992.

# UNIT 3

# THE NATION GROWS AND CHANGES

*A* brave young Shoshone woman named Sacagawea and her French-Canadian husband helped a group of explorers cross the Rocky Mountains. The group, led by Meriwether Lewis and William Clark, traveled to the Pacific Ocean. They brought exciting information about the West back to President Thomas Jefferson.

As you read Unit 3, you will learn how the nation grew larger and stronger. Find out why Americans fought wars in 1812 and 1848. Learn how Americans moved west when gold was found in California.

## THINK ABOUT IT

- George Washington was the only President who did not join a political party. Why?
- Andrew Jackson became a war hero after the Battle of New Orleans, but this battle should not have been fought. Why?
- The invention of the cotton gin made slaves more valuable than ever. Why?
- One state was once an independent republic with its own president. Which state?

---

**1750**                    **1800**

**1789**
George Washington becomes first President.

**1791**
Bank of the United States Begins.

**1793**
Eli Whitney invents the cotton gin.

**1803**
United States buys Louisiana.

**1807**
The Embargo act stops trade with France and Great Britain.

**Lewis and Clark expedition, 1804-1806**

**1814**
Treaty of Ghent ends War of 1812.

**1823**
President Monroe delivers the Monroe Doctrine.

**1832**
South Carolina passes the Nullification Act.

**1846**
United States and Great Britain compromise over Oregon.

**1853**
Mexico agrees to the Gadsden purchase.

1850

**1812**
War of 1812 begins.

**1820**
The Missouri Compromise is written.

**1828**
Andrew Jackson is elected President.

**1836**
Texas wins independence from Mexico.

**1849**
Gold Rush begins in California.

137

# Chapter 10

# THE START OF THE NEW NATION

◄ *George Washington coins from 1790*

**People**

Benjamin Banneker •
Anthony Wayne • Pierre
L'Enfant • Maurice de
Talleyrand • Napoleon
Bonaparte • Charles
Pinckney • Aaron Burr •
Richard Henry Lee

**Places**

Mount Vernon • District of
Columbia • Potomac River •

Washington, D.C.

**New Vocabulary**

precedents • appointed •
Cabinet • rebel •
foreign affairs •
political parties •
foreign minister •
unconstitutional •
electoral college •
electors • candidates

**Focus on Main Ideas**

1. How did Alexander Hamilton's plans help the United States pay its debts?
2. What difficult decisions did George Washington and John Adams make as Presidents?
3. Why did the House of Representatives elect the President in 1800?

In April 1789 George Washington left the home he loved in Virginia and traveled with his wife, Martha, to New York City. That city, the largest in the country, was the nation's first capital. Crowds cheered for Washington as he traveled through towns on his way to New York. On April 30, 1789, Washington was inaugurated as the nation's first President.

## The New Government Begins

In 1788 the Constitution had been ratified, and the new Congress started meeting in March 1789. The first job for Congress was to write the Bill of Rights. Congress also created executive departments to help the President carry out his duties. George Washington knew that his actions would create **precedents**, or examples, that future Presidents would follow. So he was careful about every decision he made. Washington **appointed**, or selected, people to advise him and to lead the new executive departments. These people were called the **Cabinet**. Every President has followed Washington's precedent and has had a Cabinet of leaders.

The Constitution gave Congress the power to create a federal court system.

138

To do this, Congress passed a law called the Judiciary Act. It gave the nation's highest court, the Supreme Court, six judges called justices. The leader of the Court is called the Chief Justice. Today the Supreme Court has nine justices. The Judiciary Act also created federal courts that heard cases in different parts of the nation.

## Paying the Nation's Debts

In 1789 the new government had huge war debts. To pay for the American Revolution, the Continental Congress had borrowed millions of dollars from other nations and from the American people by selling bonds. After a certain period of time, the government had to repay the money it borrowed, with interest. If the new country could not pay its debts, no nation and no person would ever lend money to the American government again.

Alexander Hamilton, secretary of the treasury, made plans for the United States to pay all its debts. He asked Congress to pass new tax laws. Hamilton also wanted to create a Bank of the United States where the federal government would keep the tax money it collected. This bank would lend money to businesses in order to help them grow. The taxes these businesses paid would help the nation grow.

The men pictured here with George Washington were members of the first Cabinet. From the right they are Attorney General Edmund Randolph, Secretary of State Thomas Jefferson, Secretary of the Treasury Alexander Hamilton, and Secretary of War Henry Knox.

*Washington chose Benjamin Banneker, a free African American, to survey the land for the nation's new capital city.*

Thomas Jefferson and James Madison believed that the Constitution did not give Congress power to create the Bank of the United States. But Hamilton said the Elastic Clause in the Constitution allowed Congress to pass laws to carry out its powers. The Bank would help Congress carry out its power to collect taxes. In 1791 Congress passed a law creating the Bank of the United States.

Alexander Hamilton's plans worked well. Slowly the government collected enough tax money to repay its debts, and the American economy grew stronger.

## Problems and Decisions for the New Government

The Northwest Ordinance of 1787 said settlers could not take land away from the Indians of the region. But American settlers moved into the Northwest Territory and settled on Indian land. There were many fights between the settlers and the Indians of the region. In 1793 George Washington sent General Anthony Wayne to the Northwest Territory to protect the settlers. After two years of fighting, the Indians surrendered and signed the Treaty of Greenville.

After Congress put a tax on whiskey in 1791, frontier farmers started the Whiskey Rebellion. The farmers grew corn that they made into whiskey. Many farmers earned most of their money from the sale of whiskey. In 1794 the farmers prepared to fight to end the whiskey tax. President Washington led about 13,000 soldiers against the frontier farmers. When they reached the frontier, none of the **rebel** farmers could be found. Unlike Shays's Rebellion in 1786, the Whiskey Rebellion ended quickly. The new government was strong enough to stop rebellions and keep order in the nation.

Washington had to make difficult decisions about the nation's **foreign affairs**. In 1793 Great Britain went to war against France. The British seized American ships that were trading with France. Many Americans wanted the United States to help France and go to war against Great Britain. But Washington felt the United States was not strong enough to fight another war against Britain. Instead he sent John Jay to Great Britain to discuss a peace treaty. Although many people thought Jay's Treaty was unfair to the United States, Washington accepted the treaty in order to avoid war. By avoiding war the United States had time to grow stronger.

By the end of his first term as President, Washington wanted to retire. But members of the Cabinet asked him to serve another term. In 1796 Washington decided not to serve a third term as President. This decision set the precedent that Presidents should serve only two terms. For the next 145 years, no President served more than two terms.

At the end of his term, Washington wrote his famous Farewell Address. He told the American people to remain united at home and to develop more trade with other nations. He warned his country to remain neutral and to not favor any foreign nation: "Tis our true policy to steer clear of permanent alliances with any portion of the foreign world."

President Washington retired to his home at Mount Vernon. On the way home, he stopped to visit the site where the nation's new capital was being built.

Congress had passed a bill that allowed the nation to build a new capital city. Washington had helped plan the District of Columbia along the Potomac River between Virginia and Maryland. He had asked Pierre L'Enfant of France to plan the capital. That city became Washington, D.C.

## The United States Under President John Adams

Disagreements between two Cabinet members, Thomas Jefferson and Alexander Hamilton, led to the development of the first **political parties**. Jefferson's party became the Democratic Republican party. Its members were often called Republicans. This is not the same as the modern Republican party, which began in the 1850s. Alexander Hamilton's party became the Federalist party. John Adams, a Federalist, was elected President in 1796.

Soon after Adams became President, he faced serious problems with France. The French had seized American ships that were trading in the West Indies. Adams sent three Americans to France to end this problem. The **foreign minister** of France, Maurice de Talleyrand, sent three men to meet secretly with the

*In 1795 the chiefs of 12 Indian nations in the Northwest Territory signed the Treaty of Greenville. In this treaty the Indians agreed to give the United States a large part of what is now the state of Ohio.*

141

Americans. The French men said France would stop seizing ships if the United States paid ten million dollars to France. The three French men were called Mr. X, Mr. Y, and Mr. Z, so the problem with the French became known as the XYZ Affair.

The American people were furious about the XYZ Affair. The words "Millions for defense, but not one cent for tribute" were heard everywhere. In other words, Americans would spend money to defend their nation, but they would not spend money to pay for favors. Adams made an agreement with the new French leader, Napoleon Bonaparte, without paying the money. France agreed to stop seizing American ships.

In 1798 the Federalists in Congress passed several unfair laws called the Alien and Sedition Acts. The Alien Act forced people from foreign countries to wait 14 years instead of 5 years to become American citizens. The Sedition Act said it was a crime to write or print anything against the government. This law took away rights that were protected by the First Amendment of the Constitution.

Thomas Jefferson and James Madison believed the new laws were **unconstitutional**. So in 1798 Jefferson wrote the Kentucky Resolution. It said Kentucky did not have to obey a federal law that was unconstitutional. Madison wrote almost the same thing in the Virginia Resolution. Because of these resolutions, many people wondered if state governments should have more power or less power than the federal government. This question would continue to be a problem for the next 65 years of American history.

## The Election of 1800

The Constitution states that the President must be elected by the **electoral college**. Each state chooses delegates called **electors** for the electoral college. The number of electors chosen by a state is the same as the number of representatives and senators the state sends to Congress. Electors meet to vote for the President and the Vice President. During the nation's early years, the person who received the most electoral votes became President. The person who received the second largest number of votes became Vice President.

In the election of 1800, John Adams and Charles Pinckney were the Federalist **candidates**. Thomas Jefferson and Aaron Burr were the Republican candidates. Adams lost the election when Jefferson and Burr received more votes. But Jefferson and Burr received the same number of votes.

The Constitution said the House of Representatives must elect the President when there is a tie vote. For six days members of the House voted, and each time there was a tie vote. Then Alexander Hamilton advised other Federalists to vote for Jefferson because he would be a better leader than Burr. Jefferson was elected President, and Burr became Vice President. Because of this election, the Twelfth Amendment was added to the Constitution in 1804. It required separate voting for President and Vice President.

The election of 1800 gave power to the Republican party. Thomas Jefferson, the man who wrote the Declaration of Independence, became the nation's third President.

## George Washington 1732-1799

George Washington has been called the "father of our country." He earned that honor by leading the United States during the country's difficult early years.

Washington was born in Virginia. He led soldiers from Virginia against the French during the French and Indian War. He spent 16 years as a farmer after the war. He also became a judge in a Virginia court. He was elected to the Virginia House of Burgesses where he helped write laws for the colony.

Washington married Martha Custis. Martha had been married before, and Washington adopted Martha's children, John and Patsy.

Washington was a delegate to the First and Second Continental Congresses. He was chosen as commander in chief of the American Army. Washington led Americans to victory in 1781.

After the war Washington was glad to return to his plantation at Mount Vernon. He studied ways to grow better crops and raise healthier farm animals. But when the United States needed a Constitution, Washington agreed to lead the Constitutional Convention. When the new nation chose its first President, Americans wanted Washington. He became President, and Congress passed a law that gave him a salary of $25,000 each year. That was a large salary in 1789.

Washington disliked political parties, and he was the only President who never belonged to one. Some people complained that he behaved like a king. He rode white horses, wore expensive clothes, and had many servants. But he never wanted more power. In 1797 he retired and became a farmer again. Washington died in 1799. The new capital city was named Washington, D.C., to honor the nation's first President.

After his death, Washington's close friend Richard Henry Lee said that Washington was "first in war, first in peace, and first in the hearts of his countrymen."

## In Your Own Words

Write a paragraph in your notebook that tells how George Washington served his country in war and in peace.

# REVIEW AND APPLY

## CHAPTER 10 MAIN IDEAS

- After the Constitution was ratified in 1788, the new government was started.

- George Washington, the country's first President, selected people to advise him. These people became known as the President's Cabinet.

- The challenges that faced the new government included paying the debt from the American Revolution, stopping the rebellion against taxes by frontier farmers, and settling the Northwest Territory.

- George Washington served two terms as President. He was followed by President John Adams and President Thomas Jefferson.

- The election of 1796 saw the creation of the country's first political parties, the Democratic Republicans and the Federalists.

## VOCABULARY

Finish the Sentence ■ Choose one of the words or phrases from the box to complete each sentence. You will not use all the words in the box.

1. George Washington set a _____ , or example, for future Presidents by not serving a third term as President.

2. President Washington's _____ advised him on issues such as the national debt and foreign affairs.

3. The Democratic Republicans and the Federalists were the

   country's first _____ .

4. Thomas Jefferson and James Madison believed that Americans

   should not obey laws that were _____ , or went against

   the Constitution.

5. The Constitution states that the President must be elected by the

   _____ .

> unconstitutional
> precedent
> candidates
> Cabinet
> political parties
> electoral college

## USING INFORMATION

Writing an Opinion ■ The election of 1800 was decided by a vote in the House of Representatives. Who would you have voted for if you had been a member of the House of Representatives in 1800?

## COMPREHENSION CHECK

**Who Said It?** ■ Read each statement in Group A. Then look in Group B for the person who might have said it. You will not use all the words in Group B.

### Group A

_____ 1. "I was the first President of the United States."

_____ 2. "My plan for paying off the country's debts included creating the Bank of the United States."

_____ 3. "I was sent to the Northwest Territory to protect settlers."

_____ 4. "I planned the city of Washington, D.C."

_____ 5. "As President, I refused to pay the French any bribe money."

_____ 6. "I wrote the Declaration of Independence."

_____ 7. "I surveyed the land for the nation's capital."

### Group B

A. Pierre L'Enfant

B. John Jay

C. George Washington

D. Thomas Jefferson

E. Benjamin Banneker

F. Alexander Hamilton

G. John Adams

H. Anthony Wayne

## CRITICAL THINKING

**Categories** ■ Read the words in each group. Write a title for each group on the line above each group. You may use the words in the box for all or part of each title. There is one title in the box that you will not need to use.

| Political Parties | The Bank of the United States | The XYZ Affair |
| The President's Cabinet | The Electoral College | |

1. _____

   included Secretary of Treasury
      Alexander Hamilton
   advised President Washington
   every President has had one to
      give advice

2. _____

   created to pay off country's debts
   first proposed by Alexander Hamilton
   lent money to American businesses

3. _____

   occurred with the country of France
   made the American people very angry
   America was asked to pay ten million
      dollars

4. _____

   has representatives from each state
   created in the Constitution
   meets to elect the President and
      the Vice President

# A TIME OF GROWTH AND WAR

◀ Scales of Justice

## People

James Monroe • William
Marbury • John Marshall •
Meriwether Lewis • William
Clark • York • Shoshone •
Sacagawea • William Henry
Harrison • Tecumseh •
Henry Clay • Dolley
Madison • Francis Scott Key
• Andrew Jackson •
Seminoles • Simón Bolívar •
José de San Martín

## Places

New Orleans • St. Louis •
Tippecanoe Creek • Fort
McHenry • Latin America

## New Vocabulary

repealed •judicial
review •impressed •
Embargo Act •
War Hawks • anthem

### Focus on Main Ideas

1. Why was *Marbury v. Madison* an important Supreme Court case?
2. How did the Louisiana Purchase help the United States?
3. Why did the United States fight in the War of 1812?
4. What important ideas were in the Monroe Doctrine?

The years between 1800 and 1825 were a time of growth, war, and change for the United States. During these twenty-five years, the nation was led by three Virginians—Thomas Jefferson, James Madison, and James Monroe.

## The Age of Jefferson Begins

The election of Jefferson in 1800 was a victory for his Democratic Republican party. But Jefferson did not want the differences between Republicans and Federalists to tear the nation apart. In his first speech as President, Jefferson said, "We are all Republicans, we are all Federalists." He kept many of the laws and ideas of the Federalists. Jefferson continued Hamilton's program of paying off the nation's debts. He also kept the Bank of the United States. But Jefferson also made changes. During his first term, the Alien and Sedition Acts ended, and the Whiskey Tax was **repealed**.

## The Louisiana Purchase

Louisiana was a huge region to the west of the Mississippi River. Louisiana and New Orleans belonged to France until France gave them to Spain in 1762. Spain allowed American farmers to use the port of New Orleans. Farmers west of the Appalachian Mountains would send their products down the river to the port. In New Orleans, products were moved from river boats to oceangoing ships.

In 1800 Napoleon Bonaparte, the ruler of France, won control of Louisiana. Jefferson wanted the United States to control New Orleans. So he sent James Monroe to France to buy the important port. Napoleon needed money for his wars in Europe, so he offered to sell Louisiana and New Orleans for $15 million. In 1803 Jefferson signed a treaty agreeing to purchase, or buy, Louisiana.

The Louisiana Purchase doubled the size of the United States. The nation now owned all the land between the Atlantic Ocean and the Rocky Mountains. Jefferson wanted to learn about the land of the Louisiana Purchase. He hired Meriwether Lewis and William Clark to explore Louisiana. In May 1804 the Lewis and Clark expedition left from St. Louis, Missouri, with about 40 men. One of these men, York, was Clark's African American slave. York was a great help to the expedition because he had the ability to make friends with the Indians they met. The expedition traveled northwest until cold weather forced them to spend the winter in North

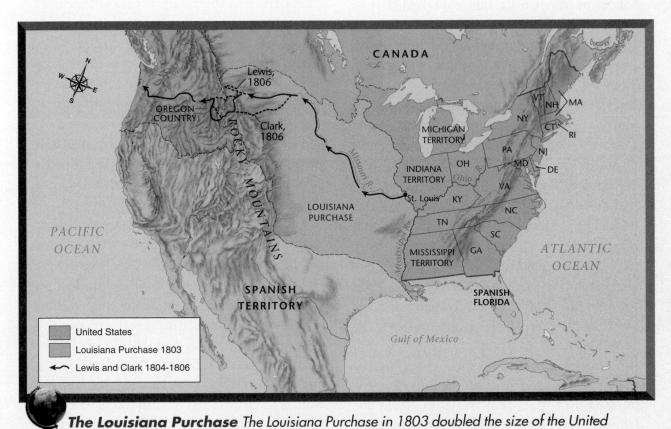

**The Louisiana Purchase** *The Louisiana Purchase in 1803 doubled the size of the United States. President Jefferson sent Meriwether Lewis and William Clark on an expedition to explore this area. After leaving St. Louis, on what river did the expedition travel into Louisiana?*

Dakota. There they met a young Shoshone woman named Sacagawea. She and her French Canadian husband agreed to join the expedition and help them cross the Rocky Mountains. In November 1805 they finally reached the Pacific Ocean. Then the group began the long trip home. They reached St. Louis in September 1806. York became free at the end of the expedition. Lewis and Clark gave Jefferson new maps and information about Louisiana.

## Marbury v. Madison

The *Marbury* v. *Madison* case of 1803 became one of the most important cases the Supreme Court has ever heard. Just before leaving office, President Adams had appointed William Marbury to be a judge. The Judiciary Act that Congress passed in 1789 allowed President Adams to do this. But the new secretary of state, James Madison, refused to give Marbury this job. Marbury took his case to the United States Supreme Court.

At the time, John Marshall was Chief Justice of the United States. Marshall and the other justices decided that the Judiciary Act of 1789 was unconstitutional. Because that law was used to appoint Marbury as a judge, Marbury could not have the job given to him. Marshall's decision was important because it gave the Supreme Court the power of **judicial review**. This means that the United States Supreme Court has the power to decide if any federal or state law is unconstitutional. This decision made the federal government more powerful because the Supreme Court could decide if state laws had to be changed.

## Problems that Led to the War of 1812

When Napoleon went to war against Britain, it became difficult for the United States to be neutral. Both Britain and France seized hundreds of American trading ships, but the large British Navy captured most of them. The British often **impressed**, or forced, American sailors from these captured ships into the British Navy. The United States insisted that both nations respect America's right to have freedom of the seas.

In 1807 President Jefferson asked Congress to pass the **Embargo Act**. This law stopped all American trade with other countries. New England lost money because it depended on trade. The Embargo Act hurt Americans far more than it hurt Britain or France. The Embargo Act made so many Americans unhappy that Congress repealed it.

By the end of 1808, Thomas Jefferson had served two terms as President. He followed Washington's precedent and retired. James Madison was elected President.

While Americans tried to solve their problems with the British, they also faced problems with Indians in the Northwest Territory. As Americans moved onto Indian lands in Indiana, they faced new Indian attacks. In 1809 the governor of the Indiana Territory, General William Henry Harrison, pressured the Indians into signing an unfair treaty. In this treaty the Indians sold a large amount of Indiana land to the United States for very little money.

A Shawnee chief, Tecumseh, became furious when he learned about the treaty.

Tecumseh had fought the Americans during the American Revolution. Since then he had fought to slow the spread of settlers onto Indian lands. In 1811 General Harrison prepared to attack Tecumseh's village on Tippecanoe Creek in Indiana. Tecumseh was away, but his brother was defeated when he led an attack against Harrison. After defeating the Shawnees in the Battle of Tippecanoe, Harrison destroyed their village. Tecumseh would fight against the United States again later.

## The War of 1812

The British continued to seize American ships and impress American sailors. The question of going to war against Britain divided the nation. People in New England did not want war because war would prevent trade with other nations. People in the South and in the West favored going to war. These people, called **War Hawks**, were led by Senator Henry Clay of Kentucky. They wanted to end British attacks on American ships. In June 1812 President Madison asked Congress to declare war against Great Britain. The War of 1812 had begun.

The United States was not prepared for war in 1812. Its army and navy were small. But the war was difficult for Britain, too. Until 1814 most British soldiers and sailors were fighting a war against Napoleon.

In 1813, American troops captured the Canadian city of York, which is now called Toronto. Americans burned the government buildings in York. But Canada remained part of Great Britain. Later that year, Tecumseh was killed while fighting Americans in Canada.

Tecumseh fought to slow the spread of settlers onto Indian lands. He tried to unite several Indian nations into a confederation that would not sell land to settlers.

In 1814 Napoleon was defeated in Europe, and British soldiers stopped fighting the French. The British sent many more ships, sailors, and soldiers to fight against the United States. In August 1814 the British prepared to attack Washington, D.C.

President Madison was with the army in Maryland when the British attacked Washington. Madison sent a message to his wife, Dolley, telling her to escape from the capital as quickly as possible. Dolley packed important government papers in trunks. She packed a famous painting of George Washington that had been hanging in the White House dining room. Then she left the capital. The British entered the city and burned many buildings.

Next the British planned to capture Baltimore, but the city's harbor was protected by Fort McHenry. Francis Scott Key, an American who watched the battle at Fort McHenry, was filled with joy when he saw the American flag flying over the fort after the long battle. He wrote a poem about the flag called "The Star Spangled Banner." That poem became our country's national **anthem**.

Peace talks to end the war began in August 1814. On December 24, 1814, the United States and Great Britain signed a peace treaty called the Treaty of Ghent.

The last battle of the War of 1812 was actually fought in January 1815, not long after the peace treaty was signed. News about the treaty did not reach the United States until February. General Andrew Jackson had learned that the British wanted to capture New Orleans. So he gathered more than 5,000 soldiers to defend the city. Many free African Americans joined Jackson's army. During the Battle of New Orleans, 2,200 British soldiers were wounded or killed, and only 8 Americans died. Jackson became a war hero.

The United States did not win new land in the War of 1812. But the United States did win respect from Great Britain and other European nations.

*Many of the battles during the War of 1812 were fought along the border of Canada. In the Battle of Lake Erie, Oliver Hazard Perry defeated a British fleet and took control of Lake Erie. His ship was damaged during the battle, and he had to take a rowboat to get to another American ship.*

## The Era of Good Feelings

The Republican party was so popular after the War of 1812 that the Federalist party lost most of its members. In the election of 1816, the Republican candidate, James Monroe, won 183 out of 217 electoral votes.

The years when Monroe was President have been called the Era of Good Feelings. During this time the nation grew larger. By 1821 the nation had 24 states. Businesses were growing, and many Americans were earning more money.

While Monroe was President, many slaves in the South ran away to Spanish Florida to hide among the Seminole Indians. Monroe sent General Jackson to Florida to attack the Seminoles and capture runaway slaves. Jackson fought battles against the Seminoles and destroyed their villages. But he also captured two Spanish forts. The Spanish were too weak to fight back. In 1819 Spain signed the Adams-Onís Treaty, which gave Florida to the United States for about $5 million.

## The Monroe Doctrine

For a few hundred years, Spain had ruled a large empire in America. But in the early 1800s, Spain's colonies began to fight for independence. The fight for freedom in Latin America began in Mexico in 1810. In South America Simón Bolívar and José de San Martín helped Spanish colonies win freedom. By 1822 most nations in Central and South America were independent.

President Monroe feared that other European nations might try to start colonies in Latin America. To prevent this

*Simón Bolívar led five South American nations to independence from Spain. He is known as the George Washington of South America.*

from happening, Monroe gave a speech to Congress that is now called the Monroe Doctrine. Monroe stated that the United States would not allow European countries to start new colonies in Latin America. The United States might even go to war to prevent new European colonies. European nations must stay out of the Americas. In return the United States would stay out of Europe's affairs. The Monroe Doctrine helped many future Presidents decide how to handle problems with Latin America.

The United States had grown stronger, larger, and more powerful when Jefferson, Madison, and Monroe served as Presidents. In the next chapter, you will learn about other changes that took place in the nation during this time.

# BIOGRAPHY

## Sacagawea

Sacagawea helped Lewis and Clark reach the Pacific Ocean. Most of what is known about this woman comes from the journals that Lewis and Clark wrote during their expedition.

Sacagawea was born a Shoshone, but she was kidnapped at about age 12 by the Minnetaree Indians. She lived with them in what is now North or South Dakota. Toussaint Charbonneau, a French Canadian fur trapper, was also living with the Minnetarees. He bought Sacagawea from them when she was about 14 years old and married her in an Indian ceremony.

Sacagawea met Lewis and Clark during the winter that they spent in North Dakota. They hired her husband to be an interpreter for them because he knew Indian sign language. Sacagawea was also hired because she knew the Shoshone language.

During the winter in North Dakota, Sacagawea gave birth to a baby boy. Although she had to care for a baby, Sacagawea kept up with the expedition.

As the expedition traveled through Shoshone country, Lewis and Clark met the Shoshone chief Cumeahwait. To Sacagawea's surprise, the chief was her brother. She had not seen him since the day she had been kidnapped.

Sacagawea's knowledge of the plants of the region helped her to show the men which plants were safe to eat. Because Sacagawea and her baby were traveling with Lewis and Clark, the Indian groups that they met were friendly towards the expedition. Sacagawea helped Lewis and Clark cross the Rocky Mountains and reach the Pacific. When the expedition ended, Sacagawea, her husband, and her son returned to live with the Shoshone. No one is certain what happened to Sacagawea later in life. Some believe she died of illness when she was only 25. Others believe Sacagawea lived with the Shoshones in Wyoming until she died in 1884. She would have been almost 100 years old.

### In Your Own Words

Write a paragraph in the journal section of your notebook explaining how Sacagawea helped Lewis and Clark.

# REVIEW AND APPLY

- The early 1800s was a time of growth, war, and change for the United States.

- The United States nearly doubled its size when it purchased the Louisiana Territory from France for $15 million.

- The War of 1812 was fought because the British had seized American ships and impressed American sailors.

- James Monroe was elected President in 1816 and brought in the Era of Good Feelings. American businesses and the nation were growing.

- The Monroe Doctrine offered Latin American countries help from the United States if European nations tried to make colonies in Latin America.

## VOCABULARY

Choose the Meaning ■ Write the letter of the word or phrase that best completes each sentence.

1. A **republic** is a _____ .

   a. form of government
   b. political party
   c. branch of government

2. **Repeal** means to _____ .

   a. fight against
   b. do away with
   c. declare something unconstitutional

3. The **Embargo Act** _____ .

   a. stopped other countries from trading with the United States
   b. stopped the United States from trading with other countries
   c. stopped all trade to and from the United States

4. To **impress** means to _____ .

   a. sign
   b. fight
   c. draft

5. **War Hawks** were people who _____ .

   a. wanted war
   b. opposed war
   c. wanted to remain neutral

6. Our country's national **anthem** is a _____ .

   a. book
   b. song
   c. flag

## USING INFORMATION

Writing an Essay ■ During the early 1800s, the United States went through a period of growth, war, and change. Select one of these three areas and write an essay relating it to the United States during this time.

## COMPREHENSION CHECK

**Understanding Events in History** ■ Complete the graphic organizer below with information about the Louisiana Purchase.

*What two leaders were involved?*

_____

_____

*Why did France sell this land?*

_____

_____

**The United States Bought the Louisiana Territory**

*In what year did it happen?*

_____

*What are two results of this event?*

_____

_____

_____

## CRITICAL THINKING

**Cause and Effect** ■ Choose a cause or an effect from Group B to complete each sentence in Group A. Group B has one more answer than you need.

**Group A**

1. The Supreme Court decided that the Judiciary Act of 1789 was unconstitutional, so _____ .

2. _____ , so France sold Louisiana to the United States for $15 million.

3. News of the peace treaty ending the War of 1812 did not reach the United States until two months later, _____ .

4. _____ , so his time as President became known as the Era of Good Feelings.

5. President Monroe was afraid that European nations would try to set up colonies in Latin America, _____ .

**Group B**

A. so Jay's Treaty was signed

B. France needed to pay off its war debts

C. While James Monroe was President, the country grew

D. the *Marbury* v. *Madison* court case gave the Supreme Court the power of judicial review

E. so he gave a speech that is now called the Monroe Doctrine

F. so the Battle of New Orleans was fought after the war was over

154

# Chapter 12

# GROWTH AND SECTIONALISM

◀ *Eli Whitney's cotton gin*

## People

Samuel Slater • Robert Fulton • John Quincy Adams • John C. Calhoun • Creek • Cherokee • Choctaw • Chickasaw • Sequoya • Osceola • Black Hawk • Sauk • Fox

## Places

Erie Canal • Rock River

## New Vocabulary

Industrial Revolution • textile mills • fibers • cotton gin • sectionalism • tariffs • Union • majority • spoils system • states' rights • nullify

## Focus on Main Ideas

1. How did the Industrial Revolution affect the North and the South?
2. How did North, South, and West differ in their ideas about slavery, building roads, and tariffs?
3. What important decisions did Andrew Jackson make as President?

**D**uring the Era of Good Feelings, feelings of unity among Americans grew stronger. While events like the War of 1812 united most Americans, other forces were dividing the nation.

## The Industrial Revolution

The **Industrial Revolution** was a change from making products by hand at home to making products by machine in factories. It began in the 1700s in Great Britain with the invention of machines that could spin cotton thread. Then weaving machines were invented. Factories called **textile mills** were built where workers used these new machines to spin thread and weave cloth. In 1789 Samuel Slater came to America from England. In Rhode Island Slater built factories that had spinning machines. Before long, there were many textile mills in the North.

The textile mills in the North needed the cotton **fibers** taken from cotton plants that were grown in the South. It took many hours of work to remove the cotton seeds from the cotton fibers. Eli Whitney helped solve this problem when he invented the **cotton gin** in 1793. This machine quickly separated the cotton seeds from the fibers.

One cotton gin could do the work of many people. Because of the cotton gin, southern planters could grow and harvest large amounts of cotton. As more factories were built in the North, more cotton was needed. Soon cotton became the most important southern crop, and people began saying "Cotton is king."

Southern planters wanted to start new plantations in the West to grow more cotton. They insisted on bringing their slaves to work on these new cotton plantations. The spread of slavery was one of several issues that would divide the nation.

## The Growth of Sectionalism

In each section of the nation—the North, the South, and the West—people cared more about the needs and interests of their part of the country than about what was good for the entire nation. This division of the nation into regions with different interests has been called **sectionalism**.

By 1820 three important issues were dividing the nation. The first issue was the use of **tariffs**, or taxes on goods brought into the country from other countries. Tariffs helped industries in the North and West because they encouraged people to buy less expensive American-made products. Southerners did not want tariffs that would make European products more expensive.

A second issue was that states in the North and West wanted to use federal money to build roads across the country. The South had less need for roads. It had many rivers that it used for transportation and shipping. A National Road was built from Maryland to Illinois.

During this time other improvements in transportation were made. Steamboats and canals improved water transportation. Robert Fulton's invention of the steamboat in 1807 made it possible for ships to sail upstream quickly. The Erie Canal was built to create a water route from the Great Lakes to the Hudson River. Trade between New York City and the West increased greatly.

The most serious issue that divided the nation was slavery. The slave trade from Africa had ended in 1808, but buying and selling slaves continued within the United States. Americans argued about allowing slavery in the new territories in the West. The people in these territories wanted to join the **Union** as new states. The South wanted slavery in these new states. The North and the West wanted these new states to be free from slavery.

## The Missouri Compromise

The issue of slavery almost tore the nation apart in 1820. Missouri wanted to join the Union as a slave state. At that time there were 11 slave states and 11 free states. If Missouri joined the Union, the slave states would have more representation than the free states in the Senate. The slave states would have more power to pass laws that favored slavery. In 1820 Henry Clay suggested a compromise.

In this compromise, Missouri joined the Union as a slave state and Maine joined as a free state. Then a line was drawn from Missouri's southern border across the Louisiana Purchase. All land north of that line would be free territory. All land south of that line would be slave territory.

*The invention of the cotton gin and the new textile mills in the North increased the demand for cotton grown on plantations in the South. Greater demand for cotton led southern planters to use more slaves to work in the fields.*

The compromise provided a way to allow Missouri to join the Union and still keep the balance between slave and free states.

## The Elections of 1824 and 1828

James Monroe had served two terms as a very popular President. In the election of 1824, the candidates were all Republicans. They represented different sections of the nation. John Quincy Adams was the candidate from the North. His father, John Adams, had been the second President. William H. Crawford came from the South. Henry Clay and Andrew Jackson were both candidates from the West. Although Clay was respected in Congress, he was far less popular than Jackson. In the election of 1824, more people voted for Jackson than for the other candidates, but none of the candidates won a **majority** of electoral votes. So the House of Representatives had to elect the President. The House elected John Quincy Adams.

As President, John Quincy Adams tried to improve roads, canals, and industry. But Adams was not popular, and Congress would not pass laws to put his plans into action.

In the election of 1828, Jackson and Adams were the main candidates. Jackson and his followers from the Republican party formed a new political party, the Democratic party. Jackson won the election.

Jackson's opponents became known as the Whigs. The Federalist party and the Republican party had lost all their power.

## The Age of Jackson

The inauguration of Andrew Jackson was an exciting event. People traveled hundreds of miles to watch the man they loved become President. Jackson, who was from Tennessee, became the first President from west of the Appalachian Mountains. After the inauguration people crowded into the White House to meet the new President. They broke furniture and dishes as they pushed to get close to Jackson. He spent the night in a hotel to get away from the crowds.

Because Jackson favored the common people, he was called the "people's President." He believed that the common people should have power in government. While he was President, more white men in the western states won the right to vote because voting rules about owning property were removed.

Jackson created a **spoils system** that gave government jobs to the people who supported him. Although other Presidents had also given jobs to their supporters, Jackson was the first to brag about his actions.

Before Jackson became President, Congress had passed high tariffs. The southern states were angry because these tariffs made products from Europe more

**The Missouri Compromise** In this compromise, Maine and Missouri became states, and a line was drawn to separate free territory from slave territory. According to the Missouri Compromise, is the Unorganized Territory supposed to be free or slave territory?

expensive. John C. Calhoun, Jackson's Vice President, led the fight against the tariffs. He believed in **states' rights,** which meant that the state governments should have more power than the federal government. He said states had the right to **nullify** laws they believed were unconstitutional.

Many people thought President Jackson, a man who owned slaves, would agree with Calhoun. But Jackson strongly disagreed. At a dinner party, Jackson stood up and said, "Our Union—it must be preserved." In other words the United States could be a nation only if all states obeyed its laws.

In 1832 South Carolina passed a law that said the tariff laws were unconstitutional. The new law said South Carolina would leave the Union if it was forced to pay the tariffs. Jackson said he would send soldiers to South Carolina to force that state to obey the tariff law. He said that no state had the right to nullify the laws of Congress or leave the Union. Henry Clay wrote a compromise law that lowered the tariffs. South Carolina agreed to pay the tariffs. "Do states have the right to disobey federal laws that they believe are unconstitutional?" would continue to be a question that would trouble the nation.

The Bank of the United States had been started by Alexander Hamilton. Jackson disliked the Bank because he felt it favored the wealthy. In 1832 Congress wrote a bill to give the Bank a new charter, but Jackson

*Andrew Jackson had fought in the American Revolution at age 13. He had become a lawyer and a senator. Jackson became a hero by winning the Battle of New Orleans at the end of the War of 1812. In this painting, Jackson is giving a speech while running for President.*

**159**

vetoed that bill. After he was reelected, Jackson had the government take its money out of the Bank. The Bank could not do its work without government money. In 1836 the Bank no longer existed.

## The Trail of Tears

In 1830 Congress passed the Indian Removal Act, which forced Indians to move west across the Mississippi River. From 1830 to the early 1840s, the United States Army forced about 100,000 Indians—such as Creek, Cherokee, Choctaw, Chickasaw, and Seminole—to leave their homes. Because thousands of Indians died along the way from hunger, disease, and cold weather, the trip west has been called the "Trail of Tears."

The Cherokee had become farmers, built schools and churches, and had a representative government. One Cherokee, Sequoya, had developed an alphabet for the language of his people. The Cherokee took their case to the Supreme Court. The Supreme Court decided that the Cherokee should keep their land. But Jackson refused to obey the Supreme Court's decision.

In Florida the Seminole, led by Osceola, fought against the American Army. After winning several battles, Osceola was captured. Other Seminole continued the fight, but by 1840 there were few Indians east of the Mississippi River.

*About 100,000 Indians were forced to leave their homes and travel hundreds of miles to settle in Oklahoma. Because thousands of Indians died from hunger, disease, and cold weather, the trip west has been called the "Trail of Tears."*

# IOGRAPHY

## Black Hawk 1767–1838

Black Hawk, a leader of the Sauk and Fox nations, decided to fight for the land that belonged to his people. Black Hawk was born near the Rock River in Illinois. Black Hawk began fighting for his people soon after the Sauk were tricked into signing an unfair treaty in 1804. Five Sauk leaders were tricked by William Henry Harrison. He gave them whiskey. While the Sauk were drunk, they signed a treaty that gave all of their land east of the Mississippi River to the United States. In return the United States would pay the Sauk about $3,000.

Black Hawk was furious when he learned about the treaty. Black Hawk decided to fight the United States. During the War of 1812, he fought with Tecumseh on the side of the British.

The United States government wanted the Sauk and Fox nations to move west to Iowa. The chief of the Sauk agreed to move. By 1830 most of the Sauk and the Fox had settled in Iowa.

Black Hawk refused to leave Illinois. Instead, in 1832 Black Hawk and his sons led a group of Sauk and Fox against the United States Army. The war became known as the Black Hawk War. Black Hawk and his men fought bravely, but the American Army had more soldiers and better weapons. The war ended in August 1832 when Black Hawk and his sons were captured. They were taken to Washington, D.C., as prisoners.

While Black Hawk was a prisoner, he told the story of his life to a soldier, and it was published as Black Hawk's autobiography. From this autobiography we know how Black Hawk fought to keep Sauk lands. Black Hawk returned to his people and settled with them in Iowa. He remained there until he died in 1838. Although Black Hawk failed to keep his land, he is now admired for his brave fight to protect the rights of his people.

## In Your Own Words

How did Black Hawk work to protect the rights of the Sauk and Fox nations? Write your answer in a paragraph of five or more sentences in your notebook.

# REVIEW AND APPLY

- Issues such as slavery, sectionalism, and states' rights were starting to divide the nation in the early part of the 1800s.

- The Industrial Revolution resulted in the invention of more machines and the growth of American factories in the North.

- The Missouri Compromise tried to keep a balance between slave states and free states.

- Andrew Jackson, the people's President, served two terms in office.

- President Jackson would not let South Carolina nullify laws. He also stopped the Bank of the United States.

- Jackson had Indians removed from the Southeast. The move west became known as the Trail of Tears.

## VOCABULARY

Matching ■ Match the vocabulary word or phrase in Group B with its definition in Group A. You will not use all the words in Group B.

**Group A**

_____ 1. This was a change from making products by hand to making products by machine.

_____ 2. These were factories where machines would spin cotton thread.

_____ 3. This invention made it easier to remove cotton seeds from the cotton fibers.

_____ 4. These are taxes on goods brought into the country.

_____ 5. This means having one more than half.

_____ 6. This was a way that politicians gave jobs to people who supported them.

_____ 7. This was a belief that the state governments should have more power than the federal government.

**Group B**

A. tariffs

B. spoils system

C. textile mills

D. sectionalism

E. Industrial Revolution

F. cotton gin

G. majority

H. states' rights

## USING INFORMATION

Journal Writing ■ What three important decisions did Andrew Jackson make as President? Would you have made the same decisions if you were President?

## COMPREHENSION CHECK

Write the Answer ■ Write one or more sentences to answer each question.

1. Who was Samuel Slater and what effect did he have on American industry?

   _____

   _____

2. What issue did the Missouri Compromise help to resolve?

   _____

   _____

3. What was Andrew Jackson's nickname as President and how did he get that name?

   _____

   _____

4. What was the Trail of Tears?

   _____

   _____

## CRITICAL THINKING

Comparing and Contrasting ■ In this chapter, you read about the differences that were dividing the sections of the United States in the 1800s. Compare North, South, and West for each topic listed below.

| TOPIC | NORTH | SOUTH | WEST |
|---|---|---|---|
| Taxes | | | |
| Building Roads | | | |
| Slavery | | | |

# SOCIAL STUDIES SKILLS

### Reading a Bar Graph

A **bar graph** uses bars of different lengths and colors to show facts. The bar graph below compares the population of three sections of the nation for the years 1800, 1820, and 1850.

To read the graph, compare the height of the bar to the numbers on the left side of the graph. Notice that each color bar represents a different part of the country—North, South, and West.

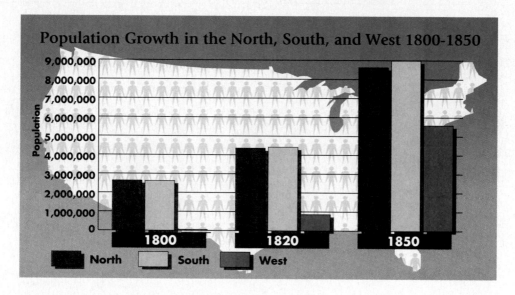

**Study the graph. Then write the answer to each question.**

1. Which section had the smallest population in 1800? _____

2. Which section showed the largest growth from 1800 to 1850?

   _____

3. Which section had less than 1 million people in 1820? _____

4. Which two sections had almost the same population for each date?

   _____ and _____

5. Based on this graph, was the total population of the United States more or less than 4

   million people in 1800? _____

# Chapter 13

# WORKING FOR REFORM AND CULTURE

◀ *Working to reform women's rights*

**People**

Horace Mann • Noah
Webster • Emma Willard •
Mary Lyon • Thomas
Gallaudet • William Lloyd
Garrison • Paul Cuffee •
Frederick Douglass •
Angelina Grimké • Sarah
Grimké • Sojourner Truth •
Lucretia Mott • Elizabeth
Cady Stanton • Dorothea
Dix • Joseph Smith

**Places**

Liberia • Great Salt Lake

**New Vocabulary**

reform • disabilities •
abolition • abolitionists •
political rights • public
office • mental illnesses •
criminals • asylums •
labor • labor unions •
transcendentalists •
persecution

**Focus on Main Ideas**

1. What were some accomplishments of the reform movements?
2. In what ways were the reform movements unsuccessful?
3. What important religious movements began in the 1800s?

In the early 1800s, most children did not go to school, thousands of people were slaves, and women did not vote. During the 1800s, **reform** movements took on the job of correcting the nation's problems. Some goals of these reform movements were to improve education, end slavery, and win more rights for women.

## Working for Better Education

Before 1820 most American children did not go to school. Wealthy people paid to send their children to private schools, but there were few free public schools. Children who lived on the frontier went to church schools or were taught by their parents at home. In towns and cities, many children went to dame schools that women ran in their homes.

A better education system was needed as more men were allowed to vote. A democracy needs educated people who can read about the nation's problems and make wise voting decisions. In the 1820s a law was passed in New York that required elementary schools for all children.

Horace Mann worked to reform education in Massachusetts. He worked with the state's lawmakers to pass laws requiring children to attend school. He believed that schools needed well-trained teachers, so three colleges were opened to train teachers. Other states copied Horace Mann's ideas. By the 1860s most white boys in the North went to free public elementary schools. There were few public high schools in the country, and there were few schools for girls or for African American children.

Noah Webster improved American education by writing the first American dictionary. His *Spelling Book* and *Reader* became best sellers that helped children throughout the nation learn how to read and to spell. Women had fewer opportunities than men in education. In 1821 Emma Willard opened the nation's first high school for girls. In 1837 Mary Lyon opened the first college for women, Mount Holyoke Seminary, in Massachusetts. By 1900 some colleges for men began accepting female students.

Schools for children with **disabilities** were started. In Connecticut, Reverend Thomas Gallaudet opened the nation's first school for deaf children. Dr. Samuel Gridley Howe started a school for blind children.

*The reform movement to change education led to more free public elementary schools. Leaders like Horace Mann convinced lawmakers to build more elementary schools and to pay teachers better salaries. These children are in the schoolyard of a public school in New York City.*

## The Abolition Movement

In 1776 the writers of the Declaration of Independence had written that "all men are created equal," but slavery had always been allowed in the United States. The Constitution allowed slavery. Slavery ended in the North by the early 1800s because slaves were not needed for northern businesses, factories, and small farms. The Industrial Revolution caused slavery to become more important in the South. Laws in the South protected the rights of slave owners.

In the early 1800s, many Americans worked to end slavery. Some wanted to prevent slavery in the West. Others wanted all slaves to be freed. Some thought slavery should end slowly. Others believed all slaves should be freed at once. The movement to end slavery was called the **abolition** movement. People who worked to win freedom for all slaves were called **abolitionists**.

The abolitionists faced a very difficult fight in the South and in the North. No southern state would agree to pass laws to end slavery. Nor would the South agree to change the Constitution by passing an amendment to end slavery. Many factory owners in the North opposed the abolitionists. They wanted southern slaves to continue growing cotton for their textile mills.

The abolition movement first began with religious groups. In 1776 the Quakers were the first group to stop owning slaves. They believed it was wrong for one person to own another. Other religious groups later joined the fight against slavery.

One of the most famous abolitionists was William Lloyd Garrison. Garrison wanted all slaves to be given their freedom immediately. To spread his beliefs, he began to publish a newspaper called *The Liberator*. In the first issue he wrote powerful

*William Lloyd Garrison published* The Liberator. *This newspaper had articles calling for the abolition of slavery.*

THE LIBERATOR.

VOL. I.] WILLIAM LLOYD GARRISON AND ISAAC KNAPP, PUBLISHERS. [NO. 33

BOSTON, MASSACHUSETTS.] ...OUR COUNTRY IS THE WORLD—OUR COUNTRYMEN ARE MANKIND. [SATURDAY, AUGUST 13, 1831.

All of these women were abolitionists and leaders in the women's rights movement. Pictured from left to right are Elizabeth Cady Stanton, Lucretia Mott, Susan B. Anthony, and Sojourner Truth. Stanton and Mott organized the convention in Seneca Falls, New York, where Stanton lived.

sentences about what he planned to do: "I will be as harsh as truth....I will not excuse. I will not retreat a single inch—and I will be heard."

Some abolitionists started a colony in West Africa called Liberia. Liberia became an independent African nation. Paul Cuffee, a wealthy, free African American, used his own money to send a group of freed slaves to settle in West Africa. But it was too expensive to send large groups to live in Africa. Few African Americans wanted to leave their families and move thousands of miles to live in Africa. Only a few thousand freed slaves moved to Liberia.

Frederick Douglass had been a slave, but he escaped to the North in 1838. As a free African American, he did not enjoy the same rights that white people enjoyed. So he spent several years in England where he could enjoy full freedom. Then he returned

to the United States where he published his own newspaper, *The North Star*. In *The North Star*, Douglass encouraged people to work to end slavery. Douglass also gave speeches about his experiences as a slave. Many people who heard him joined the abolition movement.

Angelina and Sarah Grimké were sisters who became abolitionists. Their parents owned slaves on their large southern plantation. The sisters had seen the evils of slavery. They gave many speeches to convince people to work to end slavery.

The abolition movement grew during the 1840s and 1850s. It made feelings of sectionalism stronger in the North and the South. However, the abolitionists did not succeed in passing laws to end slavery. They helped only some slaves escape to freedom. But they did make many Americans think more about the problem of slavery.

## The Women's Rights Movement

Many abolitionists were women. These women soon realized that they needed more **political rights** for themselves before they could help slaves win their freedom. In the 1800s women were controlled by their husbands and fathers. They could not vote, serve on juries, own property, or be elected to **public office**.

Some abolitionists began working to win more rights for women. Frederick Douglass and the Grimké sisters worked for women's rights. Angelina Grimké said that working for the rights of slaves helped her understand the rights that she needed as a woman.

Sojourner Truth had been a slave and had escaped to freedom. She became famous for her powerful speeches for the abolition of slavery and for the women's rights movement.

In 1848 Lucretia Mott and Elizabeth Cady Stanton organized the first conference to work for women's rights. At a conference in Seneca Falls, New York, they presented "The Declaration of Sentiments." This Declaration was written to sound like the Declaration of Independence. It included a sentence that said "all men and women are created equal." Then it went on to explain how women were treated unfairly by men. The Declaration of Sentiments ended by saying that women wanted the same rights as men, including the right to vote.

Frederick Douglass spoke at the conference and urged the delegates to accept the Declaration. Because of Douglass's powerful speech, delegates voted to accept it. But many delegates did not agree that women should have the right to vote.

Very slowly more schools and jobs opened for women. Some states passed laws that allowed women to own property. But it would take more than seventy years of hard work before women would win the right to vote.

## Other Reform Movements

When Dorothea Dix visited a prison in 1841, she was upset to find people with **mental illnesses** held there. Dix believed that people with mental illnesses should be treated as sick people, not as **criminals**. She visited many states and succeeded in getting special hospitals, or **asylums**, built for people with mental illnesses.

Dix visited hundreds of prisons, and she was unhappy with the terrible conditions she found. People who could not pay their debts were in jail for long periods of time. Children who were in jail for crimes were held in prison cells with adults.

Dix worked hard to reform prisons throughout the nation. She succeeded in getting lighter sentences for those who did less serious crimes. Fewer people were placed in each prison cell. Children were punished differently for crimes than adults were punished. People who could not pay their debts were not treated as criminals.

The Industrial Revolution created a need for **labor** reform. More and more people were factory workers who worked from morning to night for low salaries. Factory workers formed groups called **labor unions** so they could fight for better salaries and shorter workdays. But factory owners did not have to listen to the demands of labor unions because thousands of poor immigrants had come to America from 1820 to 1840. These immigrants were willing to work at any job to earn some money for their families. Labor unions really did not succeed in helping factory workers until the late 1800s.

## Creating an American Culture

During the early 1800s Americans began creating their own writing styles. The chart below provides information on some of the writers from this time period.

Washington Irving was the first American writer to become famous in Europe. Some New England writers, such as Ralph Waldo Emerson and Henry David Thoreau, were called **transcendentalists**. They stressed the importance of each person, and they believed in living close to nature.

American religion was also changing. A Protestant movement called the Second Great Awakening began in the 1820s. Religious leaders taught that everyone could get forgiveness for their sins from God. People became much more excited about religion. Thousands of people attended large religious gatherings called revivals, or camp meetings.

Joseph Smith started a new church called the Mormon church in New York in 1830. Smith's followers were called Mormons because Smith claimed he was given a holy book, *The Book of Mormon*, by an angel. Smith used that book to teach his new religion. One of Smith's many teachings was that a man could have more than one wife. Smith was killed by a mob of people who disliked his religious ideas. Brigham Young took over as leader of the Mormon church. To escape **persecution**, Young led his followers west to the Great Salt Lake in Utah. At that time Utah was part of Mexico. In Utah the Mormon Church grew larger each year.

Because Americans worked for reform, better schools were built, and women won more rights. Prisoners and people with mental illnesses received better treatment. But the reform movements did not win for women the right to vote. They did not end slavery in the United States. Because Americans were not able to solve the problem of slavery, that problem would continue to divide the North and the South.

### American Writers of the Early 1800s

| Writers | Title of Important Work | What was the Work About? |
|---|---|---|
| Washington Irving | "Rip Van Winkle," "The Legend of Sleepy Hollow" | Early American life in New York |
| James Fenimore Cooper | *The Last of the Mohicans* | American frontier life |
| Ralph Waldo Emerson | *Nature* | The ideas of the transcendentalists |
| Edgar Alan Poe | "The Raven" | Despair over death |
| Emily Dickinson | "Because I Could Not Stop for Death" | Living and death |
| Nathaniel Hawthorne | *The Scarlet Letter* | Life in Puritan New England |
| Herman Melville | *Moby Dick* | The struggle between good and evil during a whale hunt |
| Henry David Thoreau | *Walden* | Living close to nature |
| Walt Whitman | *Leaves of Grass* | Poems that praise America |

# BIOGRAPHY

## Elizabeth Blackwell 1821-1910

There was a time in this country when women could not be doctors. Elizabeth Blackwell faced this problem, and she became the first woman doctor in the United States.

Blackwell was born in England but moved to New York at age eleven. Although education for girls at that time stressed music, sewing, and cooking, Elizabeth's education included math, science, and history.

Blackwell worked as a teacher for a while. But her real goal was to become a doctor. So she began to study medical books. Later she was taught by a doctor. Then she began applying to medical schools.

Blackwell soon learned that no medical school wanted a female student. She applied to 29 schools but was not accepted. Finally, she was accepted to the medical school at Geneva College in New York. She graduated in 1849.

Blackwell thought she would have greater opportunities to work as a doctor in Europe. She sailed to Europe and worked in England and France.

In 1851 Blackwell returned to New York to practice medicine. Because she was a woman, male doctors refused to accept her as a doctor. She was not allowed to treat patients in any hospitals. Blackwell solved these problems by opening her own hospital in 1857. Her sister Emily, who had also become a doctor, worked with her. Together they started the New York Infirmary for Women and Children. It included a medical school to train women to be doctors. Women worked in the hospital, and most of the patients were poor.

Since 1949 an award called the Elizabeth Blackwell Medal has been given to women doctors who have done outstanding work in medicine. This award helps Americans remember that Elizabeth Blackwell made it possible for many other women to become doctors.

## In Your Own Words

In the journal section of your notebook, write what steps Elizabeth Blackwell took to become a doctor and to help other women become doctors.

## Frederick Douglass: The Life of an American Slave

Frederick Douglass was born a slave. When he was eight, his owner's wife began to teach Douglass how to read. He became a good reader and an excellent writer. In 1838 he escaped to Massachusetts where he began a new life as a free man. Although he was free, as an African American, Douglass was treated unfairly. He spent his life working to end slavery and to help African Americans and women win equal rights. Douglass told the story of his life in his autobiography, *Narrative Life of an American Slave*.

"I received my first impressions of slavery on this plantation.... Colonel Lloyd kept from three to four hundred slaves on his home plantation and owned a large number more on the neighboring farms belonging to him....

The men and women slaves received, as their monthly allowance of food, eight pounds of pork, or its equivalent in fish, and one bushel of corn meal. Their yearly clothing consisted of two coarse linen shirts, one pair of linen trousers, like the shirts, one jacket, one pair of trousers for winter, made of coarse negro cloth, one pair of stockings, and one pair of shoes; the whole of which could not have cost more than seven dollars....

I was seldom whipped by my old master, and suffered little from anything else than hunger and cold. I suffered much from hunger, but much more from cold. In hottest summer and coldest

winter, I was kept almost naked.... I had no bed.... The coldest nights, I used to steal a bag which was used for carrying corn to the mill. I would crawl into this bag, and there sleep on the cold, damp, clay floor....

I was probably between seven and eight years old when I left Colonel Lloyd's plantation. My old master [Anthony] had determined to let me go to Baltimore, to live with Mr. Hugh Auld, brother to my old master's son-in-law....

Very soon after I went to live with Mr. and Mrs. Auld, she kindly commenced to teach me the A, B, C. After I had learned this, she assisted [helped] me in learning to spell words of three or four letters. Just at this point of my progress, Mr. Auld found out what was going on, and at once forbade [would not allow] Mrs. Auld to instruct me further, telling her, among other things, that it was unlawful, as well as unsafe, to teach a

> *"You will be free
> as soon as you are
> twenty-one, but I am a
> slave for life!"*

slave to read…. I was saddened by the thought of losing the aid of my kind mistress. I set out with high hope to learn how to read.

I lived in Master Hugh's family about seven years. During this time, I succeeded in learning to read and write…. The plan which I adopted…was that of making friends of all the little white boys whom I met in the street…. I would say to them, I wished I could be as free as they would be when they got to 21…. "You will be free as soon as you are twenty-one, but I am a slave for life! Have not I as good a right to be free as you have?" These words used to trouble them….

I was not about twelve years old, and the thought of being a slave for life began to bear heavily upon my heart…. Every little while, I could hear something about the abolitionists…. If a slave ran away and succeeded in getting clear, or if a slave killed his master, set fire to a barn, or did any thing very wrong in the mind of a slaveholder, it was spoken of as the fruit of abolition….

My old master, Captain Anthony, died…. Now all the property of my old master was in the hands of strangers…. Not a slave was left free. All remained slaves, from the youngest to the olders…. [My old grandmother] had served my old master faithfully from youth to old age…. She was nevertheless left a slave—a slave for life…. She saw her children, her grandchildren, and her great grandchildren, divided like so many sheep…. My determination to run away was again revived…. When that time came, I was determined to be off."

## Write Your Answers

**Write the answer to each question in your notebook.**

1. What was the monthly allowance of food for slaves on Colonel Lloyd's plantation?

2. What did Douglass do to fight the cold?

3. Who began to teach Douglass how to read?

4. Why did Douglass's words trouble the other children?

5. What made Douglass determined to run away?

# REVIEW AND APPLY

- During the 1800s, many reform movements tried to correct the nation's problems.

- Horace Mann, Noah Webster, Emma Willard, and Thomas Gallaudet worked for better education in the United States.

- Abolitionists, such as William Lloyd Garrison and Fredrick Douglass, worked to end slavery.

- Reformers, such as Lucretia Mott and Elizabeth Cady Stanton, fought for women's rights such as the right to vote, to own property, and to be elected to public office.

- Other reform movements worked toward improving prisons, hospitals, and workplaces.

- During the 1800s, an American culture continued to develop.

## VOCABULARY

Writing with Vocabulary Words ■ Use six or more vocabulary words to write a paragraph in your social studies notebook about some of the reform movements of the 1800s.

| | | |
|---|---|---|
| committed | disabilities | asylums |
| reform | public office | labor |
| abolition | mentally ill | labor union |
| political rights | criminals | literature |

## COMPREHENSION CHECK

Choose the Answer ■ Write the letter of the word or phrase that best answers each question.

_____ 1. Which statement describes American education before 1820?

    a. Most children went to public school.

    b. Most children did not go to school.

    c. Most children went to private schools.

_____ 2. Who started the first school for deaf children?

    a. Reverend Thomas Gallaudet

    b. Emma Willard

    c. Mary Lyon

_____ 3. Where was the first conference on women's rights held?

    a. Boston, Massachusetts
    b. Seneca Falls, New York
    c. Washington, D.C.

_____ 4. In what reform movement was Dorothea Dix a leader?

    a. prison reform
    b. labor reform
    c. education reform

_____ 5. What did labor unions work for?

    a. prison reform
    b. a shorter workday
    c. to close factories

_____ 6. What religion did Joseph Smith start?

    a. Quakers
    b. Protestants
    c. Mormons

_____ 7. Which of the following people was a transcendentalist?

    a. Fredrick Douglass
    b. Henry David Thoreau
    c. Sojourner Truth

_____ 8. What was the Second Great Awakening?

    a. a religious movement
    b. a book by Ralph Waldo Emerson
    c. a prison reform group

## CRITICAL THINKING

**Distinguishing Relevant Information** ■ Imagine you are telling a friend about the reform movements of the 1800s. Read each sentence below. Decide which sentences are relevant to what you will say. Put a check in front of the relevant sentences. There are four relevant sentences.

_____ 1. In the 1800s, women had very few political and social rights.

_____ 2. Many children in the 1800s had disabilities.

_____ 3. Some abolitionists started a colony in West Africa called Liberia.

_____ 4. Many women in the 1800s wore dresses.

_____ 5. In the 1800s many people with mental illnesses were treated like criminals.

_____ 6. Ralph Waldo Emerson was a good writer.

## USING INFORMATION

**Writing an Opinion** ■ During the 1800s there were many reform movements. If you could have chosen only one of those movements to support, which one would it have been? Explain your answer.

# AMERICANS MOVE WESTWARD

◀ *Gold from California*

**People**

Moses Austin • Stephen
Austin • Antonio López de
Santa Anna • Sam Houston •
Suzanna Dickenson •
James Marshall• John Sutter

**Places**

Santa Fe • Oregon Country •
Alamo • Goliad • San
Jacinto River • Rio Grande •
American River • Houston

**New Vocabulary**

execution • Manifest
Destiny • missionaries •
fertile • parallel •
slogan • latitude •
pass • blended •
vaqueros • diverse

**Focus on Main Ideas**

1. How did Americans travel to Oregon and the Southwest in the 1800s?
2. How did Texas become an independent republic in 1836?
3. How did the ideas about Manifest Destiny affect the United States?
4. How did the United States win control of Texas, Oregon, and the Southwest?

**A**s thousands of settlers moved west in the 1800s, they often traveled in long wagon trains. At times more than 100 covered wagons formed one wagon train. As they traveled, their wheels made deep cuts in the ground that formed trails. Those cuts can still be seen in the West today.

### Americans Travel West

Thousands of Americans wanted to travel west to places like Santa Fe and the Oregon Country, but there were no roads or rivers to these areas. People had to travel in covered wagons. In 1821 a group of settlers met in St. Louis, Missouri. They formed a wagon train with their covered wagons, and together they traveled slowly to Santa Fe. The route they followed was known as the Santa Fe Trail. Thousands of people took this trail to the Southwest.

Other people headed west on the Oregon Trail to reach the Oregon Country. There were hardships and dangers on the Oregon Trail as people traveled across rivers, the Great Plains, and the Rocky Mountains. Wagon wheels could break, wagons could turn over, and there could be attacks from Indians along the way. At times it was difficult to find food.

People often traveled 12 hours each day. The wagon trains could not go faster than a few miles an hour, so it took many months to reach Oregon. Between 1843 and 1860, about 50,000 people traveled west on the Oregon Trail.

Americans dreamed of being able to travel by railroad from the East Coast on the Atlantic Ocean to the West Coast on the Pacific Ocean. By 1840 there were many railroads throughout the Northeast. A railroad was built that went as far west as Illinois. But railroads would not connect the Atlantic and Pacific coasts until 1869.

*Many settlers headed west in covered wagons. Usually people did not ride in the slow-moving wagons because the wagons were filled with belongings.*

## Texas Becomes a Republic

Soon after Columbus reached the Americas in 1492, the Spanish explored Mexico and what is now the southwestern part of the United States. The Spanish called the region New Spain, and they ruled it for almost 300 years. Texas, Nevada, New Mexico, and California were in the northern part of New Spain. People who were born in Spain, instead of in America, held all the power. The Spanish governors who ruled New Spain did not allow representative government.

At that time Texas was part of northern Mexico. Many Indians lived in Texas, but only about 5,000 Mexicans had settled there. In 1820 Moses Austin, an American, asked the government of New Spain if he could start a colony in Texas. The government agreed because they wanted Americans to develop the area. Moses Austin died before he could start the colony.

Mexicans fought a long war to win independence from Spain. In 1821 Mexico won its freedom from Spain. The new Mexican government allowed Stephen Austin to carry out his father's plan for a colony in Texas. The Mexican government made five important rules for the American colonists. Americans had to speak Spanish, become Catholics, and become Mexican citizens. They had to obey Mexican laws, and they could not bring slaves to Texas.

Americans came to Texas because land was very cheap. By 1830 there were 20,000 settlers. There were more Americans than Mexicans in Texas. The Mexicans became angry because the Americans had brought 2,000 slaves to Texas, and the settlers were

*The battle of San Jacinto ended the Texas Revolution. Santa Anna was captured and brought to Sam Houston, who was injured during the battle.*

not obeying the five rules. Mexican leaders decided not to allow any more Americans to settle in Texas.

In 1835 the Texans decided they wanted to be free from Mexico. The president of Mexico, General Antonio López de Santa Anna, led soldiers to Texas to end the revolt. The war became known as the Texas Revolution. In March 1836, 59 delegates met in a convention in Texas. They wrote and signed the Texas Declaration of Independence. They also chose Sam Houston as their commander in chief.

While the convention was meeting, Santa Anna and 3,000 Mexican soldiers attacked a mission called the Alamo in the town of San Antonio. Inside the Alamo were only 187 Texan soldiers. Free African Americans as well as several slaves fought with the Texans. After many days of fighting, Santa Anna's soldiers forced their way into the Alamo and killed every soldier. Fifteen women and children survived the battle. Santa Anna sent one woman, Suzanna Dickenson, to warn other Texans to end the revolt.

Meanwhile part of Santa Anna's army captured the town of Goliad. Santa Anna ordered the **execution** of nearly 400 Texans who were captured at Goliad. Texans were furious about what had happened at the Alamo and at Goliad.

On April 21, 1836, Sam Houston and the Texans attacked Santa Anna's army at the San Jacinto River. "Remember the Alamo! Remember Goliad!" they shouted as they fought the Mexican Army. In only 18 minutes the battle was over. Santa Anna and the Mexicans surrendered. The next day Santa Anna signed a treaty that said Texas was free.

Texas became an independent republic. Texans elected Sam Houston as their first president. They wrote a constitution that allowed slavery.

Most Texans wanted Texas to join the Union in 1836. But Andrew Jackson, the President at that time, was worried that there would be war with Mexico if Texas became a state. Also, the North did not want another slave state to join the Union. So Texas remained a republic until 1845. In that year Congress voted for Texas to become a state.

## Manifest Destiny

During the 1840s many Americans believed that the United States should rule all the land between the Atlantic Ocean and the Pacific Ocean. This idea was called

**Manifest Destiny**. In 1845 James K. Polk became President. Before he was elected, Polk had promised to carry out the idea of Manifest Destiny. He had said that Oregon, Texas, and California would become part of the United States.

Since 1818 the United States and Great Britain had ruled the Oregon Country together. The Oregon Country was much larger than the state of Oregon today. It included what is now Idaho as well as part of Canada. At first, few Americans or British settled in Oregon. Then, in the 1830s, American **missionaries** became the first American settlers in Oregon. Their goal was to teach the Indians to be Christians.

Slowly more Americans traveled west along the Oregon Trail and settled in Oregon. People liked the **fertile** soil and pleasant climate of the Oregon Country. By 1846 there were more Americans than British in Oregon.

President Polk wanted the United States to rule all of Oregon. As you can see on the map on page 180, Oregon's northern border was at the 54°40' **parallel**. Before the election Polk said he would fight to have all of Oregon. His **slogan** became "54°40' or Fight."

In 1846 President Polk agreed to a compromise with Great Britain. The Oregon Country was divided at the 49th parallel, or 49° line of **latitude**. All of the land north of that line was part of Canada and was to be ruled by Great Britain. All of the land to the south of 49° became part of the United States and was called the Oregon Territory. This land would later become parts of three states—Oregon, Washington, and Idaho.

## War with Mexico

Texas became a state shortly before Polk became President. Polk also wanted California and all land between California and Texas to belong to the United States. But Mexico ruled this land. When Polk asked Mexico to sell the land to the United States, the Mexican government refused.

The Mexicans were very angry when Texas became a state. Their anger grew when Mexico and the United States did not agree on where the southern border of Texas should be. The United States said the Texas border was a river called the Rio Grande. Mexico insisted that Texas should be smaller. Both nations sent soldiers to the Rio Grande in 1846. The Mexicans crossed the Rio Grande, and a short battle took place. American and Mexican soldiers were killed. Polk asked Congress to declare war against Mexico. After all, Polk said, Mexico had attacked Americans in Texas. But the Mexicans believed that it was the Americans who had been on Mexican land. Congress declared war in 1846, and the Mexican War began.

During the Mexican War, Americans captured California. The American army went south into Mexico. After many months of fighting, Americans captured the Mexican capital, Mexico City. Although Mexicans had fought bravely throughout the war, they agreed to surrender.

In 1848 the leaders of Mexico and the United States signed a peace treaty called the Treaty of Guadalupe Hidalgo. The treaty said that Texas was part of the United States, and the southern border of Texas was the Rio Grande. California and the land between Texas and California belonged to the United States. The United States agreed to pay Mexico $15 million for its land. Mexico had lost half of its land to the United States. The treaty allowed all Mexicans in the Southwest to become United States citizens.

The land the United States won in 1848 was called the Mexican Cession. As you can see on the map below, the Mexican Cession would become five states—California, Nevada, Utah, Arizona, and New Mexico—as well as parts of three other states.

In 1853 Mexico agreed to sell another piece of land to the United States for $10 million. This land to the south of the Mexican Cession was called the Gadsden Purchase. The United States bought this land because there was a **pass**, or a path, through its mountains. Americans planned to build a railroad through the pass.

## The Blending of Cultures in the Southwest

Mexicans in the Southwest became American citizens after the Mexican War. Parts of Mexican culture and American culture have **blended** together in the Southwest. Many years before, the Indian and Spanish cultures had blended to form Mexican culture.

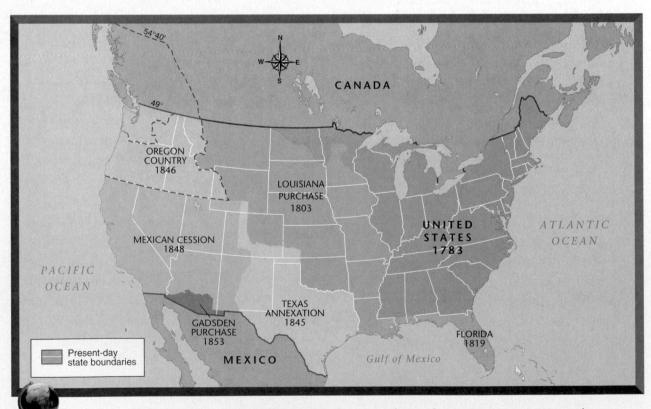

**The United States Grows 1783–1853** *The idea of Manifest Destiny came true as the nation grew to include Texas, Oregon, and the Mexican Cession. What part of the United States was added in 1853?*

*The blending of cultures and the influence of Spain and Mexico can be seen in these two photographs. The town on the left is in Mexico. The building on the right is in Oregon. Notice how both the style of the homes and the use of tiles are similar.*

The first people in the region, the Indians, had developed irrigation systems to water their crops. The Indians were the first to grow corn, wheat, beans, and cotton. They also grew spicy chili peppers.

When the Spanish conquered Mexico, the Spanish built missions where they taught the Catholic religion to the Indians. The Spanish also brought the first horses and cows to America from Europe. They built huge ranches where they forced Indians to work at caring for cattle and sheep. Years later Americans would learn these skills from Mexican cowboys, who were called **vaqueros**.

Mexican culture included great respect for parents. Mexican food included both Spanish and Indian foods. Like the Spanish, Mexicans built houses with white walls and red tiled roofs. That style continues to be popular in the Southwest today.

When the Mexican Cession became part of the United States, Americans and Mexicans learned from each other. Americans taught Mexicans to have jury trials for people who were accused of crimes. They showed Mexicans how to use better seeds and tools to grow crops.

From the Mexicans, Americans learned how to irrigate the dry desert and to mine silver and other metals. Americans also adopted two Mexican laws. One law allowed married women to own property together with their husbands. Another law said landowners could not take away their neighbor's water supply. This law helped protect the way water was used in the dry Southwest.

*Forty-niners looked for gold by separating it from gravel. The gravel was shoveled into water, which was then stirred. The lighter gravel would float, leaving the heavier gold at the bottom.*

The blend of Mexican and American cultures created a new Southwestern culture. This culture can be seen today in laws, foods, music, and houses of the region.

## There's Gold in California

In January 1848 a man named James Marshall was building a mill on the American River for John Sutter. While building Sutter's Mill, Marshall discovered gold. The news that there was gold in California spread quickly. By 1849 California had a gold rush.

The people who went to California in 1849 to find gold were called forty-niners.

Teachers left their schools and farmers left their farms as they rushed to look for gold in California. Some slave owners brought their slaves to California to help them look for gold. Free African Americans also searched for gold in California.

Some people traveled by ship all the way around South America to reach California. Most people traveled in covered wagons and followed trails over the mountains. Often they stopped along the way at the Mormon settlement at the Great Salt Lake. The Mormons grew wealthy as the forty-niners bought food and supplies for their trip to California. People from every part of the world rushed to California to find gold. Many came from Europe. Thousands came from Asia. In 1851 about 20,000 Chinese came to find gold.

Some lucky people found gold in California and became very rich. Most people did not become rich. But California's population grew quickly because of the gold rush. San Francisco grew from a small town into a busy city. By 1850 California had enough people to become a state. In that year California joined the Union as a free state.

Because of the gold rush, California's population became **diverse**. Chinese immigrants, African Americans, and white settlers went to California and stayed. More Indians and Mexicans joined the ones who were already there. Each group helped to create a special culture in California.

Americans had reached their goal of Manifest Destiny. By 1848 the United States ruled all the land between the Atlantic and Pacific oceans.

## Sam Houston 1793–1863

Sam Houston was a leader in Texas for almost thirty years. But he did many other things before arriving in Texas. Houston is the only person in American history to serve as the governor of two states.

Sam Houston ran away from his home in Tennessee to live with the Cherokees when he was 15. Later he fought in the War of 1812, opened a new school, became a lawyer, and was elected to Congress. Then he was elected governor of Tennessee. While he was governor, Houston's wife left him and returned to her family. An unhappy Houston gave up his job as governor.

Houston moved to Texas and later became a leader in the Texas Revolution. He was chosen as commander in chief of the Texas Army. He led the Texans to win the Battle of San Jacinto. Santa Anna and his soldiers had taken an afternoon nap when Houston and his soldiers made a surprise attack. The Mexican Army surrendered. Texas became an independent republic.

Houston was elected as the first president of Texas. After Texas joined the Union, Houston was elected to the United States Senate. He represented Texas for 13 years.

Sam Houston ran for governor of Texas in 1857. To win votes Houston made 67 speeches in different parts of Texas. Houston lost the 1857 election, but he ran again and won in 1859.

While Houston was governor, the battle between the North and the South over slavery grew angrier. In 1861 Texans decided to leave the Union because of the slavery issue. When Houston refused to allow Texas to leave the Union, he was forced to resign as governor. People called him a traitor. He died two years later during the Civil War.

The city of Houston, Texas, was named to honor the man who helped Texas become both an independent republic and a state.

## In Your Own Words

Use examples from Houston's biography to write a paragraph that tells what kind of person you think Houston was, a hero or a traitor?

# AMERICAN GEOGRAPHY

## Human/Environmental Interaction: The Oregon Trail

Starting in 1843, thousands of Americans traveled west on the Oregon Trail. Their wagon wheels made deep cuts in the earth that we can still see today. As they climbed into the Rocky Mountains, they had to make their wagons lighter. So they left a trail as they threw away their belongings. Forts were built on the trail to protect settlers from Indian attacks. Forts became places where people could get supplies. During the long trip, people learned how to be on their own by fixing wagon wheels and hunting buffalo.

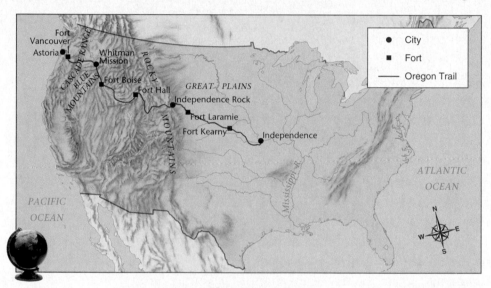

**Study the map and read the paragraphs above to learn about changes in the West as people traveled on the Oregon Trail. Then answer the questions.**

1. List four forts that were built along the trail. _____ ,

   _____ , _____ , and _____ .

2. Which three mountain ranges did the pioneers cross? _____ ,

   _____ , and _____

3. How did people change the landscape along the Oregon Trail?

   _____

4. People changed during the trip to Oregon. Give an example of how they changed.

   _____

# REVIEW AND APPLY

- In the mid-1800s, travelers formed wagon trains and traveled together to places such as Santa Fe and the Oregon Country.

- In 1836, Texas became independent of Mexico and started its own republic. Nine years later it became the forty-fifth state in the United States.

- During the 1840s, many Americans believed in Manifest Destiny, the idea that the United States should rule all the land between the Atlantic and Pacific oceans.

- The United States and Great Britain reached an agreement dividing Oregon.

- The United States and Mexico went to war in 1846. After the war the United States gained control of the Southwest.

- Parts of the Mexican and American cultures have blended together in the Southwest.

- A gold rush in California led to California becoming a state in 1850.

## VOCABULARY

Find the Meaning ■ **Write the word or phrase that best completes each sentence.**

1. In an **execution**, a person is _____.

    killed     elected to public office     made citizens

2. **Manifest Destiny** was a(n) _____.

    law     idea     new colony

3. As a result of the **Mexican Cession**, the United States _____ territory.

    gained     lost     purchased

4. The **Gadsden Purchase** was made by _____.

    Mexico     the United States     Spain

5. A **pass** is a _____.

    way out of something     way into something     way through something

6. Things that have **blended** have _____.

    come together     separated     fought against one another

7. A **vaquero** is a Mexican _____.

    cowboy     politician     soldier

8. A **diverse** population is one that has people from _____.

    all the same place     many different places     the same continent

## COMPREHENSION CHECK

Finish the Paragraph ■ Use the words in the box to finish the paragraph. There is an extra word that you will not use.

| republic | Mexico | colony | Oregon Trail |
| Manifest Destiny | Utah | forty-niners | Texas | Cession |

In the 1800s Americans were moving west. People using the _____ crossed rivers and the Rocky Mountains on their way to the Oregon Country. Some Americans followed Stephen Austin into _____ to start a colony there. Texas became an independent _____ in 1836 and a state in the United States in 1845. Many Americans of this time believed in the idea of _____ . The United States did reach from coast to coast as a result of the war in 1848 with _____ . The purchase of the Mexican _____ gave the United States land that would become the states of California, Nevada, New Mexico, Arizona, and _____ . Miners who rushed to California in 1849 became known as _____ .

## CRITICAL THINKING

Sequencing Information ■ Write the numbers 1, 2, 3, 4, 5, and 6 next to these sentences to show the correct order.

_____ Gold is discovered in California.

_____ In 1845 James Polk becomes President of the United States.

_____ California becomes a state.

_____ In 1830 there were more Americans than Mexicans living in Texas.

_____ The Mexican War begins.

_____ The Battle of the Alamo takes place during the Texas Revolution.

## USING INFORMATION

Writing an Essay ■ During the 1840s the boundaries of the United States expanded. Write an essay explaining how the United States gained one of the following: the Oregon Country, Texas, or the Mexican Cession.

# SOCIAL STUDIES SKILLS

## Using Lines of Latitude and Longitude

Lines of **latitude** and **longitude** are imaginary lines that form a grid that helps you find places on maps or globes. Lines of latitude run east and west around the earth. Lines of longitude run north and south. Lines of latitude and longitude are identified with a direction and a number that stands for the degrees, or parts, of a circle. For example, New Orleans has a latitude of 30°N, read as "thirty degrees north." The longitude of New Orleans is 90°W. We say its latitude and longitude are 30°N/90°W.

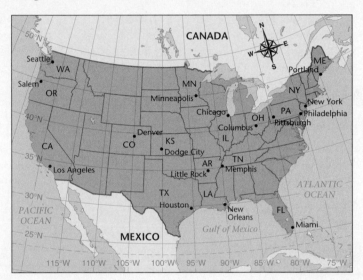

**A. Study the map. Then write the latitude for each city.**

1. Philadelphia, PA _____

2. Minneapolis, MN _____

3. Little Rock, AR _____

4. Salem, OR _____

**B. Write the longitude for each city.**

1. Philadelphia, PA _____

2. Dodge City, KS _____

3. Denver, CO _____

4. Pittsburgh, PA _____

**C. Write the latitude and the longitude for each city. Always write the latitude first.**

1. Philadelphia, PA _____

2. Memphis, TN _____

3. Houston, TX _____

# Unit 3 Review

Study the time line on this page. You may want to read parts of Unit 3 again. Then use the words or dates in the box to finish the paragraphs. Write the words or dates you choose on the correct blanks. The box has one word you will not use.

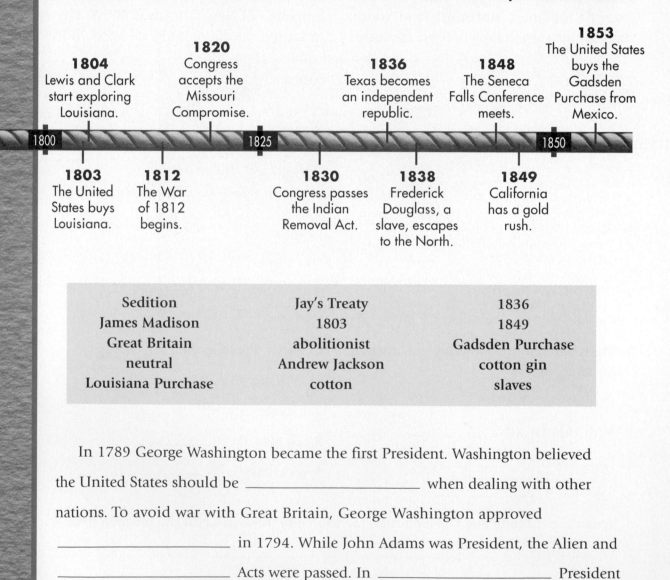

**1804**
Lewis and Clark start exploring Louisiana.

**1820**
Congress accepts the Missouri Compromise.

**1836**
Texas becomes an independent republic.

**1848**
The Seneca Falls Conference meets.

**1853**
The United States buys the Gadsden Purchase from Mexico.

1800    1825    1850

**1803**
The United States buys Louisiana.

**1812**
The War of 1812 begins.

**1830**
Congress passes the Indian Removal Act.

**1838**
Frederick Douglass, a slave, escapes to the North.

**1849**
California has a gold rush.

| | | |
|---|---|---|
| Sedition | Jay's Treaty | 1836 |
| James Madison | 1803 | 1849 |
| Great Britain | abolitionist | Gadsden Purchase |
| neutral | Andrew Jackson | cotton gin |
| Louisiana Purchase | cotton | slaves |

In 1789 George Washington became the first President. Washington believed the United States should be _____ when dealing with other nations. To avoid war with Great Britain, George Washington approved _____ in 1794. While John Adams was President, the Alien and _____ Acts were passed. In _____ President

188

Thomas Jefferson agreed to buy Louisiana from France for $15 million. Then in 1804 Jefferson asked Lewis and Clark to explore the _____. Although _____ seized many American ships at sea, Jefferson avoided going to war. Later, Henry Clay and the War Hawks urged President _____ to fight Great Britain in the War of 1812.

After the _____ was invented in 1793, southern planters grew more cotton. Planters needed more _____ to work in the cotton fields. During the Industrial Revolution, many textile mills were built in the North. These mills needed _____ from the South.

President _____ approved the Indian Removal Act in 1830, and thousands of Indians were forced to move to Oklahoma. Frederick Douglass escaped to freedom and became an important _____. Texas became an independent republic in _____. Mexico lost a lot of land after the United States won the Mexican War. The population of California grew rapidly during the gold rush of _____.

## Looking Ahead to Unit 4

The differences between North and South grew stronger as western territories wanted to became states. The question of whether the new states should be free states or slave states continued to tear the nation apart. After 1850 the North and South grew farther apart. From 1861 to 1865 the North and South fought the Civil War.

As you read Unit 4, think about the people who led the North and South during the Civil War. Find out why the North defeated the South. Find out how life changed for African Americans during this time period. Read on to learn how events led the North and South to fight the terrible Civil War.

# Unit 4

# THE CIVIL WAR AND RECONSTRUCTION

**A**s they marched into battle, many Northern soldiers asked themselves, "Will I be fighting against my Southern cousin or best friend today?" Southern soldiers shared the same worries. The Civil War divided American families and friends in both the North and the South. In 1865, after 600,000 soldiers died, the North and the South became one nation again.

As you read Unit 4, you will learn how slavery and other problems divided the nation. Find out how the long Civil War changed the United States. Discover how Americans rebuilt their nation.

| 1850 | | 1860 | | | |
|------|------|------|------|------|------|

**1852**
Harriet Beecher Stowe writes *Uncle Tom's Cabin*.

**1857**
The Supreme Court makes the Dred Scott Decision.

**1860**
Abraham Lincoln is elected President.

**1861**
The Civil War begins at Fort Sumter.

**1862**
The battle of Antietam is fought

**1863**
Lincoln signs the Emancipation Proclamation

## THINK ABOUT IT

- Abraham Lincoln said he would not end slavery in the South. So why did Southern states form their own country after Lincoln was elected?

- The South had far less soldiers, weapons, and money, but they defeated the North many times. How?

- During the years after the Civil War, thousands of African Americans in the South voted in elections. After 1877, few African Americans voted. Why did they stop voting?

▲ *Americans today act as Union soldiers marching into battle.*

**1865**
The Confederate Army surrenders.

**1867**
Congress passes its first Reconstruction Act.

**1870**
The Fifteenth Amendment is ratified.

**1881**
The first Jim Crow law is passed.

1870

**1865**
Congress passes the Thirteenth Amendment to end slavery.

**1868**
The Fourteenth Amendment is ratified.

**1877**
Reconstruction ends.

**1896**
The Supreme Court's decision in *Plessy* v. *Ferguson* allows segregation.

# Chapter 15

# NORTH AND SOUTH DISAGREE

◀ cotton plant

**People**

Gabriel Prosser • Nat Turner •
Harriet Tubman • Daniel
Webster • Harriet Beecher
Stowe • Stephen Douglas •
James Buchanan • Dred
Scott • Roger B. Taney •
John Brown • Abraham
Lincoln • Jefferson Davis

**Places**

Richmond • Harpers Ferry

**New Vocabulary**

rebellions • secede •
popular sovereignty •
debates • novel • Free
Soilers • opposed •
arsenal • nominated •
Confederate States of
America • Confederacy

**Focus on Main Ideas**

1. How did the Compromise of 1850 keep peace in the United States for ten years?
2. How did Bleeding Kansas, John Brown, and the Dred Scott decision further divide the North and the South?
3. What caused some Southern states to form their own nation?

As the years passed, the differences between the North and the South grew stronger. By 1861 those differences were so serious that some Southern states decided they could no longer be part of the United States.

## Differences Between the North and the South

By 1850 the North and the South had grown further apart. The North had changed into a region of factories, railroads, and large cities. Millions of immigrants had settled throughout the North. African Americans in the North were not allowed to vote in most states. People in the North believed that the nation needed a strong federal government.

The South, with its smaller population, small farms, and large plantations, was very different from the North. The South had fewer cities, immigrants, factories, and railroads. The South's economy depended on slaves to work on cotton, sugar, and tobacco plantations. Most Southerners believed in states' rights and wanted the federal government to have less power.

The biggest problem between the North and the South was over the issue of slavery.

Northern abolitionists wanted to end slavery. Most Southerners were against all efforts to end slavery.

## Slaves Struggle for Freedom

Slave owners lived in fear that their slaves might rebel against them. Sometimes **rebellions** did happen. One slave rebellion was led by a slave named Gabriel Prosser in 1800. He gathered about 1,000 slaves and planned to attack Richmond, Virginia. The rebellion failed, and Prosser and 36 of his followers were hanged. Nat Turner led a slave rebellion in Virginia in 1831 that frightened slave owners in the South.

Some slaves won their freedom by running away to the North and to Canada. They received help from a secret organization called the Underground Railroad. Members, or "conductors," hid runaway slaves in homes and barns as they escaped to the North.

Most slaves never returned to the South after they escaped, but a few brave people came back to help others. Harriet Tubman returned many times and led about 300 slaves to freedom. Another slave, Arnold Cragston, escaped to the North. He returned to the South many times and rowed hundreds of runaway slaves across the Ohio River to freedom.

*Nat Turner led a slave rebellion in Virginia in 1831. Turner and his followers killed 57 slave owners on several plantations. It took about two months for soldiers to capture Turner. He and about 20 of his followers were hanged.*

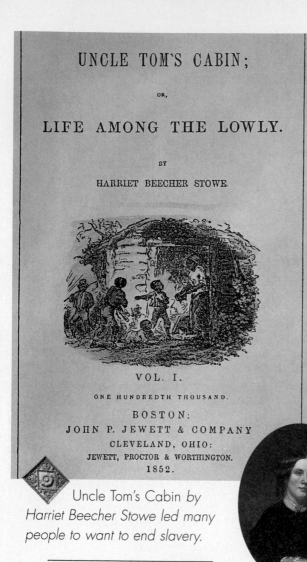

UNCLE TOM'S CABIN;

OR,

LIFE AMONG THE LOWLY.

BY

HARRIET BEECHER STOWE.

VOL. I.

ONE HUNDREDTH THOUSAND.

BOSTON:
JOHN P. JEWETT & COMPANY
CLEVELAND, OHIO:
JEWETT, PROCTOR & WORTHINGTON.
1852.

Uncle Tom's Cabin by Harriet Beecher Stowe led many people to want to end slavery.

## The Compromise of 1850

As Americans moved west, slavery became an issue in the territories of the Mexican Cession. California wanted to join the Union as a free state. The South did not want this to happen. If California joined the Union as a free state, there would be more free states than slave states. Since the North would then have more power in the Senate, it could pass laws against slavery. Some Southern states threatened to **secede**, or leave the Union, if slavery was not allowed in the Western territories.

Southerners were also angry because Northerners were helping slaves escape to freedom. When Northerners wanted to abolish slavery in the nation's capital, people in the South grew angrier.

Once again the nation turned to Senator Henry Clay. In 1820 he had written the Missouri Compromise. Clay was now old and sick, but he wanted to save his country. So he put together another compromise plan that became known as the Compromise of 1850.

The Compromise of 1850 had four main parts. First, California would join the Union as a free state. Second, the people's vote, or **popular sovereignty**, would be used to decide if there would be slavery in the New Mexico and Utah territories. Third, a stricter Fugitive Slave Act would force people in the North to return runaway slaves to the South. Fourth, slaves would no longer be bought and sold in Washington, D.C., but slavery was still allowed in the capital.

No one was really happy with the Compromise of 1850. But it seemed to be the only way to keep the nation together. Senator Daniel Webster of Massachusetts urged Congress to pass the Compromise in order to save the nation. After seven months of **debates**, Congress passed the laws that formed the Compromise of 1850.

## Uncle Tom's Cabin

In 1852 a new **novel** called *Uncle Tom's Cabin* turned thousands of people against slavery. Harriet Beecher Stowe, an abolitionist, wrote the book to show the evils of slavery. The book quickly became a bestseller. It was made into a play and performed in theaters across the country. After reading the book or seeing the play, many Northerners wanted to end slavery. People in the South accused Stowe of telling lies about slave owners. This paragraph from *Uncle Tom's Cabin* shows how cruel slavery could be:

"My master bought my oldest sister. At first I was glad she was bought, for I had one friend near me. I was soon sorry for it…. I have stood at the door and heard her whipped, when it seemed as if every blow cut into my naked heart, and I couldn't do anything to help her…."

## Trouble in Kansas

Senator Stephen Douglas wanted to build a railroad across the West through his state of Illinois. But Douglas needed votes from Southern states to pass the bill that would approve the railroad. Douglas knew that the Southern states wanted slavery to be allowed in every state. However, the Missouri Compromise prevented slavery on land north of Missouri's southern border. To get the votes from Southern states, Douglas wrote the Kansas-Nebraska Act of 1854. This law created two new territories, Kansas and Nebraska. The new law allowed popular sovereignty to decide if slavery would be allowed in these territories. The Kansas-Nebraska Act repealed the Missouri Compromise.

Kansas would be the first territory to vote on whether or not to allow slavery. People who favored slavery and people who were against slavery quickly moved into Kansas. Each side was determined to have a majority of voters. When the election took place, there were enough votes to allow slavery in Kansas. The people who were against slavery, the **Free Soilers**, refused to accept this decision. They started their own government in Kansas. Kansas then had two governments, one that favored slavery and another that **opposed** it. Terrible fighting broke out between the two sides. By 1856 more than 200 people had been killed and so many others were hurt that the Kansas territory became known as "Bleeding Kansas."

Eventually the Free Soilers won control of the government in Kansas. They passed laws to end slavery. Kansas wanted to join the Union as a free state, but Southerners in Congress voted against it.

"Bleeding Kansas" affected the presidential election in 1856. A new party, the Republican party, was formed. Its goal was to stop the spread of slavery into the West. This party was not the same Republican party of Thomas Jefferson.

The Democratic party, once Andrew Jackson's party, was now a divided party. It was split between Southern Democrats who favored slavery and Northern Democrats who opposed slavery. James Buchanan, a Northern Democrat, was elected President in 1856. Buchanan supported popular sovereignty.

## The Dred Scott Decision

The North and the South moved even further apart when the United States Supreme Court ruled on the court case of Dred Scott in 1857. Dred Scott was a slave

*Although the Supreme Court ruled in 1857 that Dred Scott was property, his owner freed him shortly after the decision.*

The decision in the Dred Scott case told the nation that slavery must be allowed in all territories. The Supreme Court used its power of judicial review in this decision. The Court decided that the Missouri Compromise was unconstitutional because it prevented slaveholders from bringing their property, in the form of slaves, into the Western territories. The Dred Scott decision pleased Southerners, but it made Northerners furious.

After the Dred Scott decision, some Americans felt that only fighting would end slavery. One of these people was an abolitionist named John Brown. In 1859 Brown captured the federal **arsenal** and its weapons in Harpers Ferry, Virginia. He planned to give the weapons to slaves so they could attack their owners. Brown was captured before he could carry out his plans. Brown and his followers were put on trial, found guilty, and hanged.

To many abolitionists in the North, John Brown was a great hero. When Southerners saw how much abolitionists admired Brown, they were convinced that the North wanted to end slavery.

## The Republican Party Wins Power

The main goal of the Republican party was to stop the spread of slavery into the West. Republicans also wanted high tariffs to protect Northern industries. Most party members were from the North and the West. One member was a tall, thin lawyer from Illinois named Abraham Lincoln.

In 1858 the Republican party in Illinois **nominated** Lincoln to be its candidate for the United States Senate. When Lincoln

in Missouri. He had worked for his owner in a free territory and in the free state of Illinois. After they moved back to Missouri, Scott's owner died. In 1846 Scott sued for his freedom. Scott said that he should be free because he had lived on free soil. The Dred Scott case went to the Supreme Court.

In 1857 the Supreme Court ruled against Scott and said he was still a slave. Chief Justice Roger B. Taney wrote that Scott was not a citizen because African Americans were not citizens and did not have the right to bring their cases to court. Taney added that since Scott was a slave, he was the property of his owner. The Fifth Amendment to the Constitution protects a person's right to own property. Taney concluded that the Fifth Amendment allowed people to take their property, including their slaves, anywhere in the nation.

agreed to run for the Senate, he made a speech that said the nation could not continue to be divided over slavery:

"A house divided against itself cannot stand. I believe this government cannot endure permanently half slave and half free...."

In the election for the Senate, Lincoln ran against Senator Stephen Douglas. Douglas agreed to be in debates with Lincoln throughout Illinois. Because newspapers throughout the nation had stories about the debates, the two candidates became famous in every part of the country. Douglas won the Senate election in 1858.

In 1860 there were four candidates for President. The Republican party chose Abraham Lincoln as its candidate. The Democratic party split into Northern Democrats and Southern Democrats. Stephen Douglas, promising to allow popular sovereignty, was the candidate of the Northern Democrats. The Southern Democrats chose John C. Breckinridge who supported slavery. A new political party, the Constitutional-Union party, nominated John Bell of Tennessee. Bell did not favor or oppose slavery.

Lincoln won the election of 1860. He received a majority of electoral votes, but none were from the South.

## The South Secedes

Southerners had threatened to secede if Lincoln won the election. Although Lincoln won the election in November 1860, he would not be inaugurated until March 1861.

South Carolina did not wait until March. In December 1860 South Carolina

# CHARLESTON
# MERCURY
## EXTRA:

Passed unanimously at 1.15 o'clock, P. M. December 20th, 1860.

### AN ORDINANCE

To dissolve the Union between the State of South Carolina and other States united with her under the compact entitled "The Constitution of the United States of America."

We, the People of the State of South Carolina, in Convention assembled, do declare and ordain, and it is hereby declared and ordained,

That the Ordinance adopted by us in Convention, on the twenty-third day of May, in the year of our Lord one thousand seven hundred and eighty-eight, whereby the Constitution of the United States of America was ratified, and also, all Acts and parts of Acts of the General Assembly of this State, ratifying amendments of the said Constitution, are hereby repealed; and that the union now subsisting between South Carolina and other States, under the name of "The United States of America," is hereby dissolved.

# THE
# UNION
# IS
# DISSOLVED!

*This headline from a newspaper in Charleston, South Carolina, announced that South Carolina had seceded from the Union.*

seceded. Before Lincoln's inauguration, six more Southern states seceded. Their leaders formed a new nation, the **Confederate States of America**. They wrote a constitution that protected slavery and favored states' rights. Jefferson Davis was elected president of the **Confederacy**.

The struggle between the North and the South had finally caused the Union to divide. No one knew how very difficult it would be to unite the North and the South into one nation again.

---

### Harriet Tubman  1820(?)–1913

Harriet Tubman was an escaped slave who helped groups of slaves escape to the North. She was one of the most famous leaders of the Underground Railroad that helped slaves escape to freedom.

Tubman grew up as a slave in Maryland. When she was about 13 years old, she received a terrible blow on her head when she tried to save another slave from punishment. After that Tubman suffered from sleeping spells that could cause her to fall asleep at any time of the day or night.

Harriet Tubman grew up to be a short but very strong woman. Her father taught her how to survive in the woods. From him she learned which plants were safe to eat. She had also learned how to use the North Star to travel north at night. In 1849, with help from the Underground Railroad, Harriet Tubman escaped to freedom in Philadelphia.

Congress passed a strict Fugitive Slave Act as part of the Compromise of 1850. It became more dangerous than ever to help runaway slaves. But danger did not stop Tubman. She made 19 trips back to Maryland. She helped more than 300 slaves, including her parents, escape to the North and to Canada.

Slave catchers throughout the South tried to find and capture Tubman. A reward in the amount of $40,000 would go to the person who caught her. But Tubman used many disguises, and she was never caught.

Harriet Tubman knew John Brown, and she admired him. But she did not join him when he attacked the arsenal at Harpers Ferry in 1859.

During the Civil War, Tubman worked as a nurse. She also served as a spy and a scout for the Union Army.

Tubman lived to be more than ninety years old. Many Americans called this brave woman Moses. Like Moses in the Bible, Tubman led her people from slavery to freedom.

### In Your Own Words

In the journal section of your notebook, write a paragraph that explains why Harriet Tubman earned the name "Moses."

# REVIEW AND APPLY

## CHAPTER 15 MAIN IDEAS

- By 1850 slavery was the biggest issue separating the North and the South.

- The Compromise of 1850 was an agreement that kept the nation together.

- The Kansas Territory became known as "Bleeding Kansas" because so many people were hurt or killed while trying to settle the issue of slavery in the territory.

- In 1857 the Supreme Court decided in the Dred Scott case that slaves were property of their owners and could be taken by their owners anywhere in the nation.

- In 1860 Abraham Lincoln won the presidential election. As a result, seven Southern states seceded from the Union and created the Confederate States of America.

## VOCABULARY

Finish the Sentence ■ Choose one of the words or phrases from the box to complete each sentence. You will not use all the words in the box.

1. Some slaves, like Gabriel Prosser, led
_____ against their slave owners.

2. Some Southern states threatened to
_____ , or leave, the Union if slavery
was not allowed in the West.

3. Harriet Beecher Stowe wrote the _____
called *Uncle Tom's Cabin*.

4. John Brown captured the federal _____
in Harpers Ferry, Virginia, where weapons were stored.

5. In 1860, the Republican Party _____
Abraham Lincoln to be its candidate for President.

6. _____ , or the people's vote, was used
in many places to decide on the issue of slavery.

7. _____ was the name given to people who opposed the spread
of slavery into new states and territories.

> novel
> rebellions
> opposed
> secede
> nominated
> popular sovereignty
> arsenal
> Free Soilers

## USING INFORMATION

Writing an Opinion ■ The Dred Scott Decision was a major setback for people who opposed slavery. Considering the time period in which it was made, do you think it was the correct decision to make? Explain your answer.

**Who Said It?** ■ Read each statement in Group A. Then match the name of the person in Group B who might have said it. You will not use all the names in Group B.

| Group A | Group B |
|---|---|
| _____ 1. "I wrote the Compromise of 1850." | A. Stephen Douglas |
| _____ 2. "My book showed the evils of slavery." | B. John Brown |
| _____ 3. "I was elected senator from Illinois in 1858." | C. Henry Clay |
| _____ 4. "I was the Northern Democrat who was elected President in 1856." | D. Abraham Lincoln |
| | E. Harriet Beecher Stowe |
| _____ 5. "I helped many slaves to freedom through the Underground Railroad." | F. Jefferson Davis |
| _____ 6. "I was elected president of the Confederate States of America." | G. James Buchanan |
| _____ 7. "My raid on Harpers Ferry made me a hero to many Northern abolitionists." | H. Harriet Tubman |

## CRITICAL THINKING

**Categories** ■ Read the words in each group. Write a title for each group on the line above each group. You may use the words in the box for all or part of each title. One of the titles in the box is not used.

| Dred Scott Decision | Underground Railroad | Compromise of 1850 |
| Confederate States of America | Nat Turner's Rebellion | |

1. _____

took place in Virginia in 1831
57 slave owners were killed
its leader was captured and hanged

2. _____

made up of seven Southern states
opposed President Lincoln
their constitution protected slavery and
    favored states' rights

3. _____

admitted California to the Union as
    a free state
forced Northerners to return
    runaway slaves
allowed people in New Mexico
    and Utah territories to vote on
    the slavery issue

4. _____

a secret organization
leaders included Arnold Cragston
helped many slaves escape to freedom

## Reading an Election Map

An **election map** shows how different areas vote in an election. The map on this page shows for each state the number of electoral votes each candidate won in the Election of 1860. The key identifies which color represents each candidate. For example, Breckenridge won Florida's three electoral votes. This map shows us that sectionalism and slavery affected the Election of 1860.

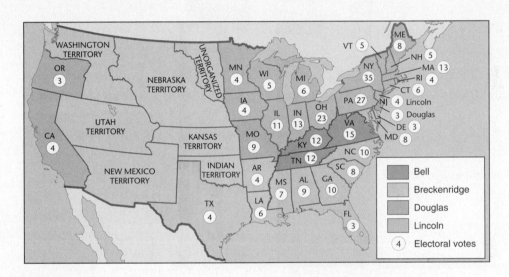

**Study the map and its map key. Then answer the questions.**

1. In which states did John Bell win electoral votes? _____ ,

   _____ , and _____

2. How many electoral votes did Douglas win? _____

3. How many states voted for Breckenridge? _____

4. In which part of the nation did Breckenridge win electoral votes?

   _____

5. In which part of the nation did Lincoln win electoral votes? _____

6. Did Lincoln win electoral votes in any Southern states? _____

7. How did the question of slavery affect the Election of 1860? _____

   _____

# Chapter 16

# THE BEGINNING OF THE CIVIL WAR

◀ Civil War cannon

### People

Robert E. Lee • Thomas "Stonewall" Jackson • George McClellan • David Farragut • Ulysses S. Grant

### Places

Fort Sumter • Manassas • Bull Run • Antietam Creek • Sharpsburg

### New Vocabulary

rejoin • ammunition border states • draft • Anaconda Plan • prey • income tax • defensive war

## Focus on Main Ideas

1. How did the Civil War begin?
2. What were the different goals of the Union and the Confederacy during the Civil War?
3. What advantages did each side have during the Civil War?
4. What happened during the early battles of the war?

In 1861 Americans began to fight the worst war the nation had ever known. From the first days of the Civil War, families and friends were divided about which side to support. During this bitter war, brothers, friends, fathers, and sons fought on opposite sides and attacked each other in battles. Even President Lincoln's wife, Mary, had brothers who were Confederate soldiers.

### Shots Fired at Fort Sumter

Seven Southern states had formed a new nation called the Confederate States of America shortly before Abraham Lincoln became President. Southerners felt that their differences with the North were too great to allow them to remain part of the United States. The Confederates wanted to leave the Union peacefully. Although Lincoln did not want a war between North and South, he said that he would fight to keep the United States together.

On March 4, 1861, Lincoln became the President of a divided nation. In his inaugural speech, he asked the South to **rejoin** the Union and to avoid war. He told the South, "We are not enemies, but friends. We must not be enemies." But within a few weeks they were at war.

Fort Sumter in Charleston Harbor, South Carolina, belonged to the United States Army. But the Confederates said that the United States must give Fort Sumter to them because it was on Confederate land. Lincoln refused to surrender the fort. Instead he sent ships with supplies for the Union soldiers at Fort Sumter.

The Confederates said that it was an act of war for the Union to send supplies to a fort on Confederate land. So on April 12, 1861, the Civil War began with the Confederate attack on Fort Sumter. On April 13, the Union soldiers at the fort ran out of **ammunition** and surrendered. The Confederates had won the first battle.

## Taking Sides in the Civil War

Each side had different goals during the Civil War. The Confederates were fighting to have their own independent nation. The North was fighting so that the South would remain part of the United States. Ending slavery was not Lincoln's goal in 1861. Lincoln did not talk about the issue of slavery because eight slave states still remained in the Union. These states were called **border states** because they were between the Union and the Confederacy.

Soon after Fort Sumter surrendered, four border states seceded and joined the Confederacy. Virginia, Tennessee,

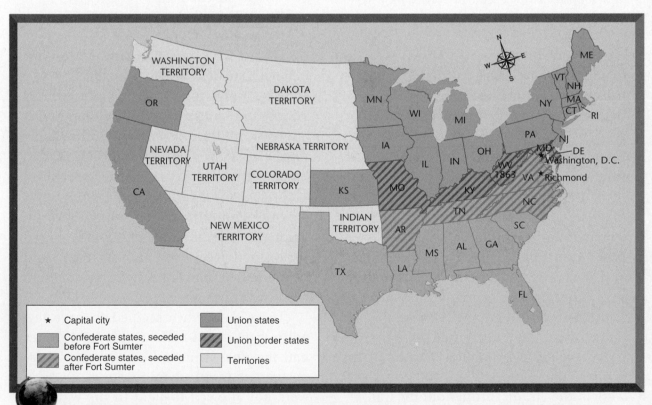

**The Nation Divides** *Before shots were fired on Fort Sumter, seven states had left the Union. After Fort Sumter, four more states left the Union. Part of Virginia would not secede and became West Virginia, a Union state, in 1863. What city was the Confederate capital?*

The North was able to produce more war supplies than the South because there were more factories in the North.

North Carolina, and Arkansas gave the Confederacy 11 states. Richmond, Virginia, became the Confederate capital. People in the western part of Virginia did not want to secede with the rest of Virginia. They formed the new state of West Virginia when they joined the Union in 1863.

Four other border states—Delaware, Maryland, Kentucky, and Missouri—decided to remain in the Union. These states were very important to the Union. Maryland and Delaware were close to Washington, D.C., the Union's capital. Missouri and Kentucky controlled the Mississippi and Ohio rivers. The North used these rivers to move soldiers and supplies. Because of the border states, more than 400,000 slaves were in the Union throughout the war.

As soon as the Civil War began, both sides began to form armies. Union soldiers wore blue uniforms. Soldiers in the Union army were often called "Yankees" or "Yanks." People called Confederate soldiers "Rebels" or "Johnny Reb." Confederates wore gray uniforms.

In 1861 the Union and the Confederacy asked for thousands of men to volunteer to be soldiers. At first many men on both sides wanted to fight. They believed that the war would end quickly. As men left home to become soldiers, they often joked that they would be "home in time for dinner." But as the war dragged on and thousands died, many more soldiers were needed. Both the Union and the Confederacy passed **draft** laws that required men to be soldiers.

## Each Side Had Advantages

Union soldiers had many reasons to believe that they would win the war and soon be "home for dinner." The Union had almost four times as many soldiers. With almost 23 million people, the Union had a much larger population. The Union also had more money to pay for the war. Union farms grew more food. Most of the nation's factories and railroads were in the North. During the war, the North's factories produced its needed weapons, ammunition, and supplies. The North used its railroads to move its troops and supplies.

The Confederacy seemed to have few advantages in 1861. The Confederate states had less than nine million people. Forty percent of those people were slaves who were not allowed to fight in the war. The Confederacy had less food and fewer factories, soldiers, and railroads. But the people in the Confederacy were fighting to have their own nation. They were willing to fight very hard for their cause. Southerners fought on their own land, which they knew well.

The Confederacy's greatest advantage was its excellent generals. Generals on both sides of the war had been trained at the United States Military Academy at West Point, New York. But many of the Southern generals had more experience. The greatest Confederate general was Robert E. Lee of Virginia. Lee had led American soldiers in the Mexican War. He had captured John Brown after Brown's attack on the arsenal at Harpers Ferry. President Lincoln admired Lee and asked him to lead the Union army. But Lee would not fight against his own state of Virginia. Instead he led Confederate armies.

## Planning and Paying for War

To defeat the South, the North decided to use the **Anaconda Plan**. It was named for the South American anaconda snake that crushes its **prey** to death. The North planned to capture the Mississippi River and divide the Confederacy in half. The Union also planned to capture Richmond, the Confederate capital. Northern ships would blockade Southern ports to stop the Confederacy from receiving supplies from Europe. The blockade would also prevent the South from selling its cotton to Great Britain and other nations.

To pay for the war, Congress passed the nation's first **income tax** laws. Americans had to give some of the money they earned to the federal government. The government also sold war bonds to raise money to help pay for the war.

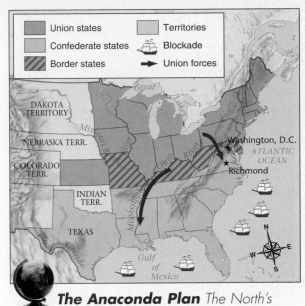

**The Anaconda Plan** *The North's plan to win the war called for dividing the South and using a blockade on Southern ports.*

The South planned to fight a **defensive war**. Southerners would fight on their own land and defend it. The South thought that the Union would grow tired of fighting and would decide to surrender. The Confederates were also hopeful that Great Britain would provide them with supplies during the war.

To pay for the war, the Confederacy placed taxes on many different products. The Confederate government also sold war bonds. But as the war destroyed farms and businesses, few Southerners had money to buy bonds or to pay taxes. The South did not have enough money to pay for the war, so there was not enough food and ammunition. The lack of supplies weakened the Southern army.

## Confederate Victories in the East

The first major battle of the Civil War took place in Virginia, near a town called Manassas and a stream called Bull Run.

On July 21, 1861, 30,000 Union soldiers fought 22,000 Confederates in this battle. Union troops seemed to be winning early in the day. But Confederate troops led by Thomas J. Jackson held their position and helped turn the battle into a victory. "Stonewall" Jackson became one of the South's best generals. After this battle the Union knew the war would not end quickly.

President Lincoln asked General George McClellan to command the Union Army in the East. McClellan trained 150,000 men to fight against Lee's army. But McClellan was too cautious. He refused to attack Lee's army at times when he could have defeated the Confederates.

General McClellan's goal was to capture Richmond, Virginia. He tried to do this in the Battle of Seven Days in June 1862. But Lee defeated McClellan, and the Confederate

capital would be safe for more than two years. In September 1862 the Union army fought the Confederates again at the Second Battle of Bull Run. Once again Lee defeated the Union army.

While the Confederates held back the Union forces in the East, the Union was winning battles in the West along the Mississippi. The Union navy captured the port of New Orleans. After capturing New Orleans, the Union controlled the southern part of the Mississippi River.

## Antietam

Confederate leaders hoped that Great Britain would help them fight the Union

The Battle of New Orleans took place in April 1862. David Farragut led a fleet of ships on the Mississippi River in a battle against forts on the shore and ships in the river. Farragut's ships sank most of the Confederate ships, and New Orleans surrendered.

*The Second Battle of Bull Run was fought in September, 1862. Like the first battle fought at Manassas, this battle was a Confederate victory. In this painting, Confederate soldiers from Louisiana defend their position, throwing stones when they ran out of ammunition.*

because the British bought cotton from the South. If the South won a major battle in the North, the British might support the South. So President Davis and General Lee decided to invade Maryland. Unfortunately for Lee, his battle plans were found by one of McClellan's soldiers.

On September 17, 1862, Lee led his army against the Union near Antietam Creek outside the small town of Sharpsburg, Maryland. It was the bloodiest day of the Civil War. Thousands of Confederate and Union soldiers died, and thousands more were wounded during that one day of fighting.

The Battle of Antietam became a Union victory. Lee was forced to retreat to Virginia. But General McClellan foolishly

waited 19 days before he attacked Lee's army again. President Lincoln was furious with McClellan for waiting. He believed McClellan should have followed Lee's army, destroyed it, and forced Lee to surrender. If McClellan had done that, the war might have ended in 1862. Soon after Antietam, Lincoln chose another general to command the Union army.

The Union victory at the Battle of Antietam made Great Britain and other European nations decide not to aid the Confederacy. Because the Union had won an important battle, Lincoln felt the time was right to act against slavery. Read on in Chapter 17 to learn how Lincoln took steps to end slavery and how the Civil War ended.

# BIOGRAPHY

## Robert E. Lee 1807–1870

"Make your sons Americans," Robert E. Lee told Southerners after the Civil War. Although Lee led the Confederate Army for four years, he had a strong love for the United States.

Lee attended the United States Military Academy at West Point. After graduating from West Point, second in his class, Lee worked as an army officer. Lee fought bravely in the Mexican War. He fought in the same unit with Ulysses S. Grant, George McClellan, and Thomas "Stonewall" Jackson. All of these men became important generals in the Civil War.

As the disagreements between the North and the South grew stronger, Lee hoped the Southern states would not secede. Lee loved the South, but he hated slavery. He had freed the few slaves he owned long before the Civil War began.

After the Civil War began, Abraham Lincoln asked Lee to lead the Union army. Lee decided that he could not go to war against his own state. Lee believed the Southern states had the same right to leave the Union that the 13 colonies had when they separated from Great Britain in 1776.

As general of the Army of Northern Virginia, Lee became famous for his brilliant battle plans. Although his army was much smaller than the Union army, Lee defeated the Union Army again and again. When he won battles, Lee praised the work of his soldiers. When battles were lost, he took full blame upon himself.

By April 1865 Lee knew that it would not be possible for the South to win the war. So General Lee surrendered. Although many Confederates wanted to continue fighting, Lee told them to go home and become good American citizens again. After the war ended, Lee tried to heal the anger between the North and the South.

Robert E. Lee's birthday, January 19, is a legal holiday in most Southern states. Lee continues to be respected as one of the nation's greatest generals.

## In Your Own Words

Write a paragraph in your notebook that explains why Robert E. Lee is considered a great general and a hero.

# REVIEW AND APPLY

- By the time Abraham Lincoln became President, the nation was divided and preparing for war.

- The first battle of the Civil War took place in April 1861 at Fort Sumter, South Carolina.

- The Confederacy grew from seven states to eleven states when the border states of Virginia, Tennessee, North Carolina, and Arkansas seceded from the Union.

- Each side had its advantages in the war. The North had more people and more industries. The South had better generals and knowledge of the land.

- Early Confederate victories included the Battle of Bull Run and the Second Battle of Bull Run. The Union army won the Battle of Antietam.

## VOCABULARY

Matching ■ Match the vocabulary word or phrase in Group B with its definition in Group A. You will not use all the words in Group B.

| Group A | Group B |
|---|---|
| _____ 1. This was the name of the war between the North and the South. | A. draft |
| _____ 2. Union soldiers ran out of this and were forced to surrender Fort Sumter. | B. Anaconda Plan |
| _____ 3. These were states that were between the Union and the Confederacy. | C. Civil War |
| _____ 4. This was the way that the North planned to win the war. | D. income tax |
| _____ 5. Congress used this to raise money for the war. | E. defensive war |
| _____ 6. This was the way that the Confederacy planned to fight the war. | F. border states |
|  | G. ammunition |

## USING INFORMATION

Journal Writing ■ Imagine that you are General Lee or General McClellan. You are writing a report to President Lincoln or President Davis about your victory at Bull Run or Antietam. Explain the importance of your victory to your commander in chief.

## COMPREHENSION CHECK

Write the Answer ■ Write one or more sentences to answer each question.

1. Why did the Union and the Confederacy fight over Fort Sumter?

   _____

   _____

2. Explain the North's plan for winning the war.

   _____

   _____

3. Explain the South's plan for winning the war.

   _____

   _____

4. Who was Robert E. Lee, and why did he decide to fight for the Confederacy?

   _____

   _____

## CRITICAL THINKING

Comparing and Contrasting ■ In this chapter, you read about the early years of the Civil War. Compare the North and the South in the early part of the war for each topic listed below.

| TOPIC | NORTH | SOUTH |
|---|---|---|
| Reasons for Fighting | | |
| Nicknames and Uniform Colors | | |
| Advantages | | |
| Early Victories | | |

# SOCIAL STUDIES SKILLS

## Comparing Circle Graphs

A **circle graph**, also called a **pie graph**, is a circle that has been divided into sections that look like pieces of a pie. All the pie sections add up to 100 percent of the circle. Percent means parts of 100. The two circle graphs below give percents of the populations of the Union and the Confederacy in 1860. The two graphs can be compared.

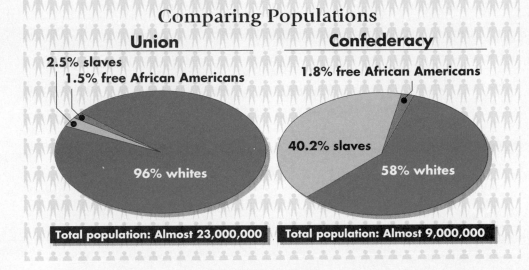

Comparing Populations

Union

2.5% slaves
1.5% free African Americans
96% whites
Total population: Almost 23,000,000

Confederacy

1.8% free African Americans
40.2% slaves
58% whites
Total population: Almost 9,000,000

**A. Study the two graphs. Use your knowledge about multiplying percents to choose the correct answer for each question.**

_____ 1. The Union had more than _____ white people in 1860.

_____ 2. The slave population in the Confederacy was about _____ .

_____ 3. The slave population in the Union was about _____ .

_____ 4. There were fewer than one million African Americans in the _____ in 1860.

_____ 5. The white population in the Confederacy was about _____ .

a. 5,220,000
b. 575,000
c. 22,000,000
d. Union
e. 3,600,000
f. Confederacy

**B. Answer the following question in your notebook.**

Compare the populations in the Union and the Confederacy. How were they different?

# Chapter 17

# THE END OF THE CIVIL WAR

◀ *Young Union soldier*

### People

José Chavez • Edward Solomon • Loretta Valesquez • Judah P. Benjamin • Clara Barton • George C. Meade • William T. Sherman • Ely S. Parker • John Wilkes Booth

### Places

Gettysburg • Vicksburg • Atlanta • Savannah • Appomattox Court House

### New Vocabulary

Emancipation Proclamation • emancipated • battlefield • Gettysburg Address • unconditional surrender • laid siege • total war • malice • charity • bind up • just • assassinated • dictator

### Focus on Main Ideas

1. How did the Emancipation Proclamation help the Union during the Civil War?
2. How did events at Gettysburg and Vicksburg affect the Civil War?
3. How did Abraham Lincoln want to treat the South after the Civil War?
4. What were the consequences of the Civil War?

---

**A**fter the Battle of Antietam, both the North and the South knew the war would continue for a long time. New victories gave the Union hope of winning the war.

### The Emancipation Proclamation

President Lincoln's goal at the start of the Civil War was to keep the United States together. But Lincoln had always thought slavery was wrong. After the Battle of Antietam, he took action to end it. Lincoln wrote the **Emancipation Proclamation**. This paper said that after the date it was issued, January 1, 1863, all slaves in states that were at war with the Union would be **emancipated**, or freed. Slaves in the Confederacy were filled with joy when they learned that Lincoln said they were free.

However, the Emancipation Proclamation did not free any slaves. It did not free the slaves in the border states or in Southern territory captured by the Union. Only an amendment to the Constitution could end slavery in those areas. The Proclamation could not free slaves in the Confederate states because Lincoln had no power there.

The Emancipation Proclamation did accomplish three important things for the Union. First, it gave Union soldiers two important causes to fight for: freeing the slaves and saving the Union. Second, the Proclamation encouraged African American slaves to escape from their owners and join the Union army. Third, Great Britain and other European nations decided not to aid the Confederacy when they heard that the Union was trying to end slavery there.

## The Contributions of Many Americans

Thousands of African American slaves joined the Union army soon after the Emancipation Proclamation was written, African American soldiers faced special dangers. If captured by Confederate soldiers, African Americans could be sold into slavery or killed. Twenty-two African Americans won the Congressional Medal of Honor for their courage.

About 440,000 immigrants fought in the Union army. They came from Ireland, Germany, Italy, Sweden, Poland, and other nations. One of these immigrant soldiers was a Polish man, Wladimir Kryzanowski. He became a general after fighting at Bull Run, Gettysburg, and in other battles.

About 10,000 Hispanic Americans fought for the Union. Lieutenant Colonel José Chavez led a company of Union soldiers that captured Confederate land in the Southwest.

About 6,000 Jewish Americans also fought for the Union army. One of these soldiers was Colonel Edward Solomon. He led a large group of soldiers from Illinois at the battles of Gettysburg and Atlanta.

Fewer immigrants fought for the Confederacy because fewer immigrants lived in the South. Loretta Valesquez, a Cuban immigrant, dressed as a man and fought in the Confederate army.

Judah P. Benjamin became the most important Jewish citizen in the Confederacy. He worked in Jefferson Davis's cabinet. Benjamin was attorney general, secretary of state, and secretary of war at different times during the Civil War.

Women played an important role in the Union and in the Confederacy. As men went off to fight, women ran farms, businesses, and plantations. Women worked as nurses and ran hospitals. The nation's first woman doctor, Elizabeth Blackwell, organized a group to train

*This soldier is one of the 200,000 African Americans who fought for the Union during the Civil War.*

Union nurses. Dorothea Dix, who had helped people with mental illnesses before the war, was in charge of the Union's nurses during the war. Sojourner Truth and Harriet Tubman had once been slaves, but they served as nurses and scouts for the Union army.

Another brave woman was Clara Barton. Before the war Barton had been a teacher, but she became a Union nurse during the war. At the Battle of Antietam, Barton worked in a small hospital right on the **battlefield**. After Antietam she nursed men at other battles.

*Clara Barton was a nurse during the Civil War. After the war ended, Barton started the American Red Cross.*

## The Battle of Gettysburg

After the Union victory at Antietam, the Union lost two battles in Virginia. Lincoln appointed General George C. Meade to command the Union Army that was fighting in the East.

Robert E. Lee decided to try once again to attack the North. He hoped that a victory would convince the Union to surrender. So Lee planned to invade Pennsylvania. Lee led 75,000 Confederate soldiers and Meade led 90,000 Union soldiers. The two armies met at Gettysburg, Pennsylvania, on July 1, 1863. The Battle of Gettysburg lasted three terrible days.

During the third day, thousands of Confederate soldiers charged across open fields toward the Union forces. Using rifles and cannons, the Union soldiers shot down the Confederate soldiers. The Union won a great victory at Gettysburg. But that victory was expensive. The North lost 23,000 soldiers; the South lost 28,000.

To save his defeated army, Lee retreated to Virginia. Lincoln sent a message to General Meade ordering him to attack Lee's army before it crossed the Potomac River into Virginia. Like General McClellan, Meade waited too many days to attack. Lee's army escaped back into Virginia.

Lee had lost more soldiers than the South's small population could replace. After the Battle of Gettysburg, the South's army would never be as strong as it had once been. The Confederates would never invade the North again.

So many soldiers died at Gettysburg that a military cemetery was built for the Union soldiers who died there. On

November 19, 1863, President Lincoln dedicated the new cemetery. He gave a short speech that is now called the **Gettysburg Address**.

## War in the West and the Fall of Vicksburg

To carry out its Anaconda Plan, the Union had to win control of the entire Mississippi River. Then the Confederates would not be able to use the Mississippi to move their soldiers and supplies. The Southern states west of the river would be cut off from the eastern states. The Union controlled part of the Mississippi. Lincoln knew that to control all of the river, Vicksburg, Mississippi, had to be captured. Lincoln ordered General Ulysses S. Grant and his army to capture Vicksburg.

What kind of man was General Grant? Like Robert E. Lee, Grant had studied at West Point and had fought in the Mexican War. When the Civil War began, Grant was working in his father's business in Illinois. He rejoined the army and became a general. When Grant demanded the **unconditional surrender** of a fort early in the war, the newspapers started calling him Unconditional Surrender Grant. President Lincoln liked Grant because he would fight until he won a battle.

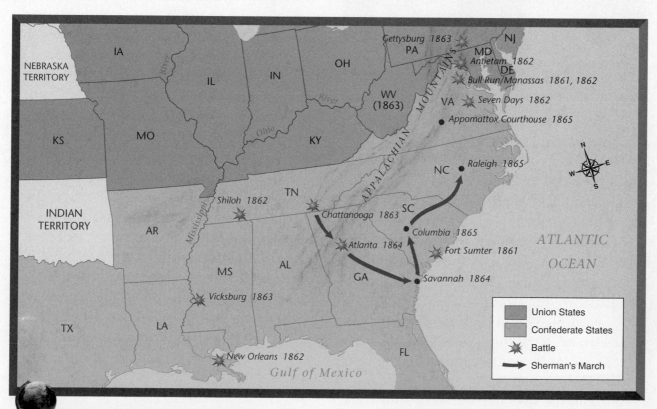

**The Civil War 1861–1865** *Some of the major battles during the Civil War are shown above. Many battles occurred in Virginia and along the Mississippi River. Which two major battles were fought in 1863?*

*Ulysses S. Grant became the first American general since George Washington to hold the rank of lieutenant general.*

From November 1862 to July 1863, Grant fought to capture Vicksburg. By May 1863 Grant's army surrounded the city. But the people of Vicksburg would not surrender. So Grant **laid siege** to the city. No food, supplies, or people could move in or out of the city. By summer the starving people of Vicksburg were eating dogs and rats in order to stay alive. On July 4, 1863, the city surrendered to Grant.

Next the Union captured Port Hudson, Louisiana. Now they controlled the entire Mississippi River. By controlling the river, the Union had split the Confederacy. Without the river the Southern army could not get food from Texas and Arkansas.

The fall of Vicksburg happened one day after the Union won the Battle of Gettysburg. The Union victories at Gettysburg and Vicksburg were turning points in the Civil War. The Confederate army was not ready to surrender, but it had become too weak to win the war.

## Sherman's March to the Sea

Early in 1864 President Lincoln appointed Grant commander of all the Union armies. Grant now commanded more than 500,000 soldiers. His goal was to crush the South to make it impossible for the Confederates to continue fighting.

Grant sent General William Tecumseh Sherman to capture the city of Atlanta, Georgia. Sherman led about 100,000 Union soldiers on a march through the South. He started by attacking Atlanta, an important manufacturing and railroad center. Sherman captured the city and set it on fire. Atlanta was completely destroyed. Sherman's actions were called **total war**. His goal was to destroy everything that the South could use to continue the war.

After burning Atlanta, Sherman led his army to Savannah, Georgia, a city near the Atlantic Ocean. Sherman and his soldiers carried out total war as they marched toward the sea. Farm animals, houses, barns, roads, railroads, and bridges were destroyed. Sherman forced the people of Georgia to surrender. But he also caused them to hate people from the North.

## Lincoln's Reelection

The news of Sherman's victory in Atlanta swept through the North. People in the Union believed the war would soon be over. The victory made Lincoln popular. In 1864 Lincoln was reelected. He defeated Democrat George McClellan.

In January 1865 Congress passed an amendment to end slavery in the nation. The Thirteenth Amendment was ratified in December 1865.

Lincoln was inaugurated for his second term as President in March 1865. He knew that the North would soon win the war and that the North and the South would be united again. He did not want Northerners to treat the Confederates as traitors. He felt that they had been punished enough by the terrible war. In his inaugural speech, Lincoln asked the Union to forgive the South. He asked the North and the South to work together to rebuild the nation. In his speech he said, "With **malice** toward none, with **charity** for all, with firmness in the right as God gives us to see the right, let us strive on to finish the work we are in, to **bind up** the nation's wounds,...to do all which may achieve and cherish a **just** and lasting peace among ourselves and with all nations."

## Final Battles of the Civil War

While Lincoln spoke of peace, the war continued. Sherman's army destroyed everything it could as it marched through South Carolina and North Carolina.

Grant fought hard to capture the Confederate capital at Richmond. To do this, he kept Lee's army under siege in the nearby town of Petersburg for almost a year. During this time, Lee's army had little food and lost many men. Finally, both Petersburg and Richmond were captured. The Union army completely surrounded Lee's army. Sadly, Lee sent a message to Grant that he was ready to surrender.

On April 9, 1865, the two generals met in a house in a town called Appomattox Court House. Lee signed the surrender papers that Grant had prepared. Grant was kind to the Confederates. All Confederate soldiers were allowed to return to their homes. They could keep their horses and mules. Officers were allowed to keep their pistols and swords. Grant sent food to feed Lee's army.

Lee was introduced to Grant's officers, including General Ely S. Parker, Grant's army secretary. Parker was also a Seneca Indian. Lee said to Parker, "I am glad to

*The Civil War ended when General Lee surrendered to General Grant in Appomattox Court House on April 9, 1865.*

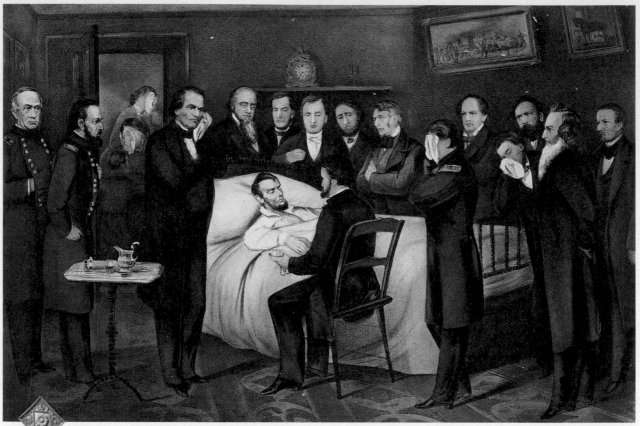

Lincoln was shot in the back of the head as he watched a play with his wife at Ford's Theater in Washington, D.C. He was taken to a room across the street where he died the next morning. John Wilkes Booth was shot and killed while Union troops tried to capture him in a barn in Virginia.

see one real American here." Parker answered, "We are all Americans." With the war over, the Confederates were Americans once again.

Five days after General Lee surrendered, President Lincoln was **assassinated.** John Wilkes Booth shot him because Booth was angry that the Confederacy had lost the war. People everywhere mourned for Abraham Lincoln.

## The Results of the Civil War

The United States had survived four terrible years of war. More than 620,000 men died during the Civil War. No other war in American history has caused so many American deaths. The Civil War ended slavery in the United States. It settled the question about whether or not states could secede. Never again would states leave the Union. As a result of the Civil War, the federal government became stronger than the state governments.

The Civil War destroyed much of the South. It created hatred between people in the North and the South. African Americans were no longer slaves, but they continued to face prejudice from Northerners and Southerners. It would take many years for the nation to recover from the Civil War.

## Abraham Lincoln 1809–1865

Abraham Lincoln was born in a small log cabin in Kentucky. His parents were poor and had never learned to read. His mother died when he was nine. After Lincoln's father remarried, Lincoln's stepmother encouraged him to read the Bible and to learn as much as possible. Throughout his life Lincoln read the Bible whenever he had to make difficult decisions. Although he only went to school for about one year, he read as many books as he could.

Lincoln moved to New Salem, Illinois, when he was 22 years old. He studied law on his own and became a lawyer. In 1834 Lincoln was elected to the Illinois state legislature. In 1846 he was elected to the House of Representatives. During his one term in Congress, Lincoln spoke out against President Polk for fighting the Mexican War. In 1858 he ran for the Senate as a Republican, but he lost to Stephen Douglas. However, in 1860 Lincoln was elected President.

No President ever faced the difficult problems that Lincoln faced in 1861. The South had seceded, the Civil War had begun, and slavery had to be ended.

Lincoln was determined to do everything possible to save the Union. He felt that the United States would be a much weaker nation without the South.

During the Civil War, Lincoln took on more power than the Constitution allowed. Some people called Lincoln a **dictator**. But he insisted that everything he did was necessary to save the Union.

Although the war took up most of his time, President Lincoln made other important decisions. He encouraged Congress to pass a law that gave free land to people who settled in the West.

Lincoln was assassinated before he could lead the nation in a time of peace. Millions wept when he died. Today, Lincoln is remembered as the great President who saved the Union.

## In Your Own Words

Write a paragraph in the journal section of your notebook that explains why Abraham Lincoln was one of the nation's great leaders.

# VOICES *from the* PAST

## The Gettysburg Address

A military cemetery was built at Gettysburg for the thousands of Union soldiers who died there. The dedication of the cemetery took place on November 19, 1863. President Lincoln was asked to give a short speech since he was not the main speaker that day. In his speech Lincoln told Americans that the purpose of the Civil War was to make the United States a democracy with freedom and liberty for all. The Gettysburg Address lasted only two minutes, but today it is considered one of the nation's greatest speeches.

Four score and seven years ago our fathers brought forth on this continent, a new nation, conceived in Liberty, and dedicated to the proposition that all men are created equal.

Now we are engaged in a great civil war, testing whether that nation, or any nation so conceived and so dedicated, can long endure. We are met on a great battlefield of that war. We have come to dedicate a portion of that field, as a final resting place for those who here gave their lives that that nation might live. It is altogether fitting and proper that we should do this.

But, in a large sense, we can not dedicate—we can not consecrate—we can not hallow—this ground. The brave men, living and dead, who struggled here, have consecrated it, far above our poor power to add or detract. The world will little note, nor long remember what we say here, but it can never forget what they did here. It is for us the living, rather, to be dedicated here to the unfinished work which they who fought here have thus far so nobly advanced. It is rather for us to be here dedicated to the great task remaining before us—that from these honored dead we take increased devotion to that cause for which they gave the last full measure of devotion—that we here highly resolve that these dead shall not have died in vain—that this nation, under God, shall have a new birth of freedom—and that government of the people, by the people, for the people, shall not perish from the earth.

## Explanation of the Gettysburg Address

*Paragraph 1* Eighty-seven years ago, in 1776, our leaders created a new nation based on the idea of liberty.

**Four score and seven years ago...**

The United States would exist to prove the statement that "all men are created equal."

*Paragraph 2* Now we are fighting a Civil War. This war is a test to see if the United States, or any other nation, can exist for a long time if it is based on the ideas of liberty and equality. We are now meeting at the battlefield of Gettysburg. We have come to dedicate part of the battlefield as a cemetery for soldiers who died here. Those soldiers died fighting so that the United States would continue to be a nation based on ideas of liberty and equality. It is correct and proper that we dedicate this cemetery to honor those dead soldiers.

*Paragraph 3* But we really do not have the power to dedicate this cemetery and make this ground holy. We cannot do this because this cemetery has already been made holy by the brave men, living and dead, who fought at Gettysburg. We cannot do anything more to make this cemetery holy than they have already done. The world will not notice or remember what we say here today. But the world can never forget what they did at Gettysburg. It must be our job to dedicate our own lives to the work these soldiers fought for so hard but could not finish. We must dedicate ourselves to the great cause for which these soldiers died. To honor them we must work harder than ever for this cause. We must prove that these soldiers did not die without a reason. We must work hard so that this nation, under God, will have a government that allows equality and liberty for all people. We must make sure that this democratic government will never be destroyed.

## Write Your Answers

**On a separate sheet of paper answer these questions.**

1. Why did people gather at Gettysburg on November 19, 1863?

2. Why did Lincoln say "we can not dedicate—we can not consecrate—we can not hallow this ground?"

3. How does Lincoln think Americans should finish the work for which the Union soldiers fought?

# AMERICAN GEOGRAPHY

### Place: Vicksburg

Place is what makes an area special and what makes it different from other areas. Landscape and culture are two of the features that tell us about a place.

Vicksburg was an important port on the Mississippi River. General Grant wanted to capture Vicksburg because its location would allow the Union to control the Mississippi River. Grant laid siege to Vicksburg. Grant would not allow the city to receive supplies from its port or its railroad. After 47 days the starving city surrendered.

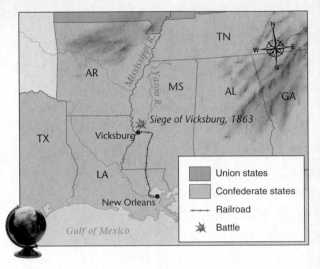

**Read the paragraph above. Then study the map of the Mississippi River and Vicksburg. Write the answer for each question.**

1. Which two rivers flowed into Vicksburg? _____ and

    _____

2. Why was control of New Orleans important to the Union's strategy? _____

    _____

3. Which two cities were connected by a railroad? _____ and

    _____

4. Which Confederate state was west of Vicksburg? _____

5. How did Grant's control of Vicksburg's railroad help the Union to win control of the city?

    _____

6. Why was control of Vicksburg important to the Union? _____

    _____

# REVIEW AND APPLY

- President Lincoln issued the Emancipation Proclamation. It said that after January 1, 1863, all slaves in the Confederate states would be freed.

- African Americans, European immigrants, Jewish Americans, and women all played important roles for both sides during the Civil War.

- The Battle of Gettysburg was fought from July 1 to July 3, 1863. As a result of this Union victory, the Confederacy would not invade the North again.

- Union victories at Vicksburg and Atlanta greatly weakened the South.

- President Lincoln was reelected in 1864.

- The Civil War came to an end on April 9, 1865, when Lee surrendered to Grant at Appomattox Court House, Virginia.

- Five days after the South's surrender, President Lincoln was assassinated.

## VOCABULARY

Writing with Vocabulary Words ■ Use six or more vocabulary words below to write a paragraph about why and how the North won the Civil War. Write your paragraph in your social studies notebook.

| | | |
|---|---|---|
| emancipated | laid siege | charity |
| battlefield | total war | just |
| unconditional surrender | malice | assassinated |

## COMPREHENSION CHECK

Choose the Answer ■ Write the letter of the word or phrase that best answers each question.

_____ 1. What was the name of President Lincoln's speech that honored the soldiers who died at Gettysburg?

    a. Farewell Address
    b. Inaugural Speech
    c. Gettysburg Address

_____ 2. What was the name given to General Sherman's actions in Atlanta?

    a. unconditional surrender
    b. total war
    c. defensive war

_____ 3. What role did Clara Barton play during the war?

    **a.** a cook
    **b.** a photographer
    **c.** a nurse

_____ 4. When did President Lincoln issue the Emancipation Proclamation?

    **a.** on January 1, 1863
    **b.** before the Battle of Antietam
    **c.** after the war was over

_____ 5. Who was the Union commander at the Battle of Gettysburg?

    **a.** George Meade
    **b.** Robert E. Lee
    **c.** Ulysses S. Grant

_____ 6. Which Constitutional amendment ended slavery in the United States?

    **a.** Thirteenth Amendment
    **b.** Fourteenth Amendment
    **c.** Fifteenth Amendment

_____ 7. Where did the Civil War come to an end?

    **a.** Richmond, Virginia
    **b.** Atlanta, Georgia
    **c.** Appomattox Court House, Virginia

_____ 8. In what battle was the Union able to split the Confederacy into two parts?

    **a.** Vicksburg
    **b.** Antietam
    **c.** Appomattox

## CRITICAL THINKING

**Sequencing Information** ■ Write the numbers 1, 2, 3, 4, and 5 next to these sentences to show the correct order.

_____ In January 1865 Congress passes an amendment to end slavery in the United States.

_____ Lincoln is assassinated in Washington, D.C.

_____ The Battle of Gettysburg is fought for three days in July 1863.

_____ On April 9, 1865, the Confederate army surrenders, ending the Civil War.

_____ Lincoln dedicates a new cemetery to the soldiers who died at the Battle of Gettysburg.

## USING INFORMATION

**Writing an Essay** ■ After President Lincoln made Ulysses S. Grant commander of all the Union armies, the tide of the war started to change in favor of the North. Explain the actions taken by General Grant that helped the Union win the war. Start your essay with a topic sentence.

224

# Chapter 18

# THE RECONSTRUCTION YEARS

◀ Carpetbag

### People

Andrew Johnson • Edwin
Stanton • Blanche Bruce •
Samuel Tilden • Rutherford
Hayes • Homer Plessy •
Booker T. Washington

### Places

Hampton Institute •
Tuskegee Institute

### New Vocabulary

Reconstruction • oath •
Radical Republicans •
freedmen • Civil Rights Act •
campaigned • due process •
public office • impeach •
carpetbaggers •
scalawags •
sharecroppers • Ku Klux
Klan • poll tax • literacy •
clauses • segregation

### Focus on Main Ideas

1. How did the Republicans help African Americans during Reconstruction?
2. Why were the Fourteenth and Fifteenth Amendments added to the Constitution?
3. What changes took place in the South after Reconstruction?

The United States faced serious problems after the Civil War. Much of the South had been destroyed. During the years known as **Reconstruction**, Southern states would rebuild their economies and become part of the United States again.

### Plans for Reconstruction

Lincoln's goals for Reconstruction were to reunite all of the states and to rebuild the country. Lincoln planned to allow Southern states to rejoin the Union if one tenth of their voters would take an **oath** to be loyal to the Union. One group in Congress, which became known as the **Radical Republicans,** disagreed with Lincoln's plan. They believed that the South was to blame for the war and should be punished. Lincoln vetoed the harsh Reconstruction plan passed by Congress. Before Lincoln and the Congress could compromise on a plan, Lincoln was assassinated.

Vice President Andrew Johnson became President. Johnson had a Reconstruction plan that was like the plan Congress had passed, but the Radical Republicans rejected it. The Radical Republicans believed that Johnson's plan did not punish the South enough.

The Radical Republicans became furious when people who had been Confederate leaders were elected to Congress and to state governments. They were also furious when Southern states passed laws called Black Codes. These laws treated African Americans as if they were still slaves. Congress created an agency called the Freedmen's Bureau to help the **freedmen,** slaves who became free after the Civil War. The Black Codes in the South said freedmen could only work as farmers or house servants. Freedmen had to carry special passes when they traveled. They could not serve on juries or vote. Since the Republicans controlled Congress, they decided to use their power to change what was happening in the South.

## Congress and Reconstruction

The Radical Republicans created their own Reconstruction plan. Their first action was to pass a **Civil Rights Act** in 1866. This law said that African Americans were American citizens and had equal rights under the law. Next the Republicans wanted to add the Fourteenth Amendment to the Constitution. President Johnson **campaigned** against the amendment and the Radical Republicans. Despite Johnson's efforts, Republicans won control of Congress in

By the end of the Civil War, much of the the South looked like the photograph below of Richmond, Virginia. Many soldiers returned to their homes to find that they had been destroyed. Throughout the South many farms, factories, railroads, bridges, and buildings would have to be rebuilt.

the election of 1866. The Fourteenth Amendment was ratified in 1868.

The Fourteenth Amendment has been called the Equal Rights Amendment. The amendment said that all people born in the United States were citizens of their state and the nation. This included African Americans. The amendment also said that states could not make laws that took away the rights of citizens. States had to give all people **due process** under the law.

In 1867 the Republicans passed the Reconstruction Act. The act had five parts. First, any state governments in the South that had been created under Lincoln's plan or Johnson's plan were not recognized by Congress. Instead federal troops would be sent to rule the South. Second, people who had been Confederate soldiers or leaders could not vote or hold **public office**. Third, all other white men and all African American men could vote and be elected to public office. Fourth, Southern states had to write new state constitutions that guaranteed African American men the right to vote. Fifth, all Southern states had to ratify the Fourteenth Amendment before they could rejoin the Union.

Johnson vetoed Congress's plan for Reconstruction, but Congress passed it again and the Reconstruction Act became law. By 1870 all Southern states had ratified the Fourteenth Amendment and had rejoined the Union.

## The Impeachment of Johnson

The Radical Republicans disliked Andrew Johnson because he opposed their Reconstruction plans. They wanted to

After the Civil War, African Americans had the right to vote. Their votes helped to elect African American leaders during the years of Reconstruction.

remove Johnson from the job of President. According to the Constitution, the House of Representatives can **impeach** a President who commits crimes. Then the President is put on trial in the Senate. If two thirds of the senators find the President guilty, the President loses his job.

In 1868 the House of Representatives voted to impeach Johnson. Congress had never before voted to impeach a President. Johnson was accused of not carrying out the Reconstruction plan of Congress and of breaking the Tenure in Office Act. Congress had passed the Tenure of Office Act to have power over the President. This law said that he could not fire anyone without the Senate's approval. When the President fired Edwin Stanton, the secretary of war, Johnson had broken the Tenure of Office Act.

After Johnson was impeached, he had a trial in the Senate that lasted three months.

The Senate needed 36 votes to find Johnson guilty. Only 35 senators voted against him. The other senators correctly believed that Johnson was a poor leader and a poor President, but he had not committed crimes. Johnson finished his term as President.

In November 1868 the popular Union war hero, General Ulysses S. Grant, was elected President. For the first time, African Americans were able to vote in an election for President. They helped Grant win. Grant did a poor job as President. Many of the people whom he appointed stole money from the government. Still, in 1872, Grant was reelected to a second term.

Under President Grant, the Fifteenth Amendment became part of the Constitution in 1870. This amendment said citizens cannot be denied the right to vote because of their race. Therefore, African American men had the right to vote. Women were not yet allowed to vote in any state, but they could vote in the Territory of Wyoming.

## The South During Reconstruction

During Reconstruction the South was controlled by three groups—**carpetbaggers**, **scalawags**, and African Americans. Carpetbaggers came from the North. They were called carpetbaggers because travelers

*Most African Americans who had been slaves remained in the South as farmers. They started small farms on land that they rented from the plantation owners. They paid for the use of the land by giving the owner part of the crops they raised.*

carried their clothing in bags made of carpet material. Some carpetbaggers really tried to help the South, but many used their power to get rich. Scalawags were white Republican Southerners. They became the largest group in Reconstruction governments. Before the war, most scalawags had been small farmers. After the war they wanted the power that had belonged to rich plantation owners. Most former Confederates hated the scalawags.

African Americans had a small role in government while the Union Army controlled the South. During Reconstruction many African Americans were elected to public office in state governments. Also, 22 African Americans were elected to Congress. Two of these men became senators. One of these two senators was Blanche Bruce from Mississippi. In the Senate, he worked to help African Americans, Indians, and Chinese immigrants win equal rights. Bruce was respected because he was an honest senator who cared about helping different groups of Americans.

## African Americans in the South After the Civil War

After the Civil War, there were four million freedmen who had no money, no land, no jobs, and no education. The Freedmen's Bureau gave African Americans and poor whites food, clothing, and medical care. It started new hospitals and more than 4,000 public schools. The Bureau also started several universities for African Americans.

Freedmen needed jobs after the war, but there were few kinds of work besides farming that they knew how to do. Since they did not have money to buy land, seeds, tools, and farm animals, they were forced to become **sharecroppers**. They rented farmland by giving landowners a share of their crops. They paid for the use of their tools, seeds, and farm animals with another share of their crops. This system forced sharecroppers to give more than half of their crops to the landowners. They had few crops left to sell or to use for themselves, so sharecroppers remained very poor year after year.

In 1866 white Southerners started a secret organization in the South called the **Ku Klux Klan**. Members wore white hoods and white robes. Their goal was to stop freedmen from using the new rights they had won. Many freedmen were beaten and many others were killed by the Klan.

## The End of Reconstruction

In 1872, while Grant was President, Congress passed a law that allowed most Confederates to vote and hold public office. Once that happened, Democrats slowly won control of the South just as they had before the Civil War.

During the election of 1876, Democratic Governor Samuel Tilden of New York ran against Republican Governor Rutherford Hayes of Ohio. To win the election, one candidate needed a majority of electoral votes. Each side said it had won a majority of electoral votes. Each side also said there had been cheating during the election. Since it was hard to decide which candidate was the real winner, Congress created a special committee to choose the President. That committee chose Hayes

The decision of the Supreme Court in the 1896 case of *Plessy v. Ferguson kept segregation in the United States until the 1950s.*

as the winner of the election after Democrats and Republicans worked out a compromise.

Under this Compromise of 1877, Hayes promised to remove all federal troops from the South. He also promised that federal money would be used to build southern railroads. The Democrats accepted this compromise.

In March 1877, Hayes became the new President. He ordered federal troops to leave the South. Reconstruction had ended.

## The South After Reconstruction

The Fifteenth Amendment was supposed to protect the right of African Americans to vote. When federal troops left, Southern governments passed laws that took away that right. One law required voters to pay a special **poll tax** in order to vote. Most African Americans were too poor to pay the tax. Another law required people to pass a difficult **literacy** test. In order to allow poor whites to vote, these laws had grandfather **clauses.** These clauses said that people whose grandfather had voted in 1867 did not have to pay poll taxes or pass literacy tests to vote. These laws allowed poor whites to vote but made it impossible for most African Americans to vote.

Governments throughout the South also began to pass **segregation** laws called Jim Crow laws. These laws kept African Americans and whites apart in public places, such as schools, hotels, beaches, churches, and restaurants.

In 1896 the Supreme Court protected segregation in a case called *Plessy* v. *Ferguson.* Homer Plessy, an African American, wanted to ride in the same railroad cars as white people. The Court ruled against Plessy and said that states could pass segregation laws to keep African Americans and white people apart. However, the public places for African Americans had to be equal to those for whites. Whites used this decision to carry out segregation until the 1950s.

In 1776 the United States had started with the goal that this nation would allow all people to have freedom and equality. The years after Reconstruction proved that this goal had not been reached. But the Thirteenth, Fourteenth, and Fifteenth Amendments gave the nation better tools for reaching its goal. Many years later, those amendments would finally allow all Americans to have equal rights.

# BIOGRAPHY

## Booker T. Washington 1856–1915

Booker T. Washington was born a slave, but he became an important African American leader. He advised governors, Congressmen, and two Presidents on how to help African Americans.

Washington became free when he was nine years old. He wanted an education very badly, so he went to school at the Hampton Institute, a school for African American students. He became a teacher.

In 1881 Washington started the Tuskegee Institute in Alabama. Washington's goal was to teach African Americans different trades at the school so they could get better jobs. Many students at Tuskegee became teachers who later started their own schools for African Americans. Washington was the principal at Tuskegee for 33 years.

While Washington worked at Tuskegee, he often thought about the problems African Americans had in the South. Washington wanted to help African Americans have a better life even though they were not treated fairly. He believed that African Americans needed good jobs so they could earn more

money and then buy their own land. By doing this, they would slowly have more power to improve their civil rights.

Washington said these ideas in a famous speech, the Atlanta Compromise. He asked whites to be fair and to give African Americans better jobs. He said that African Americans must accept segregation and not ask for equal rights. As they earned more money, they would receive better treatment. Not all African Americans agreed with Washington's ideas. Some believed African Americans should demand equal rights.

Booker T. Washington succeeded in helping many African Americans get a good education. Today Washington is remembered as one of the most important African American leaders during the years after Reconstruction.

## In Your Own Words

Write a paragraph in your notebook that tells how Booker T. Washington tried to help African Americans.

# REVIEW AND APPLY

■ The years after the Civil War were called Reconstruction.

■ After Abraham Lincoln was assassinated, Andrew Johnson became President.

■ Radical Republicans, members of Congress who blamed the South for the war and felt the South should be punished, opposed President Johnson's Reconstruction plan.

■ Radical Republicans tried, but failed, to impeach President Johnson.

■ Reconstruction came to an end in March 1877 when President Hayes ordered federal troops to leave the South.

■ After Reconstruction, Southern states passed laws that took many rights away from African Americans. Segregation laws separated African Americans and whites in many public places.

## VOCABULARY

**Choose the Meaning** ■ Write the letter of the word or phrase that best completes each sentence.

1. An **oath** is a _____ .

   a. promise to be loyal
   b. a proposed law
   c. a plan

2. **Freedmen** were people who _____ .

   a. passed the Black Codes
   b. wanted to stop slaves from gaining their freedom
   c. became free after the Civil War

3. The **Civil Rights Act** said that African Americans _____ .

   a. were American citizens
   b. had to pay for their freedom
   c. could not hold any public offices

4. To **impeach** means to _____ .

   a. be elected to a public office
   b. be charged with a crime in order to be removed from public office
   c. be chosen to run for political office

5. **Sharecroppers** rented land from landowners in return for _____ .

   a. money
   b. labor
   c. crops

6. A **poll tax** had to be paid so that a person could _____ .

   a. own land
   b. move to another place
   c. vote

## COMPREHENSION CHECK

Understanding Events in History ■ Complete the graphic organizer below with information about Reconstruction.

What was President Lincoln's plan for Reconstruction?

_____

_____

_____

_____

What was the Radical Republicans' plan for Reconstruction?

_____

_____

_____

_____

Reconstruction

What effect did the Black Codes have on Reconstruction?

_____

_____

_____

How did the Freedmen's Bureau help the South during Reconstruction?

_____

_____

_____

## CRITICAL THINKING

Distinguishing Relevant Information ■ Imagine you are telling a friend about Reconstruction in the South after the Civil War. Read each sentence below. Decide which sentences are relevant to what you will say. Put a check in front of the relevant sentences. There are four relevant sentences.

_____ 1. President Lincoln cared about Southerners.

_____ 2. President Johnson and the Radical Republicans disagreed over Reconstruction plans.

_____ 3. The Fourteenth and Fifteenth amendments were added to the Constitution.

_____ 4. Radical Republicans tried to impeach President Johnson.

_____ 5. Carpetbaggers, scalawags, and African American Republicans controlled the South during Reconstruction.

_____ 6. Samuel Tilden ran for President in 1876.

## USING INFORMATION

Writing an Opinion ■ After the Civil War there were different ideas about rebuilding the South and bringing the Southern states back into the Union. Write a paragraph explaining which plan of Reconstruction you would have supported.

# *Unit 4* Review

Study the time line on this page. You may want to read parts of Unit 4 again. Then use the words and dates in the box to finish the paragraphs. The box has one possible answer that you will not use.

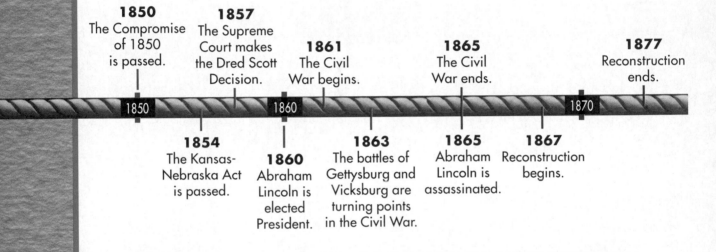

**1850**
The Compromise of 1850 is passed.

**1857**
The Supreme Court makes the Dred Scott Decision.

**1861**
The Civil War begins.

**1865**
The Civil War ends.

**1877**
Reconstruction ends.

1850    1860    1870

**1854**
The Kansas-Nebraska Act is passed.

**1860**
Abraham Lincoln is elected President.

**1863**
The battles of Gettysburg and Vicksburg are turning points in the Civil War.

**1865**
Abraham Lincoln is assassinated.

**1867**
Reconstruction begins.

| | | | |
|---|---|---|---|
| 1854 | 1861 | impeach | Supreme Court |
| secede | Dred Scott | Reconstruction | Gettysburg |
| railroads | generals | General Grant | vote |
| Union | property | Richmond | assassinated |
| Nat Turner | Vicksburg | Equal Rights | |

Slavery continued to trouble the nation during the 1800s. After

_____ led a slave rebellion, slave owners were afraid that there

would be more rebellions. The Kansas-Nebraska Act of _____

allowed the question of slavery to be decided by popular sovereignty. In 1857 the

Supreme Court made a decision about a slave named _____ .

The Court said that Scott was still a slave and all slaves were _____,
so they could be taken to any part of the country. After Abraham Lincoln was elected
President, the Southern states began to _____. Lincoln said that
his goal was to save the _____. The Civil War began in
_____ when South Carolina attacked Fort Sumter. The Confederates
had better _____, but the Union had more money, soldiers, supplies,
and _____.

In 1863 the Union won the three-day battle at _____,
Pennsylvania. To win control of the Mississippi River, General Grant laid siege to
_____, Mississippi. In April 1865 the Union captured the
Confederate capital of _____, Virginia. General Robert E. Lee knew
he could not win the war, so he surrendered to _____ at Appomattox
Court House. On April 14, 1865, Abraham Lincoln was _____.
In 1867 Congress passed the _____ Act so the South could rejoin the
Union. In 1868 the House of Representatives voted to _____
President Andrew Johnson. The Senate did not have enough votes to find Johnson
guilty, so he finished his term as President. The Fourteenth Amendment, often called
the _____ Amendment, was ratified in 1868. In 1870, the Fifteenth
Amendment gave African Americans the right to _____.
After Reconstruction ended, it became very difficult for African Americans to vote.

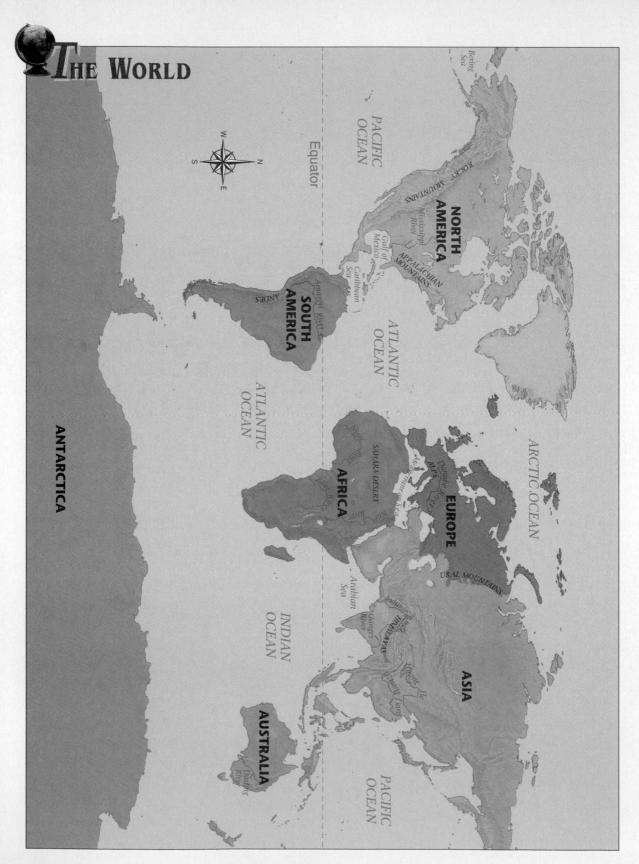

# THE WORLD

PACIFIC OCEAN

Equator

NORTH AMERICA

ROCKY MOUNTAINS

Mississippi River

Gulf of Mexico

Caribbean Sea

APPALACHIAN MOUNTAINS

Bering Sea

ATLANTIC OCEAN

SOUTH AMERICA

ANDES

Amazon River

ATLANTIC OCEAN

ARCTIC OCEAN

ANTARCTICA

AFRICA

SAHARA DESERT

Niger River

Zaire River

Nile River

Congo River

Arabian Sea

EUROPE

ALPS

Danube River

Mediterranean Sea

URAL MOUNTAINS

INDIAN OCEAN

ASIA

Indus River

Ganges River

HIMALAYAS

Huang He

Chang Jiang

PACIFIC OCEAN

AUSTRALIA

Darling River

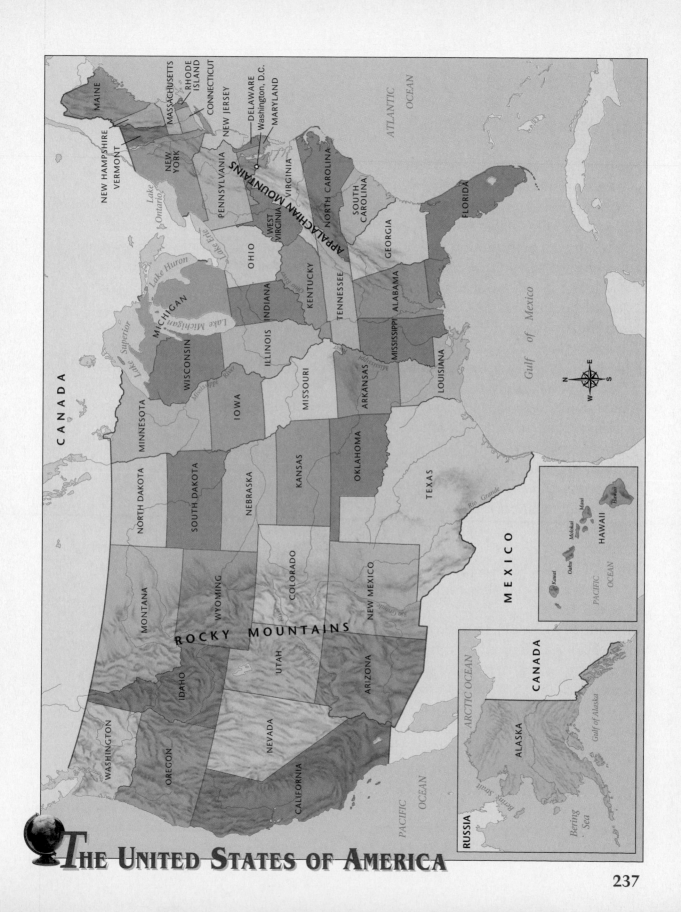

MAINE
MASSACHUSETTS
RHODE ISLAND
CONNECTICUT
NEW JERSEY
DELAWARE
Washington, D.C.
MARYLAND
NEW HAMPSHIRE
VERMONT
NEW YORK
PENNSYLVANIA
WEST VIRGINIA
VIRGINIA
NORTH CAROLINA
SOUTH CAROLINA
GEORGIA
FLORIDA

ATLANTIC OCEAN

APPALACHIAN MOUNTAINS

Lake Ontario
Lake Erie
Lake Huron
Lake Superior
Lake Michigan

OHIO
MICHIGAN
INDIANA
KENTUCKY
TENNESSEE
ALABAMA
MISSISSIPPI
LOUISIANA

Ohio River
Mississippi River

WISCONSIN
ILLINOIS
IOWA
MISSOURI
ARKANSAS

CANADA

MINNESOTA
NORTH DAKOTA
SOUTH DAKOTA
NEBRASKA
KANSAS
OKLAHOMA
TEXAS

Gulf of Mexico

N E S W

MONTANA
WYOMING
COLORADO
NEW MEXICO
ROCKY MOUNTAINS
IDAHO
UTAH
ARIZONA
NEVADA

Rio Grande

MEXICO

Kauai
Oahu
Molokai
Maui
Hawaii
HAWAII
PACIFIC OCEAN

WASHINGTON
OREGON
CALIFORNIA

PACIFIC OCEAN

ARCTIC OCEAN
CANADA
ALASKA
Gulf of Alaska
Bering Strait
Bering Sea
RUSSIA

# THE UNITED STATES OF AMERICA

# GLOSSARY

**abolition** (page 167) Abolition meant ending slavery.

**abolitionist** (page 167) An abolitionist was a person who worked to end slavery.

**ally** (page 73) An ally is a nation that promises to help another nation.

**amendment** (page 100) A law that is added to the Constitution is called an amendment.

**ammunition** (page 203) Ammunition is something that can be fired at an enemy. Cannon balls and bullets are kinds of ammunition.

**Anaconda Plan** (page 205) The Anaconda Plan was the strategy that the Union used to fight the Civil War.

**anthem** (page 150) An anthem is a song that praises a country. The "Star-Spangled Banner" is the national anthem, or official song, of the United States.

**appoint** (page 138) To appoint means to choose a person for a job or government office.

**apprentice** (page 61) An apprentice agrees to work a set amount of time for a person who is skilled at making a product. In return the apprentice learns those skills.

**archaeologist** (page 4) An archaeologist looks for bones, tools, and artifacts from people who lived long ago. These objects are studied to find out how people then.

**arsenal** (page 196) An arsenal is a place where weapons are stored.

**artifact** (page 5) An artifact is an object, such as a tool or jewelry, made by a person who lived long ago.

**assassinate** (page 218) To assassinate means to murder an important leader.

**astrolabe** (page 15) An astrolabe is an instrument that measures how high in the sky the sun, stars, and planets are. The astrolabe helped sailors locate where they were.

**asylum** (page 169) An asylum is a hospital that cares for people with mental illnesses who cannot care for themselves.

**battlefield** (page 214) A battlefield is the place where armies fight a battle.

**bind up** (page 217) To bind up means to put a bandage on a wound so that the wound will heal.

**blend** (page 180) Blend means to mix two or more things together.

**blockade** (page 79) Blockade means one nation uses its ships to block an enemy's ports so that the enemy's ships cannot sail in or out.

**border state** (page 203) A border state was one of the eight states located along the border between the Union and the Confederacy.

**boycott** (page 72) A boycott is a protest against a group or a nation's actions by not buying goods from that group or nation.

**Cabinet** (page 138) The Cabinet is the group of people that advises the President and leads the executive departments of the government.

**campaign** (page 226) To campaign means to take part in activities to gain support for a cause. The cause might be getting a person elected or keeping a law from being passed.

**candidate** (page 142) A candidate is a person who runs in an election for a government office, such as President.

**carpetbagger** (page 228) Carpetbagger was the name Southerners gave to a person from the North who came to the South during Reconstruction. Many carpetbaggers cared more about becoming rich than about helping the South.

**cash crop** (page 59) A cash crop is a crop that a farmer grows to make money.

**central government** (page 96) A central government is a government that rules an entire nation.

**charity** (page 217) Charity means kindness and love to others.

**charter** (page 45) A charter is a paper signed by a person in power that gives the owner of the charter certain rights.

**checks and balances** (page 100) Checks and balances is a system of dividing power among the branches of a government so that no branch has enough power to control the others.

**circumnavigate** (page 19) Circumnavigate means to sail all the way around.

**civilization** (page 8) A civilization is the way of life of a group of people who have a written language, laws, and a government.

**Civil Rights Act** (page 226) A Civil Rights Act is a law that protects the rights of people. Civil rights include the right to vote and the right to equal treatment under the law.

**civil war** (page 29) A civil war is a war between people who live in the same nation.

**clause** (page 230) A clause is a part of a law that gives more information about the law.

**colony** (page 17) A colony is a place ruled by another country.

**commander in chief** (page 78) The commander in chief is the leader in charge of all of a nation's armies.

**Committee of Correspondence** (page 72) A Committee of Correspondence was one of many protest groups in the 13 colonies that sent information to each other about the actions of the British.

**compass** (page 15) A compass is an instrument that shows directions.

**compromise** (page 98) A compromise is a way of solving a problem in which each side gives up something they want so that an agreement can be made.

**Confederacy** (page 197) The Southern states that seceded at the beginning of the Civil War were called the Confederacy.

**Confederate States of America** (page 197) The Southern states that seceded at the beginning of the Civil War started a new nation called the Confederate States of America.

**confederation** (page 7) A confederation is a group of nations that have joined together for a purpose.

**conquistador** (page 25) A conquistador was one of the explorers who came from Spain to the Americas in the 1500s to conquer land for Spain.

**contract** (page 39) A contract is an agreement between two or more people.

**convert** (page 36) To convert means to change to a different religion.

**cotton gin** (page 155) The cotton gin is a machine that separates cotton seeds from cotton fibers.

**Creole** (page 28) Creole was the Spanish name for a person who had Spanish ancestors but was born in the Americas.

**criminal** (page 169) A criminal is a person who has done a crime.

**culture** (page 5) Culture is the way of life of a group of people. Clothing, food, beliefs, language, and customs are all part of culture.

**dame school** (page 61) A dame school was a school for girls that was taught by a woman in her home.

**debate** (page 194) A debate is a discussion in which people tell why they are for or against an idea.

**debtor** (page 49) A debtor is a person who owes money.

**defensive war** (page 205) A defensive war is a war in which a nation tries to fight off attacks on its own land.

**delegate** (page 78) A delegate is a person who is chosen to represent others at a meeting.

**democracy** (page 59) Democracy is government that is run by the people.

**dictator** (page 219) A dictator is a leader who has complete power.

**disability** (page 166) A disability is a condition that makes it hard for part of a person's body or mind to work.

**diverse** (page 182) Diverse means made up of different kinds.

**draft** (page 204) A draft is a rule that requires men of certain ages to serve in the armed forces.

**due process** (page 227) Due process means following the law and giving everyone the same rights and treatment.

**elector** (page 142) An elector is a person chosen by his or her state to be part of the Electoral College.

**electoral college** (page 142) The Electoral College is a group of delegates from each state who elect the President and Vice President of the United States.

**emancipate** (page 212) To emancipate means to set free.

**Emancipation Proclamation** (page 212) The Emancipation Proclamation was a paper written by President Abraham Lincoln that said all slaves in Confederate States at war with the Union were free.

**Embargo Act** (page 148) The Embargo Act of 1807 was a law that stopped Americans from trading with other countries.

**empire** (page 9) An empire is a large area of land, sometimes including many nations, in which the people are ruled by one leader.

**Enlightenment** (page 80) The Enlightenment was a movement during the 1700s that encouraged new ideas about freedom and government.

**Episcopal Church** (page 60) In the United States, the Church of England was called the Episcopal Church.

**established church** (page 44) An established church is one that the government says everyone must belong to and that the people pay taxes to support.

**execution** (page 178) Execution is the killing of a person by a government as punishment for breaking the law.

**executive** (page 100) Executive means having to do with carrying out the nation's laws. The executive branch of the federal government is led by the President and carries out the laws of Congress.

**fare** (page 39) A fare is the cost a passenger is charged for a journey on a ship.

**favorable balance of trade** (page 62) A favorable balance of trade means that a nation sells more products to other nations than it buys from other nations.

**federal** (page 99) Federal means having to do with a central, or national, government.

**federalism** (page 99) Federalism is a type of government in which power is divided between a national government and state governments.

**fertile** (page 179) Fertile means good for growing crops.

**fiber** (page 155) A fiber is a thin, thread-like part of a plant that can be spun into yarn.

**flexibility** (page 100) Flexibility is the quality of being able to change to fit new conditions.

**foreign affairs** (page 140) Foreign affairs means a nation's relationships with other nations.

**foreign minister** (page 141) A foreign minister is the person in some governments who handles problems and creates treaties with other countries.

**freedman** (page 225) A freedman was a slave who was set free.

**Free Soiler** (page 195) A Free Soiler was a person who believed that slavery should not be allowed in the western territories.

**frontier** (page 70) The frontier is an area in a country that has not been settled yet.

**gatherer** (page 5) A gatherer was a person from long ago who found and collected foods such as fruit, nuts, and roots. Gatherers did not know how to grow their own food.

**Gettysburg Address** (page 215) The Gettysburg Address is a short speech given by Abraham Lincoln to dedicate the military cemetery built for the Union soldiers who died at the Battle of Gettysburg during the Civil War.

**grammar school** (page 61) A grammar school is an elementary school.

**Great Awakening** (page 61) The Great Awakening was a religious movement that started in New England in the early 1700s.

**Huguenot** (page 29) Huguenot was the name for French Protestants during the 1500s and 1600s.

**human sacrifice** (page 8) Human sacrifice means killing human beings as a gift to a god. Some ancient peoples believed that their gods needed human sacrifices or the gods would become angry and punish the people.

**impeach** (page 227) To impeach means to charge a government leader with a crime.

**impress** (page 148) To impress means to force a person to serve in the navy.

**income tax** (page 205) An income tax is a law saying that people must give a certain amount of the money they earn to the government.

**indentured servant** (page 39) An indentured servant was a person who agreed to work a set number of years for a person who would pay the cost of the trip to the English colonies .

**indigo** (page 60) Indigo is a plant that was raised as a cash crop in the 13 colonies. A blue dye can be made from indigo.

**Industrial Revolution** (page 155) The Industrial Revolution was a change from making products by hand at home to making products by machine in factories.

**Intolerable Acts** (page 70) The Intolerable Acts were laws that Parliament passed to punish the American colonists. Intolerable means hard to put up with. The colonists called them the Intolerable Acts because the laws were so unfair.

**irrigation canal** (page 5) An irrigation canal is a ditch that carries water from a river to a farm to water crops.

**Islam** (page 36) Islam is a religion based on the teachings of Muhammad. People who follow Islam are called Muslims. They worship a god called Allah.

**joint stock company** (page 45) A joint-stock company is a business that is owned by many people. If the company makes money, all the people who own stock in the company share the money.

**journeyman** (page 62) A journeyman is a person who has learned enough skills by working for another person to be able to work on his or her own. A person cannot become a journeyman until he or she has been an apprentice for a number of years.

**judicial** (page 100) Judicial means having to do with judges and courts of law. The judicial branch of the federal government is made up of courts. The judges in these courts use the laws made by Congress to make decisions.

**judicial review** (page 148) Judicial review is the power of the United States Supreme Court to decide if a state or federal law is unconstitutional, or says something different from the laws in the Constitution.

**just** (page 217) Just means fair to all.

**Ku Klux Klan** (page 229) The Ku Klux Klan, or KKK, was a secret organization started by Southerners after the Civil War. The KKK attacked, frightened, and killed African Americans to stop them from using the rights they had won.

**labor** (page 169) Labor means people who work.

**labor union** (page 169) A labor union is a group of workers who join together, often to demand better pay and working conditions.

**latitude** (page 179) A latitude is an imaginary line circling the globe. Latitudes are used to measure distance north or south of the equator. Lines of latitude are also known as parallels.

**lay siege** (page 216) To lay siege means to try to conquer an area by surrounding it with an army so that no food, supplies, or people can go in or out.

**legislative** (page 100) Legislative means having to do with making laws. The legislative branch of the federal government is Congress.

**literacy** (page 230) Literacy means the ability to read and write.

**log** (page 20) A log is a journal written by the captain of a ship to record the events that happen on the trip.

**Loyalist** (page 80) A Loyalist was a colonist who wanted the 13 colonies to remain part of Great Britain.

**Magna Carta** (page 68) The Magna Carta was the first set of laws in England to limit the king's power. English nobles forced King John I to sign the Magna Carta in 1215.

**mainland** (page 17) The mainland is the land that is part of a continent.

**majority** (page 157) A majority is more than half. If 100 people vote, at least 51 votes are needed to make a majority.

**malice** (page 217) Malice means wanting to hurt others.

**Manifest Destiny** (page 179) Manifest Destiny was the belief that the United States should rule all of the land between the Atlantic and the Pacific oceans.

**manufacture** (page 59) Manufacture means to make products, usually by machine in factories.

**mental illness** (page 169) A mental illness is a disease of the mind. A person with a mental illness is sick and needs medicine or special care.

**mercantilism** (page 62) Mercantilism is the idea that nations become wealthy by selling more goods to other countries than they buy from other countries. Mercantilism was popular in Europe during the 1600s and 1700s.

**mestizo** (page 28) Mestizo was the Spanish name for a person whose parents were Indian and Spanish.

**Middle Passage** (page 37) The Middle Passage was the step in the slave trade when slaves were sent by ship from Africa to America.

**militia** (page 73) A militia is a group of people who train themselves to act as soldiers during a war.

**mission** (page 28) A mission was a place where Spanish priests taught their religion to Indians.

**missionary** (page 179) A missionary is a person who tries to teach his or her religion to a group of people who do not yet believe in that religion.

**monarch** (page 15) A monarch is a king or queen.

**morale** (page 83) Morale is a feeling of excitement and purpose shared by a group.

**mulatto** (page 28) Mulatto was the Spanish name for a person who had African and Spanish or African and Indian parents.

**Muslim** (page 35) A Muslim is a person who follows the religion of Islam.

**Navigation Acts** (page 62) The Navigation Acts were trade laws that Parliament began to pass in 1651. These laws forced England's colonies to trade only with England using English ships.

**neutral** (page 80) Neutral means not taking sides during a war or disagreement.

**nominate** (page 196) To nominate means to name person to run for an office as a a candidate in an election.

**novel** (page 194) A novel is a long story that a writer invented.

**nullify** (page 159) To nullify means to make a law no longer exist.

**oath** (page 225) An oath is a promise.

**oppose** (page 195) To oppose means to be against or act against something.

**pamphlet** (page 79) A pamphlet is a short booklet.

**parallel** (page 179) A parallel is an imaginary line circling the globe. Parallels measure the distance north or south of the equator. Parallels are also known as lines of latitude.

**Parliament** (page 68) Parliament is the group of people who make laws for Great Britain. British people vote for people to represent them in Parliament.

**pass** (page 180) A pass is a way between or through mountains.

**Patriot** (page 80) A Patriot was an American colonist who wanted independence from Great Britain.

**peasant** (page 29) In some European countries, a poor person who does farm work is called a peasant.

**persecution** (page 170) Persecution means causing a person to suffer, often because of his or her race, religion, or ideas.

**plantation** (page 27) A plantation is a large farm where one or two cash crops are grown.

**planter** (page 59) A planter is the owner of a plantation.

**political party** (page 141) A political party is a group of people who work together to get people elected who agree with their ideas.

**political right** (page 169) A political right allows a person to be involved with government. Political rights include the right to vote, the right to serve on a jury, and the right to hold a public office.

**poll tax** (page 230) A poll tax is a tax people pay when they vote.

**popular sovereignty** (page 194) Popular sovereignty means the vote of the people decides an issue.

**precedent** (page 138) A precedent is an action that sets an example for others to follow.

**prejudice** (page 39) Prejudice is an unfair dislike or hatred of a person who belongs to a certain group or looks a certain way.

**prey** (page 205) Prey is an animal that is hunted for food by another animal.

**principle** (page 99) A principle is an important idea that shapes and guides people's choices and decisions.

**proclamation** (page 70) A proclamation is an order that is written by a government leader.

**proprietary colony** (page 46) A proprietary colony was a colony that was owned and ruled by one person or a small group of people.

**proprietor** (page 46) A proprietor is an owner of a business or land.

**public office** (page 169) A public office is an elected or appointed job in the government.

**pursuit of happiness** (page 80) The pursuit of happiness means the right to earn a living and to own property.

**pyramid** (page 8) A pyramid is a large stone building made of four triangle-shaped walls that meet at the top in a point.

**Radical Republican** (page 225) A Radical Republican was a member of a group in Congress who wanted to punish the South for starting the Civil War.

**ratify** (page 96) To ratify means to approve by a vote.

**rebel** (page 140) A rebel is a person who fights the government and refuses to obey its laws.

**rebellion** (page 193) A rebellion is a fight against the government or the people in power.

**Reconstruction** (page 225) Reconstruction was the period after the Civil War when the Southern states became part of the United States again.

**reform** (page 165) Reform is a change to improve something.

**rejoin** (page 202) To rejoin means to join again.

**religious freedom** (page 44) Religious freedom is the right to belong to any religion.

**repeal** (page 146) To repeal means to end or to remove a law.

**representation** (page 71) Representation means standing in someone's place. Having representation in the government means having people in the government who will fight for the needs of the people who voted for them.

**representative** (page 45) A representative is a person who is elected to work in the government for the people who voted for him or her.

**representative government** (page 45) In a representative government, people vote for leaders to work for them in the government and make the laws.

**retreat** (page 81) To retreat means to back away from danger.

**revolt** (page 28) A revolt is a fight in which people turn against the ruling government or the people in power.

**royal colony** (page 46) A royal colony was a colony owned by a king or a queen.

**rum** (page 37) Rum is an alcoholic drink that is made from sugar or molasses.

**scalawag** (page 228) Scalawag was the name used by Southern Democrats for white Southern Republicans who worked in Reconstruction governments.

**secede** (page 194) To secede means to leave an organization.

**sectionalism** (page 156) Sectionalism is caring more about one's section of the nation and less about the entire nation.

**segregation** (page 230) Segregation means separating people because of their race.

**self-governing colony** (page 47) A self-governing colony was a colony in which people voted for their own leaders.

**senator** (page 98) A senator is a member of a senate.

**separation of powers** (page 100) Separation of powers divides power between the branches of government. Giving some power to each branch prevents one part of the government from having too much power.

**settlement** (page 26) A settlement is a small, new place to live, usually in an area where other people do not live.

**sharecropper** (page 229) A sharecropper was a poor farmer who rented farmland from a landowner and paid rent with a share of the crops.

**slogan** (page 179) A slogan is a group of words that expresses an idea. The person who makes up a slogan wants people to hear and remember the idea.

**smallpox** (page 26) Smallpox is a sickness that causes tiny pocks, or blisters. Smallpox spreads easily from one person to another.

**spoils system** (page 158) The spoils system is the custom of allowing a President who wins an election to give government jobs to the people who helped him or her.

**states' rights** (page 159) States' rights is the idea that state governments, not the federal government, should have control over how their state is run.

**surrender** (page 70) To surrender means to give up fighting.

**survive** (page 6) To survive means to stay alive.

**tariff** (page 156) A tariff is a tax on goods that a nation buys from other nations. Tariffs protect a nation's businesses because tariffs make foreign goods more expensive, so people will buy goods made in their own nation.

**taxation** (page 71) Taxation is the act of requiring people to pay a certain amount of money to the government.

**technology** (page 15) Technology is the knowledge that people use to improve their way of life. For example, technology helps people find new ways to travel and to make new foods and medicines.

**tepee** (page 6) A tepee is an Indian tent made of animal skins.

**terrace** (page 9) A terrace is a flat place made on the side of a hill or mountain to keep rain from washing away plants and soil.

**textile mill** (page 155) A textile mill is a factory where machines spin thread and make cloth.

**total war** (page 216) Total war means destroying everything in the enemy's area in order to force the enemy to surrender.

**totem pole** (page 6) A totem pole is a wooden post carved and painted with symbols of the owner's family. Some Native American tribes made totem poles.

**traitor** (page 81) A traitor is a person who works against his or her own nation.

**transcendentalist** (page 170) A transcendentalist was a person in the 1800s who believed in the importance of each individual and in living close to nature.

**treaty** (page 70) A treaty is an agreement between two or more nations.

**triangular trade route** (page 63) A triangular trade route was a trip to three different places on the globe to trade one or two products for another product.

**tributary** (page 19) A tributary is a river or stream that runs into a larger river or stream.

**turning point** (page 82) A turning point is a time when an important change takes place.

**unalienable right** (page 80) An unalienable right is a right that belongs to all people and should never be taken away.

**unconditional surrender** (page 215) Unconditional surrender means giving up completely.

**unconstitutional** (page 142) A law that says something other than what the laws in the Constitution say is unconstitutional.

**Union** (page 156) The Union is the United States of America.

**vaquero** (page 181) A vaquero is a Mexican cowboy.

**viceroy** (page 28) A viceroy is a governor who rules in the place of a king or queen.

**War Hawk** (page 149) A War Hawk was an American who wanted to fight a war.

# INDEX

## A

Adams, Abigail, 86–87
Adams, John, 72, 80, 85, 86–87, 141, 142, 148
Adams, John Quincy, 157–158
Adams, Sam, 72, 74, 86, 101
Africa, 16, 63
African Americans, 72, 84, 140, 150, 168, 172–173, 178, 182, 192, 196, 213, 218, 226, 227, 228, 229, 230
Africans, 28, 35–39, 45
Alien and Sedition Acts, 142, 146
American culture, 170
American Revolution, 73, 74, 80, 81–84, 85, 86, 96, 139, 149
Antietam, Maryland, 206, 212, 214
Arnold, Benedict, 84
Asia, 14–15, 16, 17, 18
Austin, Stephen, 177
Aztec Empire, 9, 25–26

## B

Bank of the United States, 139–140, 146, 159–160
Battle of Gettysburg, 214–215, 216
Battle of Vicksburg, 215–216
Bill of Rights,
    English, 69, 100
    United States, 100, 102, 103, 138
Black Hawk, 164

Blackwell, Elizabeth, 171, 213–214
Bonaparte. *See* Napoleon.
Booth, John Wilkes, 218
Boston, 63, 72, 78, 80
Brown, John, 196, 198, 205

## C

California, 28, 177, 179–180, 182, 194
Canada, 19, 70, 80, 84, 149, 179, 193, 198
Cartier, Jacques, 19
Catholics, 28, 29, 30, 49, 177
Central America, 8, 9, 27, 28, 151
Champlain, Samuel de, 19, 29, 30
Church of England, 44, 47, 48, 50, 60
Civil War, 198, 202–207, 208, 212–218, 219
Clark, William, 147, 152
Classes of people, 28, 60–61
Clay, Henry, 149, 156, 157, 159, 194
Colonies, 17, 46–47, 58–63
    English, 43–49
    French, 29–30
    Netherlands, 30, 48
    slavery in the, 38–39
    Spanish, 25–29, 151
Columbus, Christopher, 16–17, 20–21, 31
Compromise of 1850, 194, 198

Confederate(s), 202–207, 214–218, 227, 229
Confederate States of America, 197, 202, 204
Congress, 98, 100, 138, 139, 140, 142, 143, 148, 149, 157, 159–160, 179, 205, 217, 225, 226–227, 229
Constitution, 64, 96–102, 103, 108–135, 138, 140, 167, 196, 228
Continental Congress,
    First, 72, 85, 86, 143
    Second, 78, 79, 80, 85, 86, 96, 139, 143
Coronado, Francisco de, 27
Cortés, Hernan, 25–26

## D

Da Gama, Vasco, 15, 16
Davis, Jefferson, 197, 207, 213
Declaration of Independence, 80, 81, 84, 85, 91–95, 167
De Soto, Hernando, 26–27
Diseases, 26, 27, 30, 37, 38, 46, 70
Dix, Dorothea, 169, 214
Douglas, Stephen, 195, 197, 219
Douglass, Frederick, 168, 169, 172–173

## E

Education, public, 61–62, 165–166, 170
Elizabeth I, (Queen), 43, 44
Emancipation Proclamation, 212–213

Louisiana, 19, 70, 83,
146–147
Louisiana Purchase, 147, 156
Loyalists, 80

## M

Madison, James, 98, 101,
103, 140, 148, 149, 151
Magellan, Ferdinand, 18–19
Manifest Destiny, 178–179,
182
Mann, Horace, 165–166
Mansa Musa, 35–36
Marbury, William, 148
Marshall, John, 148
Maryland, 49, 204, 207
Massachusetts, 45, 48, 61,
72, 86, 165
Maya Empire, 8–9
Mayflower Compact, 45–46
McClellan, George, 206, 207,
208, 214, 217
Meade, George C., 214
Mexican Cession, 180, 181,
194
Mexican War, 179–180, 194,
208, 215, 219
Mexico, 8, 9, 25–26, 27, 38,
151, 177–178, 179–180,
181
Minutemen, 56, 73, 74, 84
Mississippi River, 19, 27, 70,
84, 160, 161, 205, 206,
215, 216
Missouri, 156, 158, 195,
196, 204
Missouri Compromise,
156–157, 158, 194, 195,
196

Moctezuma, 25–26
Monroe, James, 147, 151,
157
Monroe Doctrine, 151
Mormons, 170, 182
Mott, Lucretia, 168, 169

## N

Napoleon Bonaparte, 142,
147, 148, 149
Native Americans. *See also*
Indians. 4–9, 17
Navigation Acts, 62–63
Netherlands, 30, 37, 48
New France, 29–30, 70
New Mexico, 28, 177, 180,
194
New Orleans, Louisiana,
147, 150, 206
New Spain, 25–26, 177
New York, 30, 48, 78, 82,
101, 102, 165
New York City, 59, 72, 138
North Carolina, 49, 204, 217
North Dakota, 147–148,
152
Northwest Passage, 19, 30
Northwest Territory, 96, 140,
141, 148

## O

Osceola, 160
Oregon, 176, 178
Oregon Trail, 176–177, 178

## P

Paine, Thomas, 79
Parliament, 68–69, 70, 71,
72, 73, 98
Patriots, 80, 85

Penn, William, 48, 50
Pennsylvania, 48, 50, 70, 83,
214
Philadelphia, Pennsylvania,
50, 59, 63, 64, 78, 79, 82,
97
Philip II, (King), 43–44
Pilgrims, 45–46
Plantations, 27, 38, 39,
59–60, 156, 192
Political parties, 141, 143,
151, 157–158, 195, 197
Polk, James K., 179, 219
Ponce de Léon, 26
Pontiac, 70–71
Popular sovereignty, 194,
195, 197
Portugal, 16, 17, 30, 37
Protestants, 29, 48, 170
Pueblos, 5–6, 28
Puritans, 47–48, 58–59, 61,
62

## Q

Quakers, 48, 50, 167

## R

Radical Republicans,
225–227
Reconstruction, 225–230
Reform movements,
165–170
Religious freedom, 44,
47–48, 49, 50, 102
Revere, Paul, 73, 74
Rhode Island, 47–48, 155
Richmond, Virginia, 193,
204, 205, 206, 217, 226
Roanoke, Virginia, 44–45